Microsoft® POWERPOINT® 2013

INTRODUCTORY

Susan L. Sebok

CENGAGE
Learning®

SHELLY
CASHMAN
SERIES®

Australia • Brazil • Japan • Korea • Mexico • Singapore • Spain • United Kingdom • United States

Microsoft® PowerPoint® 2013: Introductory
Susan L. Sebok

Executive Editor: Kathleen McMahon

Product Manager: Caitlin Womersley

Associate Product Manager: Crystal Parenteau

Editorial Assistant: Sarah Ryan

Print Buyer: Julio Esperas

Director of Production: Patty Stephan

Content Project Manager: Matthew Hutchinson

Development Editor: Deb Kaufmann

Senior Brand Manager: Elinor Gregory

Market Development Manager: Kristie Clark

Market Development Manager: Gretchen Swann

Marketing Coordinator: Amy McGregor

QA Manuscript Reviewers: Jeffrey Schwartz, John Freitas, Serge Palladino, Susan Pedicini, Danielle Shaw, Susan Whalen

Art Director: GEX Publishing Services, Inc.

Text Design: Joel Sadagursky

Cover Design: Lisa Kuhn, Curio Press, LLC

Cover Photo: Tom Kates Photography

Compositor: PreMediaGlobal

Copyeditor: Harold Johnson

Proofreader: Kim Kosmatka

Indexer: Rich Carlson

For product information and technology assistance, contact us at
Cengage Learning Customer & Sales Support, 1-800-354-9706

For permission to use material from this text or product, submit all requests online at **cengage.com/permissions**
Further permissions questions can be emailed to
permissionrequest@cengage.com

Library of Congress Control Number: 2013937015

ISBN-13: 978-1-285-16786-2
ISBN-10: 1-285-16786-4

Cengage Learning
20 Channel Center Street
Boston, MA 02210
USA

Cengage Learning is a leading provider of customized learning solutions with office locations around the globe, including Singapore, the United Kingdom, Australia, Mexico, Brazil, and Japan. Locate your local office at:
international.cengage.com/region

Cengage Learning products are represented in Canada by Nelson Education, Ltd.

To learn more about Cengage Learning, visit **www.cengage.com**

Purchase any of our products at your local college bookstore or at our preferred online store at **www.cengagebrain.com**

Printed in the United States of America
2 3 4 5 6 7 14

Microsoft® POWERPOINT® 2013
INTRODUCTORY

Contents

Microsoft **Office 365**

Office 365 Essentials

Microsoft **PowerPoint 2013**

CHAPTER ONE
Creating and Editing a Presentation with Pictures

Preface

The Shelly Cashman Series® offers the finest textbooks in computer education. We are proud that since Mircosoft Office 4.3, our series of Microsoft Office textbooks have been the most widely used books in education. With each new edition of our Office books, we make significant improvements based on the software and comments made by instructors and students. For this Microsoft PowerPoint 2013 text, the Shelly Cashman Series development team carefully reviewed our pedagogy and analyzed its effectiveness in teaching today's Office student. Students today read less, but need to retain more. They need not only to be able to perform skills, but to retain those skills and know how to apply them to different settings. Today's students need to be continually engaged and challenged to retain what they're learning.

With this Microsoft PowerPoint 2013 text, we continue our commitment to focusing on the users and how they learn best.

Objectives of This Textbook

Microsoft PowerPoint 2013: Introductory is intended for a first course on PowerPoint 2013. No experience with a computer is assumed, and no mathematics beyond the high school freshman level is required. The objectives of this book are:

- To offer an introduction to Microsoft PowerPoint 2013

- To expose students to practical examples of the computer as a useful tool

- To acquaint students with the proper procedures to create presentations suitable for coursework, professional purposes, and personal use

- To help students discover the underlying functionality of PowerPoint 2013 so they can become more productive

- To develop an exercise-oriented approach that allows learning by doing

The Shelly Cashman Approach

A Proven Pedagogy with an Emphasis on Project Planning

Each chapter presents a practical problem to be solved within a project planning framework. The project orientation is strengthened by the use of the Roadmap, which provides a visual framework for the project. Step-by-step instructions with supporting screens guide students through the steps. Instructional steps are supported by the Q&A, Experimental Step, and BTW features.

A Visually Engaging Book that Maintains Student Interest

The step-by-step tasks, with supporting figures, provide a rich visual experience for the student. Call-outs on the screens that present both explanatory and navigational information provide students with information they need when they need to know it.

Supporting Reference Materials (Quick Reference)

With the Quick Reference, students can quickly look up information about a single task, such as keyboard shortcuts, and find page references to where in the book the task is illustrated.

Integration of the World Wide Web

The World Wide Web is integrated into the PowerPoint 2013 learning experience with (1) BTW annotations; (2) BTW, Q&A, and Quick Reference Summary Web pages; and (3) the Learn Online resources for each chapter.

End-of-Chapter Student Activities

Extensive end-of-chapter activities provide a variety of reinforcement opportunities for students to apply and expand their skills through individual and group work. To complete some of these assignments, you will be required to use the Data Files for Students. Visit www.cengage.com/ct/studentdownload for detailed access instructions or contact your instructor for information about accessing the required files.

New to this Edition

Enhanced Coverage of Critical Thinking Skills

A New Consider This element poses thought-provoking questions throughout each chapter, providing an increased emphasis on critical thinking and problem-solving skills. Also, every task in the project now includes a reason *why* the students are performing the task and *why* the task is necessary.

Enhanced Retention and Transference

A new Roadmap element provides a visual framework for each project, showing students where they are in the process of creating each project, and reinforcing the context of smaller tasks by showing how they fit into the larger project.

Integration of Office with Cloud and Web Technologies

A new Lab focuses entirely on integrating cloud and web technologies with PowerPoint 2013, using technologies like blogs, social networks, and SkyDrive.

More Personalization

Each chapter project includes an optional instruction for the student to personalize his or her solution, if required by an instructor, making each student's solution unique.

More Collaboration

A new Research and Collaboration project has been added to the Consider This: Your Turn assignment at the end of each chapter.

Instructor Resources

The Instructor Resources include both teaching and testing aids and can be accessed via CD-ROM or at www.cengage.com/login.

Instructor's Manual Includes lecture notes summarizing the chapter sections, figures and boxed elements found in every chapter, teacher tips, classroom activities, lab activities, and quick quizzes in Microsoft Word files.

Syllabus Easily customizable sample syllabi that cover policies, assignments, exams, and other course information.

Figure Files Illustrations for every figure in the textbook in electronic form.

Powerpoint Presentations A multimedia lecture presentation system that provides slides for each chapter. Presentations are based on chapter objectives.

Solutions to Exercises Includes solutions for all end-of-chapter and chapter reinforcement exercises.

Test Bank & Test Engine Test banks include 112 questions for every chapter, featuring objective-based and critical thinking question types, and including page number references and figure references, when appropriate. Also included is the test engine, ExamView, the ultimate tool for your objective-based testing needs.

Data Files for Students Includes all the files that are required by students to complete the exercises.

Additional Activities for Students Consists of Chapter Reinforcement Exercises, which are true/false, multiple-choice, and short answer questions that help students gain confidence in the material learned.

Learn Online

cengagebrain.com is the premier destination for purchasing or renting Cengage Learning textbooks, eBooks, eChapters, and study tools at a significant discount (eBooks up to 50% off Print). In addition, cengagebrain.com provides direct access to all digital products, including eBooks, eChapters, and digital solutions, such as CourseMate and SAM, regardless of where purchased. The following are some examples of what is available for this product on www.cengagebrain.com.

Student Companion Site The Student Companion Site reinforces chapter terms and concepts using true/false questions, multiple choice questions, short answer questions, flash cards, practice tests, and learning games, all available for no additional cost at www.cengagebrain.com.

SAM: Skills Assessment Manager Get your students workplace-ready with SAM, the market-leading proficiency-based assessment and training solution for Microsoft Office! SAM's active, hands-on environment helps students master Microsoft Office skills and computer concepts that are essential to academic and career success, delivering the most comprehensive online learning solution for your course! Through skill-based assessments, interactive trainings, business-centric projects, and comprehensive remediation, SAM engages students in mastering the latest Microsoft Office programs on their own, giving instructors more time to focus on teaching. Computer concepts labs supplement instruction of important technology-related topics and issues through engaging simulations and interactive, auto-graded assessments. With enhancements including streamlined course setup, more robust grading and reporting features, and the integration of fully interactive MindTap Readers containing Cengage Learning's premier textbook content, SAM provides the best teaching and learning solution for your course.

MindLinks MindLinks is a new Cengage Learning Service designed to provide the best possible user experience and facilitate the highest levels of learning retention and outcomes, enabled through a deep integration of Cengage Learning's digital suite into an instructor's Learning Management System (LMS). MindLinks works on any LMS that supports the IMS Basic LTI open standard. Advanced features, including gradebook exchange, are the result of active, enhanced LTI collaborations with industry-leading LMS partners to drive the evolving technology standards forward.

course|notes™
quick reference guide

CourseNotes

Cengage Learning's CourseNotes are six-panel quick reference cards that reinforce the most important and widely used features of a software application in a visual and user-friendly format. CourseNotes serve as a great reference tool during and after the course. CourseNotes are available for software applications, such as Microsoft Office 2013. There are also topic-based CourseNotes available for Best Practices in Social Networking, Hot Topics in Technology, and Web 2.0. Visit www.cengagebrain.com to learn more!

About Our Covers

The Shelly Cashman Series is continually updating our approach and content to reflect the way today's students learn and experience new technology. This focus on student success is reflected on our covers, which feature real students from The University of Rhode Island using the Shelly Cashman Series in their courses, and reflect the varied ages and backgrounds of the students learning with our books. When you use the Shelly Cashman Series, you can be assured that you are learning computer skills using the most effective courseware available.

Textbook Walk-Through

The Shelly Cashman Series Pedagogy: Project-Based — Step-by-Step — Variety of Assessments

Roadmaps provide a visual framework for each project, showing the students where they are in the process of creating each project.

Step-by-step instructions provide a context beyond the point-and-click. Each step provides information on why students are performing each task and what will occur as a result.

For an introduction to Windows and instruction about how to perform basic Windows tasks, read the Office and Windows chapter at the beginning of this book, where you can learn how to resize windows, change screen resolution, create folders, move and rename files, use Windows Help, and much more.

Roadmap

In this chapter, you will learn how to create the slides shown in Figure 1–1 on the previous page. The following roadmap identifies general activities you will perform as you progress through this chapter:

1. INSERT the four PRESENTATION SLIDES, using various layouts.
2. ENTER the TEXT for the slides.
3. FORMAT the TEXT on each slide.
4. INSERT GRAPHICAL ELEMENTS, including photos and an illustration.
5. SIZE AND POSITION the graphical elements.
6. ENHANCE the SLIDE SHOW by adding a closing slide and transition.
7. DISPLAY AND PRINT the SLIDES and a handout.

At the beginning of step instructions throughout the chapter, you will see an abbreviated form of this roadmap. The abbreviated roadmap uses colors to indicate chapter progress: gray means the chapter is beyond that activity; blue means the task being shown is covered in that activity, and black means that activity is yet to be covered. For example, the following abbreviated roadmap indicates the chapter would be showing a task in the 5 Size & Position activity.

1 INSERT PRESENTATION SLIDES | 2 ENTER TEXT | 3 FORMAT TEXT | 4 INSERT GRAPHICAL ELEMENTS

5 SIZE & POSITION | 6 ENHANCE SLIDE SHOW | 7 DISPLAY & PRINT SLIDES

Use the abbreviated roadmap as a progress guide while you read or step through the instructions in this chapter.

To Run PowerPoint

One of the few differences between Windows 7 and Windows 8 occurs

If you are using a computer to step through the project in this chapter and you want your screens to match the figures in this book, you should change resolution to 1366 × 768. For information about how to change a solution, refer to the Office and Windows chapter at the beginning

owing steps, which assume Windows 8 is running, use the Start search box to run PowerPoint based on a typical installation. You sk your instructor how to run PowerPoint on your computer. For mple of the procedure summarized below, refer to the Office and ter.

Start screen for a PowerPoint 2013 tile. If your Start screen contains a nt 2013 tile, tap or click it to run PowerPoint and then proceed to Step 5; if creen does not contain the PowerPoint 2013 tile, proceed to the next step for the PowerPoint app.

rom the right edge of the screen or point to the upper-right corner of the display the Charms bar and then tap or click the Search charm on the Charms display the Search menu.

werPoint as the search text in the Search box and watch the search results the Apps list.

To Change the Theme

1 INSERT PRESENTATION SLIDES | 2 ENTER TEXT | 3 FORMAT TEXT | 4 INSERT GRAPHICAL ELEMENTS

5 SIZE & POSITION | 6 ENHANCE SLIDE SHOW | 7 DISPLAY & PRINT SLIDES

A theme provides consistency in design and color throughout the entire presentation by setting the color scheme, font set, and layout of a presentation. This collection of formatting choices includes a set of colors (the Theme Colors group), a set of heading and content text fonts (the Theme Fonts group), and a set of lines and fill effects (the Theme Effects group). These groups allow you to choose and change the appearance of all the slides or individual slides in your presentation. *Why? At any time while creating the slide deck, you may decide to switch the theme so that the slides have a totally different appearance.* The following steps change the theme for this presentation from Ion to Facet.

1
- Tap or click DESIGN on the ribbon to display the DESIGN tab (Figure 1–36).

Figure 1–36

Explanatory callouts summarize what is happening on screen.

Navigational callouts in red show students where to click.

2
- Tap or click the More button (DESIGN tab | Themes group) to expand the gallery, which shows more theme gallery options (Figure 1–37).

Experiment
- If you are using a mouse, point to various document themes in the Themes gallery and watch the colors and fonts change on the title slide.

Figure 1–37

Experiment Steps within the step-by-step instructions encourage students to explore, experiment, and take advantage of the features of the Office 2013 user interface. These steps are not necessary to complete the projects, but are designed to increase confidence with the software and build problem-solving skills.

Q&A Are the themes displayed in a specific order?
They are listed in alphabetical order in two groups: Facet to Wisp beginning in the first row and Banded to Wood Type beginning in the second row. If you are using a mouse and point to a theme, a ScreenTip with the theme's name appears on the screen.

3
- Tap or click the Facet theme to apply this theme to all four slides (Figure 1–38).

Q&A The Facet theme is visible in the first row of the gallery, so why did I click the More button to expand the gallery?
While it is not necessary to view all the thumbnails, it sometimes is helpful to see all possible themes when deciding which one best fits the presentation.

If I decide at some future time that this design does not fit the theme of my presentation, can I apply a different design?
Yes. You can repeat these steps at any time while creating your presentation.

Q&A boxes anticipate questions students may have when working through the steps and provide additional information about what they are doing right where they need it.

Creating a Title Slide

When you open a new presentation, the default **Title Slide** layout appears. The purpose of this layout is to introduce the presentation to the audience. PowerPoint includes other standard layouts for each of the themes. The slide layouts are set up in **landscape orientation**, where the slide width is greater than its height. In landscape orientation, the slide size is preset to 10 inches wide and 7.5 inches high when printed on a standard sheet of paper measuring 11 inches wide and 8.5 inches high.

Placeholders are boxes with dotted or hatch-marked borders that are displayed when you create a new slide. Most layouts have both a title text placeholder and at least one content placeholder. Depending on the particular slide layout selected, title and subtitle placeholders are displayed for the slide title and subtitle; a content text placeholder is displayed for text, art, or a table, chart, picture, graphic, or movie. The title slide has two text placeholders where you can type the main heading, or title, of a new slide and the subtitle.

With the exception of the Blank slide layout, PowerPoint assumes every new slide has a title. To make creating a presentation easier, any text you type after a new slide appears becomes title text in the title text placeholder. The following steps create the title slide for this presentation.

To Enter the Presentation Title

1 INSERT PRESENTATION SLIDES | 2 ENTER TEXT | 3 FORMAT TEXT | 4 INSERT GRAPHICAL ELEMENTS
5 SIZE & POSITION | 6 ENHANCE SLIDE SHOW | 7 DISPLAY & PRINT SLIDES

The presentation title for Project 1 is Healthy Hydration. *Why? The presentation discusses the importance of drinking water while exercising, and blue is the color associated with water.* The following step creates the slide show's title.

1
• Tap or click the label, 'Tap to add title', or, 'Click to add title', located inside the title text placeholder to select the placeholder (Figure 1–5).

Figure 1–5

Chapter Summary

In this chapter you have learned how to apply and change a documen
text slides with a bulleted list, insert photos and an illustration a
and edit text, add a slide transition, view the presentation in Slide S
items listed below include all the new PowerPoint skills you have le
by activity.

Enter and Edit Text
Enter the Presentation Title (PPT 7)
Enter the Presentation Subtitle Paragraph (PPT 9)
Zoom a Slide (PPT 10)
Add a New Text Slide with a Bulleted List (PPT 15)
Enter a Slide Title (PPT 17)
Type a Multilevel Bulleted List (PPT 18)
Add a Slide with the Title Only Layout (PPT 23)
Add a New Slide and Enter a Slide Title and Headings (PPT 24)
Move to Another Slide in Normal View (PPT 29)
Duplicate a Slide (PPT 41)
Arrange a Slide (PPT 42)
Delete Text in a Placeholder (PPT 43)

Format a Slide
Choose a Document Theme and Variant (PPT 5)
Change the Theme (PPT 26)
Change the Variant (PPT 27)

Format Text
Italicize Text (PPT 11)
Increase Font Size (PPT 12, 22)

Chang
Bold T

Enhance
Insert
(PPT
Insert
Plac
Propor
Move
Add a T

Run and Print a Slide Show
Change Document Properties (PPT 48)
Start Slide Show View (PPT 49)
Move Manually through Slides in a Slide Show (PPT 50)
Print a Presentation (PPT 52)

Select Text and Slide Elements
Select a Paragraph (PPT 11)
Select a Word (PPT 12)
Select a Text Placeholder (PPT 18)
Select a Group of Words (PPT 20)

What decisions will you need to make when creating your next presentation?
Use these guidelines as you complete the assignments in this chapter and create your own slide show decks outside of this class.

1. Determine the content you want to include on your slides.

2. Determine which theme and variant are appropriate.

3. Identify the slide layouts that best communicate your message.

4. Format various text elements to emphasize important points.

   a) Select appropriate font sizes.

   b) Emphasize important words with bold or italic type and color.

5. Locate graphical elements, such as photos and illustrations, that reinforce your message.

   a) Size and position them aesthetically on slides.

6. Determine a storage location for the presentation.

7. Determine the best method for distributing the presentation.

Textbook Walk-Through

How should you submit solutions to questions in the assignments identified with a ⚙ symbol?
Every assignment in this book contains one or more questions identified with a ⚙ symbol. These questions require you to think beyond the assigned presentation. Present your solutions to the questions in the format required by your instructor. Possible formats may include one or more of these options: write the answer; create a document that contains the answer; present your answer to the class; discuss your answer in a group; record the answer as audio or video using a webcam, smartphone, or portable media player; or post answers on a blog, wiki, or website.

> **Apply Your Knowledge** This exercise usually requires students to open and manipulate a file that parallels the activities learned in the chapter.

Apply Your Knowledge

Reinforce the skills and apply the concepts you learned in this chapter.

Modifying Character Formats and Paragraph Levels and Moving an Illustration
Note: To complete this assignment, you will be required to use the Data Files for Students. Visit www.cengage.com/ct/studentdownload for detailed instructions or contact your instructor for information about accessing the required files.

Instructions: Run PowerPoint. Open the presentation, Apply 1-1 Effective Writing, from the Data Files for Students.
   The two slides in the presentation discuss steps to follow when writing a persuasive essay. The document you open is an unformatted presentation. You are to modify the document theme, indent the paragraphs, resize and move the photo, and format the text so the slides look like Figure 1–80 on this page and the next page.

Perform the following tasks:
1. Change the document theme to Ion.
2. On the title slide, use your name in place of Student Name and bold and italicize your name.
3. If requested by your instructor, change your first name to your grandmother's first name on the title slide.
4. Increase the title text font size to 60 point. Size and position the photo using the Smart Guides to align the image with the bottom of the title placeholder, as shown in Figure 1–80a.

(a) Slide 1 (Title Slide with a Picture)
Figure 1–80

Continued >

PPT 58   PowerPoint Chapter 1   Creating and Editing a Presentation with Pic...

STUDENT ASSIGNMENTS

Apply Your Knowledge *continued*

5. On Slide 2, increase the indent of the third and f... Then combine paragraphs six and seven (To chan... to read, To change readers' minds or confirm opi... the indent of this paragraph to second level.
6. Save the presentation using the file name, Apply
7. Submit the revised document in the format speci...
8. ⚙ In Step 5 you combined two paragraphs. How

Preparing to Write

▸ Assess the controversial issue
▸ Consider your audience
   ▸ What do readers know about the topic?
   ▸ Do they have opinions on this issue?
▸ Determine your purpose
   ▸ To change readers' minds or confirm opinions?

second-level paragraphs

combined paragraph

(b) Slide 2 (Multilevel Bulleted List)
Figure 1–80 (Continued)

Extend Your Knowledge

Extend the skills you learned in this chapter and experiment with new skills. You may need to use Help to complete the assignment.

Changing Slide Theme, Layout, and Text
Note: To complete this assignment, you will be required to use the Data Files for Students. Visit www.cengage.com/ct/studentdownload for detailed instructions or contact your instructor for information about accessing the required files.

Instructions: Run PowerPoint. Open the presentation that you are going to prepare for your brother's horseback riding business, Extend 1-1 Horseback Riding, from the Data Files for Students. You will choose a theme, format slides, and create a closing slide.

Perform the following tasks:
1. Apply an appropriate document theme.
2. On Slide 1 (Figure 1–81), use your name in place of Student Name. Format the text on this slide using techniques you learned in this chapter, such as changing the font size and color and bolding and italicizing words.
3. Delete the bullets in the subtitle text.
4. Resize the photo and move it to an appropriate area on the slide.
5. On Slide 2, add bullets to the paragraphs in the Beginners and Advanced boxes, and then change the look of the default bullets.

> **Extend Your Knowledge** projects at the end of each chapter allow students to extend and expand on the skills learned within the chapter. Students use critical thinking to experiment with new skills to complete each project.

6. On Slide 3, create paragraphs and adjust the paragraph levels to create a bulleted list. Edit the text so that the slide meets the 7 × 7 rule, which states that each line should have a maximum of seven words, and each slide should have a maximum of seven lines.

7. Create an appropriate closing slide using the title slide as a guide. Change the title text to, See you at the Trails!

8. The slides contain a variety of pictures downloaded from Office.com. Size and move them when necessary.

9. Apply an appropriate transition to all slides.

10. Save the presentation using the file name, Extend 1-1 Horseback Riding Lessons.

11. Submit the revised document in the format specified by your instructor.

12. If requested by your instructor, replace the word, you, with your mother's first name on the closing slide.

13. ✺ In this assignment, you changed the bullet style on Slide 2. Which bullet style did you select and why?

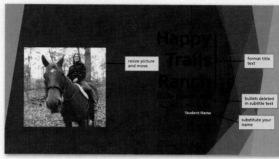

Figure 1–81

Analyze, Correct, Improve

Analyze a presentation, correct all errors, and improve it.

Correcting Formatting and List Levels

Note: To complete this assignment, you will be required to use the Data Files for Students. Visit www.cengage.com/ct/studentdownload for detailed instructions or contact your instructor for information about accessing the required files.

Instructions: Run PowerPoint. Open the presentation, Analyze 1-1 Math Tutor, from the Data Files for Students. As a part-time job while attending college, you decide to tutor students who are struggling with math. You decide to create a presentation promoting your service and begin with this document. Modify the slides by making the indicated corrections and improvements.

Continued >

In the Labs

Design and/or create a presentation using the guidelines
chapter. Labs 1 and 2, which increase in difficulty, requ
what you learned in the chapter; Lab 3 requires you to
and web technologies, by learning and investigating o

Lab 1: **Creating a Presentation wit Bulleted Lists, a Closing Slide, and**

Problem: You are majoring in accounting and work part-ti
have asked you numerous times what documents they shoul
returns. You decide to put together a presentation that woul
to organize personal documents. You develop the outline sh
the PowerPoint presentation shown in Figures 1–84a throu

Creating and Editing

Files or Piles
　　Document Storage and Retention at Home

Store and Retain
　　In Home Office Safe
　　　　Tax records for six years
　　　　Pay stubs until W2 arrives
　　　　Credit card statements
　　　　Canceled checks
　　　　Utility bills
　　In Bank Safe Deposit Box
　　　　Wills, deeds, and titles
　　　　Birth and death certificates
　　　　Passports
　　　　Military records

Keep Indefinitely
　　Personal health records
　　Medical history
　　Retirement benefit statements

General Rules
　　Shred documents showing personal information
　　Organize and store chronologically
　　Keep list of important documents
　　　　State their location
　　　　Share with relative or friend

Figure 1–83

Continued >

Textbook Walk-Through

Figure 1–87   Slide 1 (Title Slide)

✸ Consider This: Your Turn

Apply your creative thinking and problem-solving skills to design and implement a solution.

1. Design and Create a Presentation about Mars Exploration

Personal

Part 1:   Your astronomy class is studying the solar system, and you have been assigned the topic of the Mars Curiosity rover and its exploration of that planet. You have learned that the rover was launched from Cape Canaveral, Florida, on November 26, 2011, and landed in the Gale Crater on Mars on August 6, 2012. The mission was scheduled to last two years and had the major goal of assessing whether Mars was or is capable of supporting life. The Curiosity rover is the size of a car and has a MastCam equipped with two camera systems to take photos of the landscape as it maneuvers around the rocky surface. The rover also can scoop up samples of the Martian soil, fire a laser at rocks as far away as nine feet (2.7 meters), and make weather station readings. Use the concepts and techniques you learned in the chapter to create a PowerPoint presentation with a suitable theme, a title slide, and three text slides with bulleted lists. Add pictures from Office.com and apply a transition. Submit your assignment in the format specified by your instructor.

Part 2:   ✸ You made several decisions while creating the presentation in this assignment: what theme to use, where to place text, how to format the text (font, font size, paragraph alignment, bulleted paragraphs, italics, bold, color). You also decided which graphical images to use, where to position the graphical images, if a closing slide would be useful, and which transition would be most effective. What was the rationale behind each of these decisions? When you proofed the document, what further revisions did you make and why? Where would you recommend showing this slide show?

Continued >

Consider This: Your Turn
exercises call on students to apply creative thinking and problem solving skills to design and implement a solution.

Office 2013 and Windows 8: Essential Concepts and Skills

Microsoft product screen shots used with permission from Microsoft Corporation.

Objectives

You will have mastered the material in this chapter when you can:

- Use a touch screen
- Perform basic mouse operations
- Start Windows and sign in to an account
- Identify the objects in the Windows 8 desktop
- Identify the apps in and versions of Microsoft Office 2013
- Run an app
- Identify the components of the Microsoft Office ribbon

- Create folders
- Save files
- Change screen resolution
- Perform basic tasks in Microsoft Office apps
- Manage files
- Use Microsoft Office Help and Windows Help

Office 2013 and Windows 8: Essential Concepts and Skills

This introductory chapter uses PowerPoint 2013 to cover features and functions common to Office 2013 apps, as well as the basics of Windows 8.

Roadmap

In this chapter, you will learn how to perform basic tasks in Windows and PowerPoint. The following roadmap identifies general activities you will perform as you progress through this chapter:

1. SIGN IN to an account
2. USE WINDOWS
3. USE Features in PowerPoint that are Common across Office APPS
4. FILE and Folder MANAGEMENT
5. SWITCH between APPS
6. SAVE and Manage FILES
7. CHANGE SCREEN RESOLUTION
8. EXIT APPS
9. USE ADDITIONAL Office APP FEATURES
10. USE Office and Windows HELP

At the beginning of the step instructions throughout the chapter, you will see an abbreviated form of this roadmap. The abbreviated roadmap uses colors to indicate chapter progress: gray means the chapter is beyond that activity, blue means the task being shown is covered in that activity, and black means that activity is yet to be covered. For example, the following abbreviated roadmap indicates the chapter would be showing a task in the 3 USE APPS activity.

1 SIGN IN | 2 USE WINDOWS | 3 USE APPS | 4 FILE MANAGEMENT | 5 SWITCH APPS | 6 SAVE FILES
7 CHANGE SCREEN RESOLUTION | 8 EXIT APPS | 9 USE ADDITIONAL APP FEATURES | 10 USE HELP

Use the abbreviated roadmap as a progress guide while you read or step through the instructions in this chapter.

Introduction to the Windows 8 Operating System

Windows 8 is the newest version of Microsoft Windows, which is a popular and widely used operating system. An **operating system** is a computer program (set of computer instructions) that coordinates all the activities of computer hardware, such as memory, storage devices, and printers, and provides the capability for you to communicate with the computer.

The Windows operating system simplifies the process of working with documents and apps by organizing the manner in which you interact with the computer. Windows is used to run apps. An **app** (short for application) consists of programs designed to make users more productive and/or assist them with personal tasks, such as creating presentations or browsing the web.

The Windows 8 interface begins with the **Start screen**, which shows tiles (Figure 1). A **tile** is a shortcut to an app or other content. The tiles on the Start screen include installed apps that you use regularly. From the Start screen, you can choose which apps to run using a touch screen, mouse, or other input device.

Figure 1

Using a Touch Screen and a Mouse

Windows users who have computers or devices with touch screen capability can interact with the screen using gestures. A **gesture** is a motion you make on a touch screen with the tip of one or more fingers or your hand. Touch screens are convenient because they do not require a separate device for input. Table 1 on the next page presents common ways to interact with a touch screen.

If you are using your finger on a touch screen and are having difficulty completing the steps in this chapter, consider using a stylus. Many people find it easier to be precise with a stylus than with a finger. In addition, with a stylus you see the pointer. If you still are having trouble completing the steps with a stylus, try using a mouse.

Table 1 Touch Screen Gestures		
Motion	**Description**	**Common Uses**
Tap	Quickly touch and release one finger one time.	Activate a link (built-in connection) Press a button Run a program or an app
Double-tap	Quickly touch and release one finger two times.	Run a program or an app Zoom in (show a smaller area on the screen, so that contents appear larger) at the location of the double-tap
Press and hold	Press and hold one finger to cause an action to occur, or until an action occurs.	Display a shortcut menu (immediate access to allowable actions) Activate a mode enabling you to move an item with one finger to a new location
Drag, or slide	Press and hold one finger on an object and then move the finger to the new location.	Move an item around the screen Scroll
Swipe	Press and hold one finger and then move the finger horizontally or vertically on the screen.	Select an object Swipe from edge to display a bar such as the Charms bar, Apps bar, and Navigation bar (all discussed later)
Stretch	Move two fingers apart.	Zoom in (show a smaller area on the screen, so that contents appear larger)
Pinch	Move two fingers together.	Zoom out (show a larger area on the screen, so that contents appear smaller)

© 2014 Cengage Learning

BTW
BTWs
For a complete list of the BTWs found in the margins of this book, visit the BTW resource on the Student Companion Site located on www.cengagebrain.com. For detailed instructions about accessing available resources, visit www.cengage.com/ct/studentdownload or contact your instructor for information about accessing the required files.

BTW
Touch Screen Differences
The Office and Windows interfaces may vary if you are using a touch screen. For this reason, you might notice that the function or appearance of your touch screen differs slightly from this chapter's presentation.

CONSIDER THIS

Will your screen look different if you are using a touch screen?
The Windows and Microsoft Office interface varies slightly if you are using a touch screen. For this reason, you might notice that your Windows or PowerPoint screens look slightly different from the screens in this book.

Windows users who do not have touch screen capabilities typically work with a mouse that has at least two buttons. For a right-handed user, the left button usually is the primary mouse button, and the right mouse button is the secondary mouse button. Left-handed people, however, can reverse the function of these buttons.

Table 2 explains how to perform a variety of mouse operations. Some apps also use keys in combination with the mouse to perform certain actions. For example, when you hold down the CTRL key while rolling the mouse wheel, text on the screen may become larger or smaller based on the direction you roll the wheel. The function of the mouse buttons and the wheel varies depending on the app.

Table 2 Mouse Operations

Operation	Mouse Action	Example*
Point	Move the mouse until the pointer on the desktop is positioned on the item of choice.	Position the pointer on the screen.
Click	Press and release the primary mouse button, which usually is the left mouse button.	Select or deselect items on the screen or run an app or app feature.
Right-click	Press and release the secondary mouse button, which usually is the right mouse button.	Display a shortcut menu.
Double-click	Quickly press and release the primary mouse button twice without moving the mouse.	Run an app or app feature.
Triple-click	Quickly press and release the primary mouse button three times without moving the mouse.	Select a paragraph.
Drag	Point to an item, hold down the primary mouse button, move the item to the desired location on the screen, and then release the mouse button.	Move an object from one location to another or draw pictures.
Right-drag	Point to an item, hold down the right mouse button, move the item to the desired location on the screen, and then release the right mouse button.	Display a shortcut menu after moving an object from one location to another.
Rotate wheel	Roll the wheel forward or backward.	Scroll vertically (up and down).
Free-spin wheel	Whirl the wheel forward or backward so that it spins freely on its own.	Scroll through many pages in seconds.
Press wheel	Press the wheel button while moving the mouse.	Scroll continuously.
Tilt wheel	Press the wheel toward the right or left.	Scroll horizontally (left and right).
Press thumb button	Press the button on the side of the mouse with your thumb.	Move forward or backward through webpages and/or control media, games, etc.

*Note: The examples presented in this column are discussed as they are demonstrated in this chapter.

© 2014 Cengage Learning

Scrolling

A **scroll bar** is a horizontal or vertical bar that appears when the contents of an area may not be visible completely on the screen (Figure 2). A scroll bar contains **scroll arrows** and a **scroll box** that enable you to view areas that currently cannot be seen on the screen. Tapping or clicking the up and down scroll arrows moves the screen content up or down one line. You also can tap or click above or below the scroll box to move up or down a section, or drag the scroll box up or down to move to a specific location.

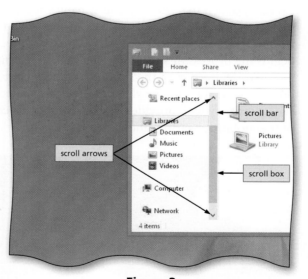

Figure 2

BTW

Pointer
If you are using a touch screen, the pointer may not appear on the screen as you perform touch gestures. The pointer will reappear when you begin using the mouse.

BTW

Minimize Wrist Injury
Computer users frequently switch between the keyboard and the mouse while creating a presentation; such switching strains the wrist. To help prevent wrist injury, minimize switching. For instance, if your fingers already are on the keyboard, use keyboard keys to scroll. If your hand already is on the mouse, use the mouse to scroll. If your hand is on the touch screen, use touch gestures to scroll.

What should you do if you are running Windows 7 instead of Windows 8?
Although Windows 8 includes several user interface and feature enhancements, many of the steps in this book work in both Windows 7 and Windows 8. If you have any questions about differences between the two operating systems or how to perform tasks in an earlier version of Windows, contact your instructor.

CONSIDER THIS

Keyboard Shortcuts

In many cases, you can use the keyboard instead of the mouse to accomplish a task. To perform tasks using the keyboard, you press one or more keyboard keys, sometimes identified as a **keyboard shortcut**. Some keyboard shortcuts consist of a single key, such as the F1 key. For example, to obtain help in many apps, you can press the F1 key. Other keyboard shortcuts consist of multiple keys, in which case a plus sign separates the key names, such as CTRL+ESC. This notation means to press and hold down the first key listed, press one or more additional keys, and then release all keys. For example, to display the Start screen, press CTRL+ESC, that is, hold down the CTRL key, press the ESC key, and then release both keys.

Starting Windows

It is not unusual for multiple people to use the same computer in a work, educational, recreational, or home setting. Windows enables each user to establish a **user account**, which identifies to Windows the resources, such as apps and storage locations, a user can access when working with the computer.

Each user account has a user name and may have a password and an icon, as well. A **user name** is a unique combination of letters or numbers that identifies a specific user to Windows. A **password** is a private combination of letters, numbers, and special characters associated with the user name that allows access to a user's account resources. An icon is a small image that represents an object, thus a **user icon** is a picture associated with a user name.

When you turn on a computer, Windows starts and displays a **lock screen** consisting of the time and date (Figure 3a). To unlock the screen, swipe up or click the lock screen. Depending on your computer's settings, Windows may or may not display a sign-in screen that shows the user names and user icons for users who have accounts on the computer (Figure 3b). This **sign-in screen** enables you to sign in to your user account and makes the computer available for use. Tapping or clicking the user icon begins the process of signing in, also called logging on, to your user account.

At the bottom of the sign-in screen is the 'Ease of access' button and a Shut down button. Tapping or clicking the 'Ease of access' button displays the Ease of access menu, which provides tools to optimize a computer to accommodate the needs of the mobility, hearing, and vision impaired users. Tapping or clicking the Shut down

Figure 3a

SC Series user icon

Note: To help you locate screen elements that are referenced in the step instructions, such as buttons and commands, this book uses red boxes to point to these screen elements.

Figure 3b

button displays a menu containing commands related to restarting the computer, putting it in a low-power state, and shutting it down. The commands available on your computer may differ.

- The Sleep command saves your work, turns off the computer fans and hard disk, and places the computer in a lower-power state. To wake the computer from sleep mode, press the power button or lift a laptop's cover, and sign in to your account.
- The Shut down command exits running apps, shuts down Windows, and then turns off the computer.
- The Restart command exits running apps, shuts down Windows, and then restarts Windows.

BTW
Q&As
For a complete list of the Q&As found in many of the step-by-step sequences in this book, visit the Q&A resource on the Student Companion Site located on www.cengagebrain.com. For detailed instructions about accessing available resources, visit www.cengage.com/ct/studentdownload or contact your instructor for information about accessing the required files.

To Sign In to an Account

1 SIGN IN | 2 USE WINDOWS | 3 USE APPS | 4 FILE MANAGEMENT | 5 SWITCH APPS | 6 SAVE FILES
7 CHANGE SCREEN RESOLUTION | 8 EXIT APPS | 9 USE ADDITIONAL APP FEATURES | 10 USE HELP

The following steps, which use SC Series as the user name, sign in to an account based on a typical Windows installation. *Why? After starting Windows, you might be required to sign in to an account to access the computer's resources.* You may need to ask your instructor how to sign in to your account. If you are using Windows 7, skip these steps and instead perform the steps in the yellow box that immediately follows these Windows 8 steps.

- Swipe up or click the lock screen (shown in Figure 3a) to display a sign-in screen (shown in Figure 3b).

- Tap or click the user icon (for SC Series, in this case) on the sign-in screen, which depending on settings, either will display a second sign-in screen that contains a Password text box (Figure 4) or will display the Windows Start screen (shown in Figure 5 on the next page).

Q&A

Why do I not see a user icon?
Your computer may require you to type a user name instead of tapping or clicking an icon.

What is a text box?
A text box is a rectangular box in which you type text.

Why does my screen not show a Password text box?
Your account does not require a password.

password text box

SC Series

Submit button

'Ease of access' button

Shut down button

Figure 4

- If Windows displays a sign-in screen with a Password text box, type your password in the text box.

2

- Tap or click the Submit button (shown in Figure 4 on the previous page) to sign in to your account and display the Windows Start screen (Figure 5).

Q&A Why does my Start screen look different from the one in Figure 5?
The Windows Start screen is customizable, and your school or employer may have modified the screen to meet its needs. Also, your screen resolution, which affects the size of the elements on the screen, may differ from the screen resolution used in this book. Later in this chapter, you learn how to change screen resolution.

How do I type if my tablet has no keyboard?
You can use your fingers to press keys on a keyboard that appears on the screen, called an on-screen keyboard, or you can purchase a separate physical keyboard that attaches to or wirelessly communicates with the tablet.

Figure 5

To Sign In to an Account Using Windows 7

If you are using Windows 7, perform these steps to sign in to an account instead of the previous steps that use Windows 8.

1. Click the user icon on the Welcome screen; depending on settings, this either will display a password text box or will sign in to the account and display the Windows 7 desktop.
2. If Windows 7 displays a password text box, type your password in the text box and then click the arrow button to sign in to the account and display the Windows 7 desktop.

The Windows Start Screen

BTW

Modern UI
The new Windows 8 user interface also is referred to as the Modern UI (user interface).

The Windows Start screen provides a scrollable space for you to access apps that have been pinned to the Start screen (shown in Figure 5). Pinned apps appear as tiles on the Start screen. In addition to running apps, you can perform tasks such as pinning apps (placing tiles) on the Start screen, moving the tiles around the Start screen, and unpinning apps (removing tiles) from the Start screen.

If you swipe up from the bottom of or right-click an open space on the Start screen, the App bar will appear. The **App bar** includes a button that enables you to display all of your apps. When working with tiles, the App bar also provides options for manipulating the tiles, such as resizing them.

CONSIDER THIS

How do you pin apps, move tiles, and unpin apps?

- To pin an app, swipe up from the bottom of the Start screen or right-click an open space on the Start screen to display the App bar, tap or click the All apps button on the App bar to display the Apps list, swipe down on or right-click the app you want to pin, and then tap or click the 'Pin to Start' button on the App bar. One way to return to the Start screen is to swipe up from the bottom or right-click an open space in the Apps list and then tap or click the All apps button again.

- To move a tile, drag the tile to the desired location.

- To unpin an app, swipe down on or right-click the app to display the App bar and then tap or click the 'Unpin from Start' button on the App bar.

Introduction to Microsoft Office 2013

Microsoft Office 2013 is the newest version of Microsoft Office, offering features that provide users with better functionality and easier ways to work with the various files they create. These features include enhanced design tools, such as improved picture formatting tools and new themes, shared notebooks for working in groups, mobile versions of Office apps, broadcast presentations for the web, and a digital notebook for managing and sharing multimedia information.

Microsoft Office 2013 Apps

Microsoft Office 2013 includes a wide variety of apps such as Word, PowerPoint, Excel, Access, Outlook, Publisher, OneNote, InfoPath, SharePoint Workspace, and Lync:

- **Microsoft Word 2013**, or Word, is a full-featured word processing app that allows you to create professional-looking documents and revise them easily.
- **Microsoft PowerPoint 2013**, or PowerPoint, is a complete presentation app that enables you to produce professional-looking presentations and then deliver them to an audience.
- **Microsoft Excel 2013**, or Excel, is a powerful spreadsheet app that allows you to organize data, complete calculations, make decisions, graph data, develop professional-looking reports, publish organized data to the web, and access real-time data from websites.
- **Microsoft Access 2013**, or Access, is a database management system that enables you to create a database; add, change, and delete data in the database; ask questions concerning the data in the database; and create forms and reports using the data in the database.
- **Microsoft Outlook 2013**, or Outlook, is a communications and scheduling app that allows you to manage email accounts, calendars, contacts, and access to other Internet content.
- **Microsoft Publisher 2013**, or Publisher, is a desktop publishing app that helps you create professional-quality publications and marketing materials that can be shared easily.
- **Microsoft OneNote 2013**, or OneNote, is a note taking app that allows you to store and share information in notebooks with other people.
- **Microsoft InfoPath Designer 2013**, or InfoPath, is a form development app that helps you create forms for use on the web and gather data from these forms.
- **Microsoft SharePoint Workspace 2013**, or SharePoint, is a collaboration app that allows you to access and revise files stored on your computer from other locations.
- **Microsoft Lync 2013** is a communications app that allows you to use various modes of communications such as instant messaging, videoconferencing, and sharing files and apps.

Microsoft Office 2013 Suites

A **suite** is a collection of individual apps available together as a unit. Microsoft offers a variety of Office suites, including a stand-alone desktop app (boxed software), Microsoft Office 365, and Microsoft Office Web Apps. **Microsoft Office 365**, or Office 365, provides plans that allow organizations to use Office in a mobile setting while also being able to communicate and share files, depending upon the type of plan selected by the organization. **Microsoft Office Web Apps**, or Web Apps, are apps that allow you to edit and share files on the web using the familiar Office interface. Table 3 on the next page outlines the differences among these Office suites.

Apps/Licenses	Office 365 Home Premium	Office 365 Small Business Premium	Office Home & Student	Office Home & Business	Office Professional
Word	✓	✓	✓	✓	✓
PowerPoint	✓	✓	✓	✓	✓
Excel	✓	✓	✓	✓	✓
Access	✓	✓			✓
Outlook	✓	✓		✓	✓
Publisher	✓	✓			✓
Lync		✓			
OneNote			✓	✓	✓
InfoPath		✓			
Licenses	5	5	1	1	1

Table 3 Office Suites

During the Office 365 installation, you select a plan, and depending on your plan, you receive different apps and services. Office Web Apps do not require a local installation and are accessed through SkyDrive and your browser. **SkyDrive** is a cloud storage service that provides storage and other services, such as Office Web Apps, to computer users.

CONSIDER THIS

How do you sign up for a SkyDrive account?

- Use your browser to navigate to skydrive.live.com.

- Create a Microsoft account by tapping or clicking the 'Sign up now' link (or a similar link) and then entering your information to create the account.

- Sign in to SkyDrive using your new account or use it in PowerPoint to save your files on SkyDrive.

Apps in a suite, such as Microsoft Office, typically use a similar interface and share features. Once you are comfortable working with the elements and the interface and performing tasks in one app, the similarity can help you apply the knowledge and skills you have learned to another app(s) in the suite. For example, the process for saving a file in Word is the same in PowerPoint, Excel, and the other Office apps. While briefly showing how to use PowerPoint, this chapter illustrates some of the common functions across the Office apps and identifies the characteristics unique to PowerPoint.

Running and Using an App

To use an app, such as PowerPoint, you must instruct the operating system to run the app. Windows provides many different ways to run an app, one of which is presented in this section (other ways to run an app are presented throughout this chapter). After an app is running, you can use it to perform a variety of tasks. The following pages use PowerPoint to discuss some elements of the Office interface and to perform tasks that are common to other Office apps.

PowerPoint

PowerPoint is a full-featured presentation app that allows you to produce compelling presentations to deliver and share with an audience. A PowerPoint **presentation** also is called a **slide show**. PowerPoint contains many features to design, develop, and organize slides, including formatting text, adding and editing video and audio clips, creating tables and charts, applying artistic effects to pictures, animating graphics, and collaborating with friends and colleagues. You then can turn your presentation into a video, broadcast your slide show on the web, or create a photo album.

To Run an App from the Start Screen

The Start screen contains tiles that allow you to run apps, some of which may be stored on your computer. *Why? When you install an app, for example, tiles are added to the Start screen for the various Office apps included in the suite.*

The following steps, which assume Windows is running, use the Start screen to run PowerPoint based on a typical installation. You may need to ask your instructor how to run PowerPoint on your computer. Although the steps illustrate running the PowerPoint app, the steps to run any Office app are similar. If you are using Windows 7, skip these steps and instead perform the steps in the yellow box that immediately follows these Windows 8 steps.

1

- If necessary, scroll to display the PowerPoint tile on the Start screen (Figure 6).

Q&A
Why does my Start screen look different?
It may look different because of your computer's configuration. The Start screen may be customized for several reasons, such as usage requirements or security restrictions.

What if the app I want to run is not on the Start screen?
You can display all installed apps by swiping up from the bottom of the Start screen or right-clicking an open space on the Start screen and then tapping or clicking the All apps button on the App bar.

How do I scroll on a touch screen?
Use the slide gesture; that is, press and hold your finger on the screen and then move your finger in the direction you wish to scroll.

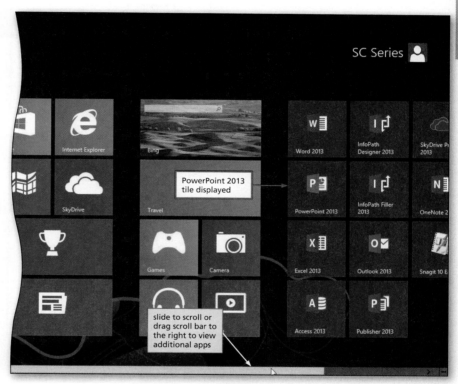

Figure 6

2

- Tap or click the PowerPoint 2013 tile to run the PowerPoint app and display the PowerPoint start screen (Figure 7).

Figure 7

• Tap or click the Blank Presentation thumbnail on the PowerPoint start screen to create a blank PowerPoint document in the PowerPoint window (Figure 8).

Q&A What happens when you run an app?

Some apps provide a means for you to create a blank document, as shown in Figure 7 on the previous page; others immediately display a blank document in an app window, such as the PowerPoint window shown in Figure 8. A **window** is a rectangular area that displays data and information. The top of a window has a **title bar**, which is a horizontal space that contains the window's name.

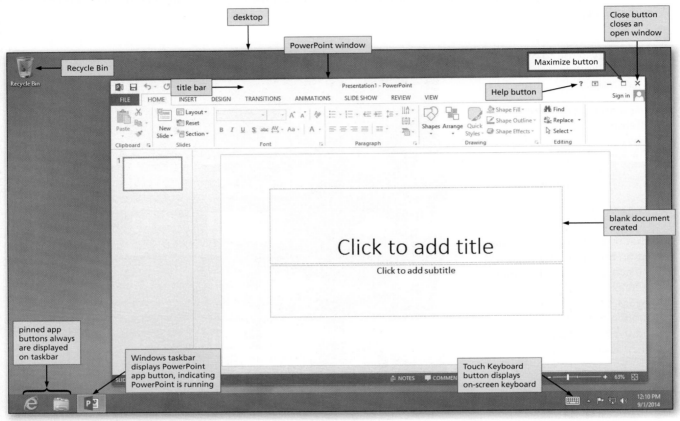

Figure 8

Other Ways

1. Tap or click Search charm on Charms bar, type app name in search box, tap or click app name in results list
2. Double-tap or double-click file created in app you want to run

BTW

Touch Keyboard

To display the on-screen touch keyboard, tap the Touch Keyboard button on the Windows taskbar. When finished using the touch keyboard, tap the X button on the touch keyboard to close the keyboard.

TO RUN AN APP USING THE START MENU USING WINDOWS 7

If you are using Windows 7, perform these steps to run PowerPoint using the Start menu instead of the previous steps that use Windows 8.

1. Click the Start button on the Windows 7 taskbar to display the Start menu.

2. Click All Programs at the bottom of the left pane on the Start menu to display the All Programs list.

3. If the PowerPoint app is located in a folder, click, or scroll to and then click, the folder in the All Programs list to display a list of the folder's contents.

4. Click, or scroll to and then click, the app name (PowerPoint, in this case) in the list to run the selected app.

Windows Desktop

When you run an app in Windows, it may appear in an on-screen work area app, called the **desktop** (shown in Figure 8). You can perform tasks such as placing objects in the desktop, moving the objects around the desktop, and removing items from the desktop.

Some icons also may be displayed in the desktop. For instance, the icon for the **Recycle Bin**, the location of files that have been deleted, appears in the desktop by default. A **file** is a named unit of storage. Files can contain text, images, audio, and video. You can customize your desktop so that icons representing apps and files you use often appear in the desktop.

To Switch between an App and the Start Screen

1 SIGN IN | 2 USE WINDOWS | 3 USE APPS | 4 FILE MANAGEMENT | 5 SWITCH APPS | 6 SAVE FILES
7 CHANGE SCREEN RESOLUTION | 8 EXIT APPS | 9 USE ADDITIONAL APP FEATURES | 10 USE HELP

While working with an app, such as PowerPoint, or in the desktop, you easily can return to the Start screen. The following steps switch from the PowerPoint app to the Start screen. *Why? Returning to the Start screen allows you to run any of your other apps.* If you are using Windows 7, read these steps without performing them because Windows 7 does not have a Start screen.

- Swipe in from the left edge of the screen, and then back to the left, or point to the lower-left corner of the PowerPoint app to display a thumbnail of the Start screen (Figure 9).

Figure 9

- Tap or click the thumbnail of the Start screen to display the Start screen (Figure 10).

- Tap or click the Desktop tile to redisplay the PowerPoint app in the desktop (shown in Figure 8).

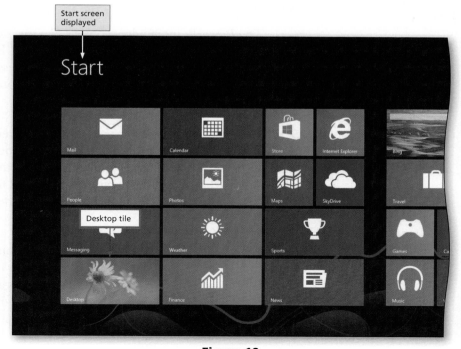

Figure 10

Other Ways

1. Press WINDOWS key to display Start screen

1 SIGN IN | 2 USE WINDOWS | 3 USE APPS | 4 FILE MANAGEMENT | 5 SWITCH APPS | 6 SAVE FILES
7 CHANGE SCREEN RESOLUTION | 8 EXIT APPS | 9 USE ADDITIONAL APP FEATURES | 10 USE HELP

To Maximize a Window

Sometimes content is not visible completely in a window. One method of displaying the entire contents of a window is to **maximize** it, or enlarge the window so that it fills the entire screen. The following step maximizes the PowerPoint window; however, any Office app's window can be maximized using this step. *Why? A maximized window provides the most space available for using the app.*

- If the PowerPoint window is not maximized already, tap or click the Maximize button (shown in Figure 8 on page OFF 12) next to the Close button on the window's title bar to maximize the window (Figure 11).

Q&A

What happened to the Maximize button?
It changed to a Restore Down button, which you can use to return a window to its size and location before you maximized it.

How do I know whether a window is maximized?
A window is maximized if it fills the entire display area and the Restore Down button is displayed on the title bar.

Figure 11

Other Ways

1. Double-tap or double-click title bar   2. Drag title bar to top of screen

PowerPoint Document Window, Ribbon, and Elements Common to Office Apps

The PowerPoint window consists of a variety of components to make your work more efficient and documents more professional. These include the document window, ribbon, mini toolbar, shortcut menus, Quick Access Toolbar, and Microsoft Account area. Most of these components are common to other Microsoft Office apps; others are unique to PowerPoint.

Scroll Bars   You use a scroll bar to display different portions of a presentation in the document window. At the right edge of the document window is a vertical scroll bar. If a slide is too wide to fit in the document window, a horizontal scroll bar also appears at the bottom of the document window. On a scroll bar, the position of the scroll box reflects the location of the portion of the presentation that is displayed in the document window.

Status Bar   The **status bar**, located at the bottom of the document window above the Windows taskbar, presents information about the presentation, the progress of current tasks, and the status of certain commands and keys; it also provides controls for viewing the presentation. As you type text or perform certain tasks, various indicators and buttons may appear on the status bar.

Figure 12

The left side of the status bar in Figure 12 shows the current slide followed by the total number of slides in the presentation and an icon to check spelling. The right side of the status bar includes buttons and controls you can use to change the view of a presentation and adjust the size of the displayed slide.

Ribbon The ribbon, located near the top of the window below the title bar, is the control center in PowerPoint and other Office apps (Figure 13). The ribbon provides easy, central access to the tasks you perform while creating a presentation. The ribbon consists of tabs, groups, and commands. Each **tab** contains a collection of groups, and each **group** contains related commands. When you run an Office app, such as PowerPoint, it initially displays several main tabs, also called default or top-level tabs. All Office apps have a HOME tab, which contains the more frequently used commands.

Figure 13

In addition to the main tabs, the Office apps display **tool tabs**, also called contextual tabs (Figure 14), when you perform certain tasks or work with objects such as pictures or tables. If you insert a picture in a PowerPoint slide, for example, the PICTURE TOOLS tab and its related subordinate FORMAT tab appear, collectively referred to as the PICTURE TOOLS FORMAT tab. When you are finished working with the picture, the PICTURE TOOLS FORMAT tab disappears from the ribbon. PowerPoint and other Office apps determine when tool tabs should appear and disappear based on tasks you perform. Some tool tabs, such as the TABLE TOOLS tab, have more than one related subordinate tab.

Figure 14

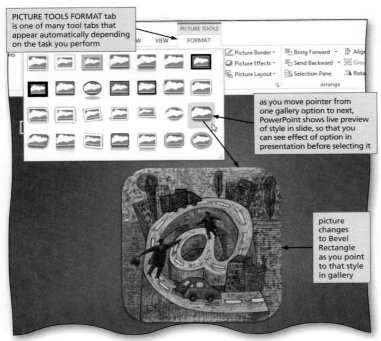

Figure 15

Items on the ribbon include buttons, boxes, and galleries (shown in Figure 13 on the previous page). A **gallery** is a set of choices, often graphical, arranged in a grid or in a list. You can scroll through choices in an in-ribbon gallery by tapping or clicking the gallery's scroll arrows. Or, you can tap or click a gallery's More button to view more gallery options on the screen at a time.

Some buttons and boxes have arrows that, when tapped or clicked, also display a gallery; others always cause a gallery to be displayed when tapped or clicked. Most galleries support **live preview**, which is a feature that allows you to point to a gallery choice and see its effect in the document — without actually selecting the choice (Figure 15). Live preview works only if you are using a mouse; if you are using a touch screen, you will not be able to view live previews.

Figure 16

Some commands on the ribbon display an image to help you remember their function. When you point to a command on the ribbon, all or part of the command glows in a shade of blue, and a ScreenTip appears on the screen. A **ScreenTip** is an on-screen note that provides the name of the command, available keyboard shortcut(s), a description of the command, and sometimes instructions for how to obtain help about the command (Figure 16).

Some groups on the ribbon have a small arrow in the lower-right corner, called a **Dialog Box Launcher**, that when tapped or clicked, displays a dialog box or a task pane with additional options for the group (Figure 17). When presented with a dialog box, you make selections and must close the dialog box before returning to the document. A **task pane**, in contrast to a dialog box, is a window that can remain open and visible while you work in the document.

BTW
Touch Mode
The Office and Windows interfaces may vary if you are using Touch mode. For this reason, you might notice that the function or appearance of your touch screen in PowerPoint differs slightly from this book's presentation.

Figure 17

Mini Toolbar The **mini toolbar**, which appears automatically based on tasks you perform, contains commands related to changing the appearance of text in a document (Figure 18). If you do not use the mini toolbar, it disappears from the screen. The buttons, arrows, and boxes on the mini toolbar vary, depending on whether you are using Touch mode versus Mouse mode. If you press and hold or right-click an item in the document window, PowerPoint displays both the mini toolbar and a shortcut menu, which is discussed in a later section in this chapter.

All commands on the mini toolbar also exist on the ribbon. The purpose of the mini toolbar is to minimize hand or mouse movement.

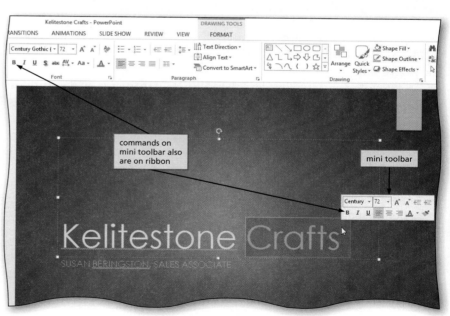

Figure 18

Quick Access Toolbar The **Quick Access Toolbar**, located initially (by default) above the ribbon at the left edge of the title bar, provides convenient, one-tap or one-click access to frequently used commands (shown in Figure 16). The commands on the Quick Access Toolbar always are available, regardless of the task you are performing. The Touch/Mouse Mode button on the Quick Access Toolbar allows you to switch between Touch mode and Mouse mode. If you primarily are using touch gestures, Touch mode will add more space between commands on menus and on the ribbon so that they are easier to tap. While touch gestures are convenient ways to interact with Office apps, not all features are supported when you are using Touch mode. If you are using a mouse, Mouse mode will not add the extra space between buttons and commands. The Quick Access Toolbar is discussed in more depth later in the chapter.

KeyTips If you prefer using the keyboard instead of the mouse, you can press the ALT key on the keyboard to display **KeyTips**, or keyboard code icons, for certain commands (Figure 19). To select a command using the keyboard, press the letter or number displayed in the KeyTip, which may cause additional KeyTips related to the selected command to appear. To remove KeyTips from the screen, press the ALT key or the ESC key until all KeyTips disappear, or tap or click anywhere in the app window.

Microsoft Account Area In this area, you can use the Sign in link to sign in to your Microsoft account. Once signed in, you will see your account information as well as a picture if you have included one in your Microsoft account.

Figure 19

To Display a Different Tab on the Ribbon

1 SIGN IN | 2 USE WINDOWS | 3 USE APPS | 4 FILE MANAGEMENT | 5 SWITCH APPS | 6 SAVE FILES
7 CHANGE SCREEN RESOLUTION | 8 EXIT APPS | 9 USE ADDITIONAL APP FEATURES | 10 USE HELP

When you run PowerPoint, the ribbon displays nine main tabs: FILE, HOME, INSERT, DESIGN, TRANSITIONS, ANIMATIONS, SLIDE SHOW, REVIEW, and VIEW. The tab currently displayed is called the **active tab**.

The following step displays the INSERT tab, that is, makes it the active tab. *Why? When working with an Office app, you may need to switch tabs to access other options for working with a document.*

1

• Tap or click INSERT on the ribbon to display the INSERT tab (Figure 20).

 Experiment

• Tap or click the other tabs on the ribbon to view their contents. When you are finished, tap or click INSERT on the ribbon to redisplay the INSERT tab.

Q&A If I am working in a different Office app, such as Word or Access, how do I display a different tab on the ribbon?
Follow this same procedure; that is, tap or click the desired tab on the ribbon.

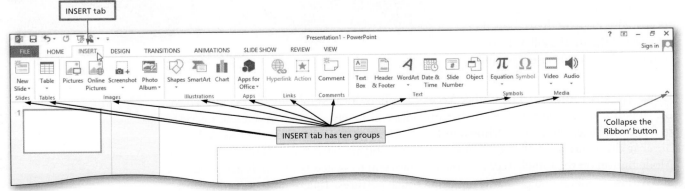

Figure 20

To Collapse and Expand the Ribbon and Use Full Screen Mode

To display more of a document or other item in the window of an Office app, some users prefer to collapse the ribbon, which hides the groups on the ribbon and displays only the main tabs, or to use **Full Screen mode**, which hides all the commands and just displays the document. Each time you run an Office app, such as PowerPoint, the ribbon appears the same way it did the last time you used that Office app. The chapters in this book, however, begin with the ribbon appearing as it did at the initial installation of Office or PowerPoint.

The following steps collapse, expand, and restore the ribbon in PowerPoint and then switch to Full Screen mode. ***Why?*** *If you need more space on the screen to work with your document, you may consider collapsing the ribbon or switching to Full Screen mode to gain additional workspace.*

❶

- Tap or click the 'Collapse the Ribbon' button on the ribbon (shown in Figure 20) to collapse the ribbon (Figure 21).

Q&A What happened to the groups on the ribbon?
When you collapse the ribbon, the groups disappear so that the ribbon does not take up as much space on the screen.

What happened to the 'Collapse the Ribbon' button?
The 'Pin the ribbon' button replaces the 'Collapse the Ribbon' button when the ribbon is collapsed. You will see the 'Pin the ribbon' button only when you expand a ribbon by tapping or clicking a tab.

Figure 21

❷

- Tap or click HOME on the ribbon to expand the HOME tab (Figure 22).

Q&A Why would I click the HOME tab?
If you want to use a command on a collapsed ribbon, tap or click the main tab to display the groups for that tab. After you select a command on the ribbon, the groups will be collapsed once again. If you decide not to use a command on the ribbon, you can collapse the groups by tapping or clicking the same main tab or tapping or clicking in the app window.

Figure 22

🔎 Experiment

- Tap or click HOME on the ribbon to collapse the groups again. Tap or click HOME on the ribbon to expand the HOME tab.

❸

- Tap or click the 'Pin the ribbon' button on the expanded HOME tab to restore the ribbon.
- Tap or click the 'Ribbon Display Options' button to display the Ribbon Display Options menu (Figure 23).

Figure 23

- Tap or click Auto-hide Ribbon to use Full Screen mode, which hides all the commands from the screen (Figure 24).
- Tap or click the ellipsis to display the ribbon temporarily.
- Tap or click the 'Ribbon Display Options' button to display the Ribbon Display Options menu (shown in Figure 23).
- Tap or click 'Show Tabs and Commands' to exit Full Screen mode.

Figure 24

Other Ways

1. Double-tap or double-click a main tab on the ribbon   2. Press CTRL+F1

To Use a Shortcut Menu to Relocate the Quick Access Toolbar

1 SIGN IN | 2 USE WINDOWS | 3 USE APPS | 4 FILE MANAGEMENT | 5 SWITCH APPS | 6 SAVE FILES
7 CHANGE SCREEN RESOLUTION | 8 EXIT APPS | 9 USE ADDITIONAL APP FEATURES | 10 USE HELP

When you press and hold or right-click certain areas of the PowerPoint and other Office app windows, a shortcut menu will appear. A **shortcut menu** is a list of frequently used commands that relate to an object. *Why? You can use shortcut menus to access common commands quickly.* When you press and hold or right-click the status bar, for example, a shortcut menu appears with commands related to the status bar. When you press and hold or right-click the Quick Access Toolbar, a shortcut menu appears with commands related to the Quick Access Toolbar. The following steps use a shortcut menu to move the Quick Access Toolbar, which by default is located on the title bar.

- Press and hold or right-click the Quick Access Toolbar to display a shortcut menu that presents a list of commands related to the Quick Access Toolbar (Figure 25).

Q&A

What if I cannot make the shortcut menu appear using the touch instruction?

When you use the press and hold technique, be sure to release your finger when the circle appears on the screen to display the shortcut menu. If the technique still does not work, you might need to add more space around objects on the screen, making it easier for you to press or tap them. Click the 'Customize Quick Access Toolbar' button and then click Touch/Mouse Mode on the menu. Another option is to use the stylus.

Figure 25

- Tap or click 'Show Quick Access Toolbar Below the Ribbon' on the shortcut menu to display the Quick Access Toolbar below the ribbon (Figure 26).

Figure 26

- Press and hold or right-click the Quick Access Toolbar to display a shortcut menu (Figure 27).

- Tap or click 'Show Quick Access Toolbar Above the Ribbon' on the shortcut menu to return the Quick Access Toolbar to its original position (shown in Figure 25).

Figure 27

Other Ways

1. Tap or click 'Customize Quick Access Toolbar' button on Quick Access Toolbar, tap or click 'Show Below the Ribbon' or 'Show Above the Ribbon'

To Customize the Quick Access Toolbar

1 SIGN IN | 2 USE WINDOWS | 3 USE APPS | 4 FILE MANAGEMENT | 5 SWITCH APPS | 6 SAVE FILES
7 CHANGE SCREEN RESOLUTION | 8 EXIT APPS | 9 USE ADDITIONAL APP FEATURES | 10 USE HELP

The Quick Access Toolbar provides easy access to some of the more frequently used commands in the Office apps. By default, the Quick Access Toolbar contains buttons for the Save, Undo, and Redo commands. You can customize the Quick Access Toolbar by changing its location in the window, as shown in the previous steps, and by adding more buttons to reflect commands you would like to access easily. The following steps add the Quick Print button to the Quick Access Toolbar in the PowerPoint window. *Why? Adding the Quick Print button to the Quick Access Toolbar speeds up the process of printing.*

- Tap or click the 'Customize Quick Access Toolbar' button to display the Customize Quick Access Toolbar menu (Figure 28).

Q&A

Which commands are listed on the Customize Quick Access Toolbar menu?
It lists commands that commonly are added to the Quick Access Toolbar.

What do the check marks next to some commands signify?
Check marks appear next to commands that already are on the Quick Access Toolbar. When you add a button to the Quick Access Toolbar, a check mark will be displayed next to its command name.

Figure 28

2

Quick Print button added
to Quick Access Toolbar

Figure 29

- Tap or click Quick Print on the Customize Quick Access Toolbar menu to add the Quick Print button to the Quick Access Toolbar (Figure 29).

Q&A How would I remove a button from the Quick Access Toolbar? You would press and hold or right-click the button you wish to remove and then tap or click 'Remove from Quick Access Toolbar' on the shortcut menu or tap or click the 'Customize Quick Access Toolbar' button on the Quick Access Toolbar and then click the button name in the Customize Quick Access Toolbar menu to remove the check mark.

To Enter Content in a Title Slide

1 SIGN IN | 2 USE WINDOWS | 3 USE APPS | 4 FILE MANAGEMENT | 5 SWITCH APPS | 6 SAVE FILES
7 CHANGE SCREEN RESOLUTION | 8 EXIT APPS | 9 USE ADDITIONAL APP FEATURES | 10 USE HELP

With the exception of a blank slide, PowerPoint assumes every new slide has a title. Many of PowerPoint's layouts have both a title text placeholder and at least one content placeholder. To make creating a presentation easier, any text you type after a new slide appears becomes title text in the title text placeholder. As you begin typing text in the title text placeholder, the title text also is displayed in the Slide 1 thumbnail in the Thumbnail pane. The title for this presentation is Kelitestone Crafts. The steps on the next page enter a presentation title on the title slide. *Why? In general, every presentation should have a title to describe what the presentation will be covering.*

1

- Tap or click the 'Click to add title' label located inside the title text placeholder to select the placeholder (Figure 30).

Q&A What are the white squares that appear around the title text placeholder as I type the presentation title? The white squares are sizing handles, which you can drag to change the size of the title text placeholder. Sizing handles also can be found around other placeholders and objects within an Office app.

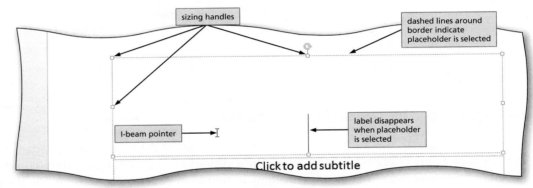

sizing handles

dashed lines around border indicate placeholder is selected

I-beam pointer

label disappears when placeholder is selected

Click to add subtitle

Figure 30

2

- Type **Kelitestone Crafts** in the title text placeholder. Do not press the ENTER key because you do not want to create a new line of text (Figure 31).

Save button

title text entered in placeholder

Kelitestone Crafts

Figure 31

Saving and Organizing Files

While you are creating a document, the computer stores it in memory. When you save a document, the computer places it on a storage medium such as a hard disk, solid state drive (SSD), USB flash drive, or optical disc. The storage medium can be permanent in your computer, may be portable where you remove it from your computer, or may be on a web server you access through a network or the Internet.

A saved document is referred to as a file. A **file name** is the name assigned to a file when it is saved. When saving files, you should organize them so that you easily can find them later. Windows provides tools to help you organize files.

CONSIDER THIS

How often should you save a document?

It is important to save a document frequently for the following reasons:

• The document in memory might be lost if the computer is turned off or you lose electrical power while an app is running.

• If you run out of time before completing a project, you may finish it at a future time without starting over.

Organizing Files and Folders

A file contains data. This data can range from a research paper to an accounting spreadsheet to an electronic math quiz. You should organize and store files in folders to avoid misplacing a file and to help you find a file quickly.

If you are taking an introductory computer class (CIS 101, for example), you may want to design a series of folders for the different subjects covered in the class. To accomplish this, you can arrange the folders in a hierarchy for the class, as shown in Figure 32.

The hierarchy contains three levels. The first level contains the storage medium, such as a hard disk. The second level contains the class folder (CIS 101, in this case), and the third level contains seven folders, one each for a different Office app that will be covered in the class (Word, PowerPoint, Excel, Access, Outlook, Publisher, and OneNote).

When the hierarchy in Figure 32 is created, the storage medium is said to contain the CIS 101 folder, and the CIS 101 folder is said to contain the separate Office folders (i.e., Word, PowerPoint, Excel, etc.). In addition, this hierarchy easily can be expanded to include folders from other classes taken during additional semesters.

The vertical and horizontal lines in Figure 32 form a pathway that allows you to navigate to a drive or folder on a computer or network. A **path** consists of a drive letter (preceded by a drive name when necessary) and colon, to identify the storage device, and one or more folder names. A hard disk typically has a drive letter of C. Each drive or folder in the hierarchy has a corresponding path.

By default, Windows saves documents in the Documents library, music in the Music library, pictures in the Pictures library, and videos in the Videos library. A **library** helps you manage multiple folders stored in various locations on a computer and devices. It does not store the folder contents; rather, it keeps track of their locations so that you can access the folders and their contents quickly. For example, you can save pictures from a digital camera in any folder on any storage location on a computer. Normally, this would make organizing the different folders difficult. If you add the folders to a library, however, you can access all the pictures from one location regardless of where they are stored.

BTW
File Type
Depending on your Windows settings, the file type .pptx may be displayed immediately to the right of the file name after you save the file. The file type .pptx is a PowerPoint 2013 document.

Figure 32

© 2014 Cengage Learning

The following pages illustrate the steps to organize the folders for this class and save a file in a folder:

1. Create the folder identifying your class.
2. Create the PowerPoint folder in the folder identifying your class.
3. Save a file in the PowerPoint folder.
4. Verify the location of the saved file.

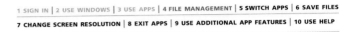

1 SIGN IN | 2 USE WINDOWS | 3 USE APPS | 4 FILE MANAGEMENT | 5 SWITCH APPS | 6 SAVE FILES
7 CHANGE SCREEN RESOLUTION | 8 EXIT APPS | 9 USE ADDITIONAL APP FEATURES | 10 USE HELP

To Create a Folder

When you create a folder, such as the CIS 101 folder shown in Figure 32 on the previous page, you must name the folder. A folder name should describe the folder and its contents. A folder name can contain spaces and any uppercase or lowercase characters, except a backslash (\), slash (/), colon (:), asterisk (*), question mark (?), quotation marks ("), less than symbol (<), greater than symbol (>), or vertical bar (|). Folder names cannot be CON, AUX, COM1, COM2, COM3, COM4, LPT1, LPT2, LPT3, PRN, or NUL. The same rules for naming folders also apply to naming files.

The following steps create a class folder (CIS 101, in this case) in the Documents library. *Why? When storing files, you should organize the files so that it will be easier to find them later.* If you are using Windows 7, skip these steps and instead perform the steps in the yellow box that immediately follows these Windows 8 steps.

- Tap or click the File Explorer app button on the taskbar to run the File Explorer app (Figure 33).

Q&A | Why does the title bar say Libraries?
File Explorer, by default, displays the name of the selected library or folder on the title bar.

Figure 33

- Tap or click the Documents library in the navigation pane to display the contents of the Documents library in the file list (Figure 34).

 Q&A What if my screen does not show the Documents, Music, Pictures, and Videos libraries?

Double-tap or double-click Libraries in the navigation pane to expand the list.

Figure 34

- Tap or click the New folder button on the Quick Access Toolbar to create a new folder with the name, New folder, selected in a text box (Figure 35).

Q&A Why is the folder icon displayed differently on my computer?

Windows might be configured to display contents differently on your computer.

Figure 35

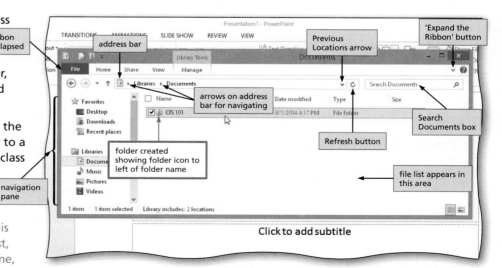

- Type CIS 101 (or your class code) in the text box as the new folder name.

- If requested by your instructor, add your last name to the end of the folder name.

- Press the ENTER key to change the folder name from New folder to a folder name identifying your class (Figure 36).

Q&A What happens when I press the ENTER key?

The class folder (CIS 101, in this case) is displayed in the file list, which contains the folder name, date modified, type, and size.

Figure 36

Other Ways

1. Press CTRL+SHIFT+N   2. Tap or click the New folder button (Home tab | New group)

To Create a Folder Using Windows 7

If you are using Windows 7, perform these steps to create a folder instead of the previous steps that use Windows 8.

1. Click the Windows Explorer button on the taskbar to run Windows Explorer.
2. Click the Documents library in the navigation pane to display the contents of the Documents library in the file list.
3. Click the New folder button on the toolbar to display a new folder icon with the name, New folder, selected in a text box.
4. Type **CIS 101** (or your class code) in the text box to name the folder.
5. Press the ENTER key to create the folder.

Folder Windows

The Documents window (shown in Figure 36 on the previous page) is called a folder window. Recall that a folder is a specific named location on a storage medium that contains related files. Most users rely on **folder windows** for finding, viewing, and managing information on their computers. Folder windows have common design elements, including the following (shown in Figure 36).

- The **address bar** provides quick navigation options. The arrows on the address bar allow you to visit different locations on the computer.
- The buttons to the left of the address bar allow you to navigate the contents of the navigation pane and view recent pages.
- The **Previous Locations arrow** displays the locations you have visited.
- The **Refresh button** on the right side of the address bar refreshes the contents of the folder list.
- The **search box** contains the dimmed words, Search Documents. You can type a term in the search box for a list of files, folders, shortcuts, and elements containing that term within the location you are searching. A **shortcut** is an icon on the desktop that provides a user with immediate access to an app or file.
- The **ribbon** contains five tabs used to accomplish various tasks on the computer related to organizing and managing the contents of the open window. This ribbon works similarly to the ribbon in the Office apps.
- The **navigation pane** on the left contains the Favorites area, Libraries area, Homegroup area, Computer area, and Network area.
- The **Favorites area** shows your favorite locations. By default, this list contains only links to your Desktop, Downloads, and Recent places.
- The **Libraries area** shows folders included in a library.

1 SIGN IN | 2 USE WINDOWS | 3 USE APPS | 4 FILE MANAGEMENT | 5 SWITCH APPS | 6 SAVE FILES
7 CHANGE SCREEN RESOLUTION | 8 EXIT APPS | 9 USE ADDITIONAL APP FEATURES | 10 USE HELP

To Create a Folder within a Folder

With the class folder created, you can create folders that will store the files you create using PowerPoint. The following steps create a PowerPoint folder in the CIS 101 folder (or the folder identifying your class). *Why?* *To be able to organize your files, you should create a folder structure.* If you are using Windows 7, skip these steps and instead perform the steps in the yellow box that immediately follows these Windows 8 steps.

- Double-tap or double-click the icon or folder name for the CIS 101 folder (or the folder identifying your class) in the file list to open the folder (Figure 37).

Figure 37

- Tap or click the New folder button on the Quick Access Toolbar to create a new folder with the name, New folder, selected in a text box folder.

- Type **PowerPoint** in the text box as the new folder name.

- Press the ENTER key to rename the folder (Figure 38).

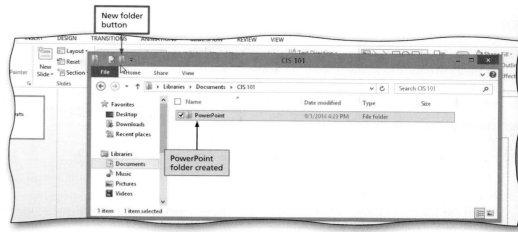

Figure 38

Other Ways

1. Press CTRL+SHIFT+N   2. Tap or click the New folder button (Home tab | New group)

TO CREATE A FOLDER WITHIN A FOLDER USING WINDOWS 7

If you are using Windows 7, perform these steps to create a folder within a folder instead of the previous steps that use Windows 8.

1. Double-click the icon or folder name for the CIS 101 folder (or the folder identifying your class) in the file list to open the folder.

2. Click the New folder button on the toolbar to display a new folder icon and text box for the folder.

3. Type **PowerPoint** in the text box to name the folder.

4. Press the ENTER key to create the folder.

To Expand a Folder, Scroll through Folder Contents, and Collapse a Folder

1 SIGN IN | 2 USE WINDOWS | 3 USE APPS | 4 FILE MANAGEMENT | 5 SWITCH APPS | 6 SAVE FILES
7 CHANGE SCREEN RESOLUTION | 8 EXIT APPS | 9 USE ADDITIONAL APP FEATURES | 10 USE HELP

Folder windows display the hierarchy of items and the contents of drives and folders in the file list. You might want to expand a library or folder in the navigation pane to view its contents, slide or scroll through its contents, and collapse it when you are finished viewing its contents. *Why? When a folder is expanded, you can see all the folders it contains. By contrast, a collapsed folder hides the folders it contains.* The following steps expand, slide or scroll through, and then collapse the folder identifying your class (CIS 101, in this case).

- Double-tap or double-click the Documents library in the navigation pane, which expands the library to display its contents and displays a black arrow to the left of the Documents library icon (Figure 39).

Figure 39

- Double-tap or double-click the My Documents folder, which expands the folder to display its contents and displays a black arrow to the left of the My Documents folder icon.

Q&A What is the My Documents folder?
When you save files on your hard disk, the My Documents folder is the default save location.

- Double-tap or double-click the CIS 101 folder, which expands the folder to display its contents and displays a black arrow to the left of the folder icon (Figure 40).

Figure 40

Experiment

- Slide the scroll bar down or click the down scroll arrow on the vertical scroll bar to display additional folders at the bottom of the navigation pane. Slide the scroll bar up or click the scroll bar above the scroll box to move the scroll box to the top of the navigation pane. Drag the scroll box down the scroll bar until the scroll box is halfway down the scroll bar.

- Double-tap or double-click the folder identifying your class (CIS 101, in this case) to collapse the folder (Figure 41).

Q&A Why are some folders indented below others?
A folder contains the indented folders below it.

Figure 41

Other Ways

1. Point to display arrows in navigation pane, tap or click white arrow to expand or tap or click black arrow to collapse

2. Select folder to expand or collapse using arrow keys, press RIGHT ARROW to expand; press LEFT ARROW to collapse.

To Switch from One App to Another

1 SIGN IN | 2 USE WINDOWS | 3 USE APPS | 4 FILE MANAGEMENT | 5 SWITCH APPS | 6 SAVE FILES
7 CHANGE SCREEN RESOLUTION | 8 EXIT APPS | 9 USE ADDITIONAL APP FEATURES | 10 USE HELP

The next step is to save the PowerPoint file containing the title text you typed earlier. PowerPoint, however, currently is not the active window. You can use the app button on the taskbar and live preview to switch to PowerPoint and then save the document in the PowerPoint document window.

Why? *By clicking the appropriate app button on the taskbar, you can switch to the open app you want to use.* The following steps switch to the PowerPoint window; however, the steps are the same for any active Office app currently displayed as an app button on the taskbar.

1

- If you are using a mouse, point to the PowerPoint app button on the taskbar to see a live preview of the open document(s) or the window title(s) of the open document(s), depending on your computer's configuration (Figure 42).

Figure 42

2

- Tap or click the PowerPoint app button or the live preview to make the app associated with the app button the active window (Figure 43).

Q&A | What if multiple documents are open in an app?
Tap or click the desired live preview to switch to the window you want to use.

Figure 43

To Save a File in a Folder

1 SIGN IN | 2 USE WINDOWS | 3 USE APPS | 4 FILE MANAGEMENT | 5 SWITCH APPS | 6 SAVE FILES
7 CHANGE SCREEN RESOLUTION | 8 EXIT APPS | 9 USE ADDITIONAL APP FEATURES | 10 USE HELP

With the PowerPoint folder created, you can save the PowerPoint document shown in the document window in the PowerPoint folder. *Why? Without saving a file, you may lose all the work you have completed and will be unable to reuse or share it with others later.* The following steps save a file in the PowerPoint folder contained in your class folder (CIS 101, in this case) using the file name, Craft Store.

1

- Tap or click the Save button (shown in Figure 43) on the Quick Access Toolbar, which depending on settings, will display either the Save As gallery in the Backstage view (Figure 44) or the Save As dialog box (Figure 45 on the next page).

Q&A | What is the Backstage view?
The **Backstage view** contains a set of commands that enable you to manage documents and data about the documents.

Figure 44

What if the Save As gallery is not displayed in the Backstage view?
Tap or click the Save As tab to display the Save As gallery.

How do I close the Backstage view?
Tap or click the Back button in the upper-left corner of the Backstage view to return to the PowerPoint window.

2

- If your screen displays the Backstage view, tap or click Computer, if necessary, to display options in the right pane related to saving on your computer; if your screen already displays the Save As dialog box, proceed to Step 3.

Q&A What if I wanted to save on SkyDrive instead?
You would tap or click SkyDrive. Saving on SkyDrive is discussed in a later section in this chapter.

- Tap or click the Browse button in the right pane to display the Save As dialog box (Figure 45).

Q&A Why does a file name already appear in the File name box?
PowerPoint automatically suggests a file name the first time you save a document. The file name normally consists of the first few words contained in the title text. Because the suggested file name is selected, you do not need to delete it; as soon as you begin typing, the new file name replaces the selected text.

Figure 45

3

- Type **Craft Store** in the File name box (Save As dialog box) to change the file name. Do not press the ENTER key after typing the file name because you do not want to close the dialog box at this time (Figure 46).

Q&A What characters can I use in a file name?
The only invalid characters are the backslash (\), slash (/), colon (:), asterisk (*), question mark (?), quotation mark ("), less than symbol (<), greater than symbol (>), and vertical bar (|).

Figure 46

4

- Navigate to the desired save location (in this case, the PowerPoint folder in the CIS 101 folder [or your class folder] in the My Documents folder in the Documents library) by performing the tasks in Steps 4a and 4b.

4a

- If the Documents library is not displayed in the navigation pane, slide to scroll or drag the scroll bar in the navigation pane until Documents appears.

- If the Documents library is not expanded in the navigation pane, double-tap or double-click Documents to display its folders in the navigation pane.

Figure 47

- If the My Documents folder is not expanded in the navigation pane, double-tap or double-click My Documents to display its folders in the navigation pane.

- If your class folder (CIS 101, in this case) is not expanded, double-tap or double-click the CIS 101 folder to select the folder and display its contents in the navigation pane (Figure 47).

Q&A What if I do not want to save in a folder?
Although storing files in folders is an effective technique for organizing files, some users prefer not to store files in folders. If you prefer not to save this file in a folder, select the storage device on which you wish to save the file and then proceed to Step 5.

4b

• Tap or click the PowerPoint folder in the navigation pane to select it as the new save location and display its contents in the file list (Figure 48).

Figure 48

5

• Tap or click the Save button (Save As dialog box) to save the document in the selected folder in the selected location with the entered file name (Figure 49).

Q&A How do I know that the file is saved?
While an Office app such as PowerPoint is saving a file, it briefly displays a message on the status bar indicating the amount of the file saved. In addition, the file name appears on the title bar.

Figure 49

Other Ways

1. Tap or click FILE on ribbon, tap or click Save As in Backstage view, tap or click Computer, tap or click Browse button, type file name (Save As dialog box), navigate to desired save location, tap or click Save button

2. Press F12, type file name (Save As dialog box), navigate to desired save location, tap or click Save button

Navigating in Dialog Boxes

Navigating is the process of finding a location on a storage device. While saving the Craft Store file, for example, Steps 4a and 4b in the previous set of steps navigated to the PowerPoint folder located in the CIS 101 folder in the My Documents folder in the Documents library. When performing certain functions in Windows apps, such as saving a file, opening a file, or inserting a picture in an existing document, you most likely will have to navigate to the location where you want to save the file or to the folder containing the file you want to open or insert. Most dialog boxes in Windows apps requiring navigation follow a similar procedure; that is, the way you navigate to a folder in one dialog box, such as the Save As dialog box, is similar to how you might navigate in another dialog box, such as the Open dialog box. If you chose to navigate to a specific location in a dialog box, you would follow the instructions in Steps 4a and 4b.

OFF 32   **Office 2013 and Windows 8 Chapter**   Essential Concepts and Skills

1 SIGN IN | **2 USE WINDOWS** | 3 USE APPS | 4 FILE MANAGEMENT | 5 SWITCH APPS | 6 SAVE FILES
7 CHANGE SCREEN RESOLUTION | 8 EXIT APPS | 9 USE ADDITIONAL APP FEATURES | 10 USE HELP

To Minimize and Restore a Window

Before continuing, you can verify that the PowerPoint file was saved properly. To do this, you will minimize the PowerPoint window and then open the CIS 101 window so that you can verify the file is stored in the CIS 101 folder on the hard disk. A **minimized window** is an open window that is hidden from view but can be displayed quickly by clicking the window's app button on the taskbar.

In the following example, PowerPoint is used to illustrate minimizing and restoring windows; however, you would follow the same steps regardless of the Office app you are using. *Why? Before closing an app, you should make sure your file saved correctly so that you can find it later.*

The following steps minimize the PowerPoint window, verify that the file is saved, and then restore the minimized window. If you are using Windows 7, skip these steps and instead perform the steps in the yellow box that immediately follows these Windows 8 steps.

- Tap or click the Minimize button on the PowerPoint window title bar (shown in Figure 49 on the previous page) to minimize the window (Figure 50).

Q&A Is the minimized window still available?
The minimized window, PowerPoint in this case, remains available but no longer is the active window. It is minimized as an app button on the taskbar.

- If the File Explorer window is not open on the screen, tap or click the File Explorer app button on the taskbar to make the File folder window the active window.

Figure 50

- Double-tap or double-click the PowerPoint folder in the file list to select the folder and display its contents (Figure 51).

Q&A Why does the File Explorer app button on the taskbar change?
A selected app button indicates that the app is active on the screen. When the button is not selected, the app is running but not active.

- After viewing the contents of the selected folder, tap or click the PowerPoint app button on the taskbar to restore the minimized window (as shown in Figure 49 on the previous page).

Figure 51

Other Ways

1. Press and hold or right-click title bar, tap or click Minimize on shortcut menu, tap or click taskbar button in taskbar button area

2. Press WINDOWS+M, press WINDOWS+SHIFT+M

To Minimize and Restore a Window Using Windows 7

If you are using Windows 7, perform these steps to minimize and restore a window instead of the previous steps that use Windows 8.

1. Click the Minimize button on the app's title bar to minimize the window.

2. If the Windows Explorer window is not open on the screen, click the Windows Explorer button on the taskbar to make the Windows Explorer window the active window.

3. Double-click the PowerPoint folder in the file list to select the folder and display its contents.

4. After viewing the contents of the selected folder, click the PowerPoint button on the taskbar to restore the minimized window.

To Save a File on SkyDrive

1 SIGN IN | 2 USE WINDOWS | 3 USE APPS | 4 FILE MANAGEMENT | 5 SWITCH APPS | 6 SAVE FILES
7 CHANGE SCREEN RESOLUTION | 8 EXIT APPS | 9 USE ADDITIONAL APP FEATURES | 10 USE HELP

One of the features of Office is the capability to save files on SkyDrive so that you can use the files on multiple computers without having to use external storage devices such as a USB flash drive. Storing files on SkyDrive also enables you to share files more efficiently with others, such as when using Office Web Apps and Office 365.

In the following example, PowerPoint is used to save a file to SkyDrive. **Why?** *Storing files on SkyDrive provides more portability options than are available from storing files in the Documents library.*

You can save files directly to SkyDrive from within Word, PowerPoint, and Excel. The following steps save the current PowerPoint file to the SkyDrive. These steps require you have a Microsoft account and an Internet connection.

• Tap or click FILE on the ribbon to open the Backstage view (Figure 52).

Q&A | What is the purpose of the FILE tab?
The FILE tab opens the Backstage view for each Office app, including PowerPoint.

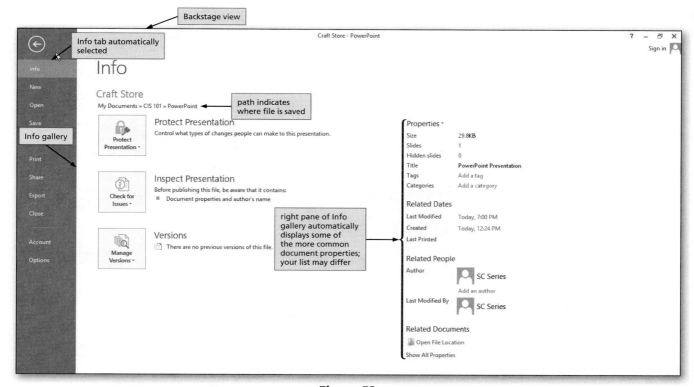

Figure 52

2

- Tap or click the Save As tab in the Backstage view to display the Save As gallery.

- Tap or click SkyDrive to display SkyDrive saving options or a Sign In button, if you are not signed in already to your Microsoft account (Figure 53).

Q&A What if my Save As gallery does not display SkyDrive as a save location?
Tap or click 'Add a Place' and proceed to Step 3.

Figure 53

3

- If your screen displays a Sign In button, tap or click it to display the Sign in dialog box (Figure 54).

Q&A What if the Sign In button does not appear?
If you already are signed into your Microsoft account, the Sign In button will not be displayed. In this case, proceed to Step 5.

Figure 54

4

- Type your Microsoft account user name and password in the text boxes and then tap or click the Sign in button (Sign in dialog box) to sign in to SkyDrive.

5

- Tap or click your SkyDrive to select your SkyDrive as the storage location (Figure 55).

Figure 55

● Tap or click the Browse button to contact the SkyDrive server (which may take some time, depending on the speed of your Internet connection) and then display the Save As dialog box (Figure 56).

Q&A
Why does the path in the address bar contain various letters and numbers?
The letters and numbers in the address bar uniquely identify the location of your SkyDrive files and folders.

● Tap or click the Save button (Save As dialog box) to save the file on SkyDrive.

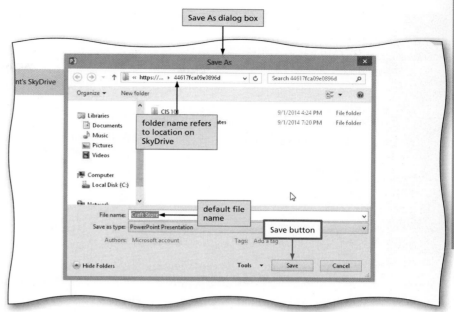

Figure 56

To Sign Out of a Microsoft Account

If you are using a public computer or otherwise wish to sign out of your Microsoft account, you should sign out of the account from the Accounts gallery in the Backstage view. Signing out of the account is the safest way to make sure that nobody else can access online files or settings stored in your Microsoft account. *Why? For security reasons, you should sign out of your Microsoft account when you are finished using a public or shared computer. Staying signed in to your Microsoft account might enable others to access your files.*

The following steps sign out of a Microsoft account from PowerPoint. You would use the same steps in any Office app. If you do not wish to sign out of your Microsoft account, read these steps without performing them.

1 Tap or click FILE on the ribbon to open the Backstage view.

2 Tap or click the Account tab to display the Account gallery (Figure 57 on the next page).

3 Tap or click the Sign out link, which displays the Remove Account dialog box. If a Can't remove Windows accounts dialog box appears instead of the Remove Account dialog box, click the OK button and skip the remaining steps.

Q&A
Why does a Can't remove Windows accounts dialog box appear?
If you signed in to Windows using your Microsoft account, then you also must sign out from Windows, rather than signing out from within PowerPoint. When you are finished using Windows, be sure to sign out at that time.

4 Tap or click the Yes button (Remove Account dialog box) to sign out of your Microsoft account on this computer.

Q&A
Should I sign out of Windows after removing my Microsoft account?
When you are finished using the computer, you should sign out of Windows for maximum security.

5 Tap or click the Back button in the upper-left corner of the Backstage view to return to the document.

Figure 57

Screen Resolution

Screen resolution indicates the number of pixels (dots) that the computer uses to display the letters, numbers, graphics, and background you see on the screen. When you increase the screen resolution, Windows displays more information on the screen, but the information decreases in size. The reverse also is true: as you decrease the screen resolution, Windows displays less information on the screen, but the information increases in size.

Screen resolution usually is stated as the product of two numbers, such as 1366 × 768 (pronounced "thirteen sixty-six by seven sixty-eight"). A 1366 × 768 screen resolution results in a display of 1366 distinct pixels on each of 768 lines, or about 1,050,624 pixels. Changing the screen resolution affects how the ribbon appears in Office apps and some Windows dialog boxes. Figure 58, for example, shows the PowerPoint ribbon at screen resolutions of 1366 × 768 and 1024 × 768. All of the same commands are available regardless of screen resolution. The app (PowerPoint, in this case), however, makes changes to the groups and the buttons within the groups to accommodate the various screen resolutions. The result is that certain commands may need to be accessed differently depending on the resolution chosen. A command that is visible on the ribbon and available by tapping or clicking a button at one resolution may not be visible and may need to be accessed using its Dialog Box Launcher at a different resolution.

Comparing the two ribbons in Figure 58, notice the changes in content and layout of the groups and galleries. In some cases, the content of a group is the same in each resolution, but the layout of the group differs. For example, the same gallery and buttons appear in the Styles groups in the two resolutions, but the layouts differ. In other cases, the content and layout are the same across the resolution, but the level of detail differs with the resolution.

(a) Ribbon at 1366 × 768 Resolution

Figure 58

not all command names visible in Clipboard and Paragraph groups

Shapes gallery is not displayed

(b) Ribbon at 1024 x 768 Resolution

Figure 58 (Continued)

To Change the Screen Resolution

1 SIGN IN | 2 USE WINDOWS | 3 USE APPS | 4 FILE MANAGEMENT | 5 SWITCH APPS | 6 SAVE FILES
7 CHANGE SCREEN RESOLUTION | 8 EXIT APPS | 9 USE ADDITIONAL APP FEATURES | 10 USE HELP

If you are using a computer to step through the chapters in this book and you want your screen to match the figures, you may need to change your screen's resolution. *Why? The figures in this book use a screen resolution of 1366 × 768.* The following steps change the screen resolution to 1366 × 768. Your computer already may be set to 1366 × 768. Keep in mind that many computer labs prevent users from changing the screen resolution; in that case, read the following steps for illustration purposes.

- Tap or click the Show desktop button, which is located at the far-right edge of the taskbar, to display the Windows desktop.

Q&A I cannot see the Show desktop button. Why not?
When you point to the far-right edge of the taskbar, a small outline appears to mark the Show desktop button.

- Press and hold or right-click an empty area on the Windows desktop to display a shortcut menu that contains a list of commands related to the desktop (Figure 59).

shortcut menu

Screen resolution command

Show desktop button

Figure 59

Q&A Why does my shortcut menu display different commands?
Depending on your computer's hardware and configuration, different commands might appear on the shortcut menu.

- Tap or click Screen resolution on the shortcut menu to open the Screen Resolution window (Figure 60).

- Tap or click the Resolution button in the Screen Resolution window to display the resolution slider.

Screen Resolution window

name of current display device

Resolution button

tapping or clicking link displays advanced settings

Figure 60

- If necessary, drag the resolution slider until the desired screen resolution (in this case, 1366 × 768) is selected (Figure 61).

Q&A

What if my computer does not support the 1366 × 768 resolution?

Some computers do not support the 1366 ×768 resolution. In this case, select a resolution that is close to the 1366 × 768 resolution.

What is a slider?

A **slider** is an object that allows users to choose from multiple predetermined options. In most cases, these options represent some type of numeric value. In most cases, one end of the slider (usually the left or bottom) represents the lowest of available values, and the opposite end (usually the right or top) represents the highest available value.

Figure 61

- Tap or click an empty area of the Screen Resolution window to close the resolution slider.

- Tap or click the OK button to change the screen resolution and display the Display Settings dialog box (Figure 62).

- Tap or click the Keep changes button (Display Settings dialog box) to accept the new screen resolution.

Q&A

Why does a message display stating that the image quality can be improved?

Some computer monitors or screens are designed to display contents better at a certain screen resolution, sometimes referred to as an optimal resolution.

Figure 62

To Exit an App with One Document Open

1 SIGN IN | 2 USE WINDOWS | 3 USE APPS | 4 FILE MANAGEMENT | 5 SWITCH APPS | 6 SAVE FILES
7 CHANGE SCREEN RESOLUTION | 8 EXIT APPS | 9 USE ADDITIONAL APP FEATURES | 10 USE HELP

When you exit an Office app, such as PowerPoint, if you have made changes to a file since the last time the file was saved, the app displays a dialog box asking if you want to save the changes you made to the file before it closes the app window. *Why?* *The dialog box contains three buttons with these resulting actions: the Save button saves the changes and then exits the Office app, the Don't Save button exits the Office app without saving changes, and the Cancel button closes the dialog box and redisplays the file without saving the changes.*

If no changes have been made to an open document since the last time the file was saved, the Office app will close the window without displaying a dialog box.

The following steps exit PowerPoint. You would follow similar steps in other Office apps.

- If necessary, tap or click the PowerPoint app button on the taskbar (shown in Figure 62) to display the PowerPoint window on the desktop.

- If you are using a mouse, point to the Close button on the right side of the PowerPoint window title bar (Figure 63).

Figure 63

②

- Tap or click the Close button to close the document and exit PowerPoint.

Q&A

What if I have more than one document open in PowerPoint?
You could click the Close button for each open document. When you click the last open document's Close button, you also exit PowerPoint. As an alternative that is more efficient, you could press and hold or right-click the PowerPoint app button on the taskbar and then tap or click 'Close all windows' on the shortcut menu to close all open documents and exit PowerPoint.

③

- If a Microsoft PowerPoint dialog box appears, tap or click the Save button to save any changes made to the document since the last save.

Other Ways

1. Press and hold or right-click the PowerPoint app button on Windows taskbar, click 'Close all windows' on shortcut menu
2. Press ALT + F4

To Copy a Folder to a USB Flash Drive

1 SIGN IN | 2 USE WINDOWS | 3 USE APPS | **4 FILE MANAGEMENT** | 5 SWITCH APPS | 6 SAVE FILES
7 CHANGE SCREEN RESOLUTION | 8 EXIT APPS | **9 USE ADDITIONAL APP FEATURES** | 10 USE HELP

To store files and folders on a USB flash drive, you must connect the USB flash drive to an available USB port on a computer. The following steps copy your CIS 101 folder to a USB flash drive. *Why? It often is good practice to have a backup of your files. Besides SkyDrive, you can save files to a portable storage device, such as a USB flash drive.* If you are using Windows 7, skip these steps and instead perform the steps in the yellow box that immediately follows these Windows 8 steps.

①

- Insert a USB flash drive in an available USB port on the computer to connect the USB flash drive.

Q&A

How can I ensure the USB flash drive is connected?
In File Explorer, you can use the navigation bar to find the USB flash drive. If it is not showing, then it is not connected properly.

②

- Tap or click the File Explorer app button on the taskbar to make the folder window the active window.

- If necessary, navigate to the CIS 101 folder in the File Explorer window (see Step 4a on page OFF 30 for instructions about navigating to a folder location).

- Press and hold or right-click the CIS 101 folder to display a shortcut menu (Figure 64).

Figure 64

③

- Tap or point to Send to, which causes a submenu to appear (Figure 65).

Figure 65

4

- Tap or click the USB flash drive to copy the folder to the USB flash drive (Figure 66).

Q&A Why does the drive letter of my USB flash drive differ?
Windows assigns the next available drive letter to your USB flash drive when you connect it. The next available drive letter may vary by computer, depending on the number of storage devices that currently are connected.

Figure 66

TO COPY A FOLDER TO A USB FLASH DRIVE USING WINDOWS 7

If you are using Windows 7, perform these steps to copy a folder to a USB flash drive instead of the previous steps that use Windows 8.

1. Insert a USB flash drive in an available USB port on the computer to open the AutoPlay window.
2. Click the 'Open folder to view files' link in the AutoPlay window to open the Windows Explorer window.
3. Navigate to the Documents library.
4. Right-click the CIS 101 folder to display a shortcut menu.
5. Point to Send to, which causes a submenu to appear.
6. Click the USB flash drive to copy the folder to the USB flash drive.

Break Point: If you wish to take a break, this is a good place to do so. To resume at a later time, continue to follow the steps from this location forward.

Additional Common Features of Office Apps

The previous section used PowerPoint to illustrate common features of Office and some basic elements unique to PowerPoint. The following sections continue to use PowerPoint to present additional common features of Office.

In the following pages, you will learn how to do the following:

1. Run PowerPoint using the search box.
2. Open a document in PowerPoint.
3. Close the document.
4. Reopen the document just closed.
5. Create a blank PowerPoint document from Windows Explorer and then open the file.
6. Save a document with a new file name.

To Run an App Using the Search Box

1 SIGN IN | 2 USE WINDOWS | 3 USE APPS | 4 FILE MANAGEMENT | 5 SWITCH APPS | 6 SAVE FILES
7 CHANGE SCREEN RESOLUTION | 8 EXIT APPS | 9 USE ADDITIONAL APP FEATURES | 10 USE HELP

The following steps, which assume Windows is running, use the search box to run the PowerPoint app based on a typical installation; however, you would follow similar steps to run any app. *Why? Sometimes an app does not appear on the Start screen, so you can find it quickly by searching.* You may need to ask your instructor how to run apps for your computer. If you are using Windows 7, skip these steps and instead perform the steps in the yellow box that immediately follows these Windows 8 steps.

1

- Swipe in from the right edge of the screen or point to the upper-right corner of the screen to display the Charms bar (Figure 67).

Figure 67

2

- Tap or click the Search charm on the Charms bar to display the Search menu (Figure 68).

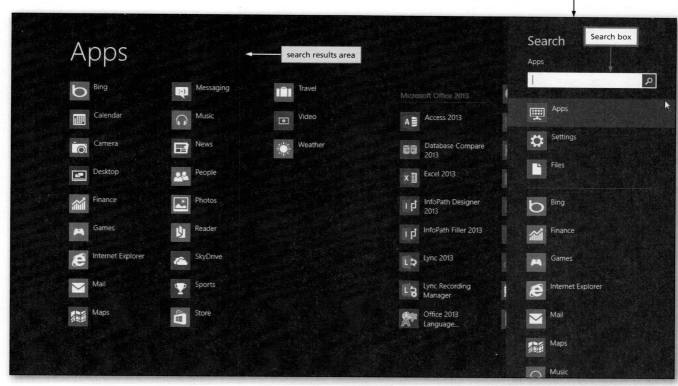

Figure 68

3

- Type **PowerPoint 2013** as the search text in the Search box and watch the search results appear in the Apps list (Figure 69).

Q&A Do I need to type the complete app name or use correct capitalization?

No, you need to type just enough characters of the app name for it to appear in the Apps list. For example, you may be able to type PowerPoint or powerpoint, instead of PowerPoint 2013.

Figure 69

- Tap or click PowerPoint 2013 in the search results to run PowerPoint.

- Tap or click the Blank Presentation thumbnail to create a blank presentation and display it in the PowerPoint window.

- If the PowerPoint window is not maximized, tap or click the Maximize button on its title bar to maximize the window (Figure 70).

Figure 70

To Run an App Using the Search Box Using Windows 7

If you are using Windows 7, perform these steps to run an app using the search box instead of the previous steps that use Windows 8.

1. Click the Start button on the Windows 7 taskbar to display the Start menu.

2. Type **PowerPoint 2013** as the search text in the 'Search programs and files' text box and watch the search results appear on the Start menu.

3. Click PowerPoint 2013 in the search results on the Start menu to run PowerPoint.

4. Click the Blank Presentation thumbnail to create a blank presentation and display it in the PowerPoint window.

5. If the PowerPoint window is not maximized, click the Maximize button on its title bar to maximize the window.

To Open an Existing File

As discussed earlier, the Backstage view contains a set of commands that enable you to manage documents and data about the documents. *Why? From the Backstage view in PowerPoint, for example, you can create, open, print, and save documents. You also can share documents, manage versions, set permissions, and modify document properties. In other Office 2013 apps, the Backstage view may contain features specific to those apps.* The following steps open a saved file, specifically the Craft Store file, that recently was saved.

- Tap or click FILE on the ribbon to open the Backstage view and then tap or click Open in the Backstage view to display the Open gallery in the Backstage view.

- Tap or click Computer to display recent folders accessed on your computer.

- Tap or click the Browse button to display the Open dialog box.

- If necessary, navigate to the location of the file to open as described in Steps 4a and 4b on pages OFF 30 and OFF 31.

- Tap or click the file to open, Craft Store in this case, to select the file (Figure 71).

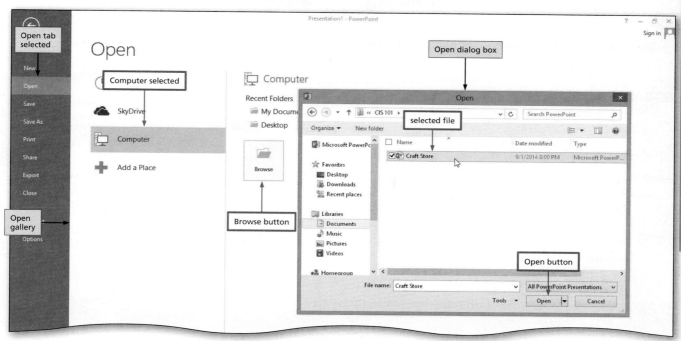

Figure 71

2

- Tap or click the Open button (Open dialog box) to open the file (shown in Figure 49 on page OFF 31).

Other Ways	
1. Press CTRL+O	2. Navigate to file in File Explorer window, double-tap or double-click file

To Create a New Document from the Backstage View

1 SIGN IN | 2 USE WINDOWS | 3 USE APPS | 4 FILE MANAGEMENT | 5 SWITCH APPS | 6 SAVE FILES
7 CHANGE SCREEN RESOLUTION | 8 EXIT APPS | 9 USE ADDITIONAL APP FEATURES | 10 USE HELP

You can open multiple documents in an Office program, such as PowerPoint, so that you can work on the documents at the same time. The following steps create a file, a blank presentation in this case, from the Backstage view. **Why?** *You want to create a new document while keeping the current document open.*

1

- Tap or click FILE on the ribbon to open the Backstage view.

- Tap or click the New tab in the Backstage view to display the New gallery (Figure 72).

Q&A Can I create documents through the Backstage view in other Office apps?
Yes. If the Office app has a New tab in the Backstage view, the New gallery displays various options for creating a new file.

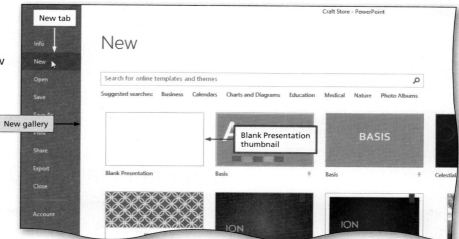

Figure 72

2

- Tap or click the Blank Presentation thumbnail in the New gallery to create a new presentation (Figure 73).

Figure 73

Other Ways

1. Press CTRL+N

To Enter Content in a Title Slide of a Second PowerPoint Presentation

The presentation title for this presentation is Elephant Habitat Opening. The following steps enter a presentation title on the title slide.

1 Tap or click the title text placeholder to select it.

2 Type **Elephant Habitat Opening** in the title text placeholder. Do not press the ENTER key (Figure 74).

Figure 74

To Save a File in a Folder

The following steps save the second presentation in the PowerPoint folder in the class folder (CIS 101, in this case) in the My Documents folder in the Documents library using the file name, Elephant Habitat Opening.

1 Tap or click the Save button on the Quick Access Toolbar (shown in Figure 74), which depending on settings will display either the Save As gallery in the Backstage view or the Save As dialog box.

2 If your screen displays the Backstage view, tap or click Computer, if necessary, to display options in the right pane related to saving on your computer; if your screen already displays the Save As dialog box, proceed to Step 4.

3 Tap or click the Browse button in the right pane to display the Save As dialog box.

4 If necessary, type **Elephant Habitat Opening** in the File name box (Save As dialog box) to change the file name. Do not press the ENTER key after typing the file name because you do not want to close the dialog box at this time.

5 If necessary, navigate to the desired save location (in this case, the PowerPoint folder in the CIS 101 folder [or your class folder] in the My Documents folder in the Documents library). For specific instructions, perform the tasks in Steps 4a and 4b on pages OFF 30 and OFF 31.

6 Tap or click the Save button (Save As dialog box) to save the presentation in the selected folder on the selected drive with the entered file name.

BTW

Customizing the Ribbon
In addition to customizing the Quick Access Toolbar, you can add items to and remove items from the ribbon. To customize the ribbon, click FILE on the ribbon to open the Backstage view, click Options in the Backstage view, and then click Customize Ribbon in the left pane of the Options dialog box. More information about customizing the ribbon is presented in a later chapter.

To Close a File Using the Backstage View

1 SIGN IN | 2 USE WINDOWS | 3 USE APPS | 4 FILE MANAGEMENT | 5 SWITCH APPS | 6 SAVE FILES
7 CHANGE SCREEN RESOLUTION | 8 EXIT APPS | **9 USE ADDITIONAL APP FEATURES** | **10 USE HELP**

Sometimes, you may want to close an Office file, such as a PowerPoint presentation, entirely and start over with a new file. ***Why else would I close a file?*** *You also may want to close a file when you are finished working with it so that you can begin a new file.* The following steps close the current active PowerPoint file, that is, the Elephant Habitat Opening presentation, without exiting the active app (PowerPoint, in this case).

- Tap or click FILE on the ribbon (shown in Figure 74) to open the Backstage view (Figure 75).

- Tap or click Close in the Backstage view to close the open file (Elephant Habitat Opening, in this case) without exiting the active app.

Q&A What if PowerPoint displays a dialog box about saving?
Tap or click the Save button if you want to save the changes, tap or click the Don't Save button if you want to ignore the changes since the last time you saved, and tap or click the Cancel button if you do not want to close the document.

Can I use the Backstage view to close an open file in other Office apps, such as Word and Excel?
Yes.

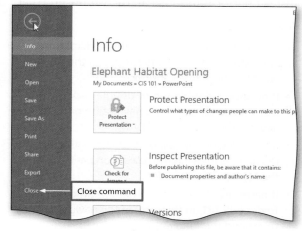

Figure 75

Other Ways

1. Press CTRL+F4

To Open a Recent File Using the Backstage View

You sometimes need to open a file that you recently modified. *Why? You may have more changes to make, such as adding more content or correcting errors.* The Backstage view allows you to access recent files easily. The following steps reopen the Elephant Habitat Opening file just closed.

- Tap or click FILE on the ribbon to open the Backstage view.

- Tap or click the Open tab in the Backstage view to display the Open gallery (Figure 76).

- Tap or click the desired file name in the Recent Presentations list, Elephant Habitat Opening in this case, to open the file (shown in Figure 74 on page OFF 44).

Figure 76

Q&A Can I use the Backstage view to open a recent file in other Office apps, such as Word and Excel?
Yes, as long as the file name appears in the list of recent files.

Other Ways

1. Tap or click FILE on ribbon, tap or click Open in Backstage view, tap or click Computer, tap or click Browse, navigate to file (Open dialog box), tap or click Open button

---

To Create a New Blank Document from File Explorer

File Explorer provides a means to create a blank Office document without running an Office app. The following steps use File Explorer to create a blank PowerPoint document. *Why? Sometimes you might need to create a blank document and then return to it later for editing.* If you are using Windows 7, skip these steps and instead perform the steps in the yellow box that immediately follows these Windows 8 steps.

- Double-tap or double-click the File Explorer app button on the taskbar to make the folder window the active window.

- If necessary, double-tap or double-click the Documents library in the navigation pane to expand the Documents library.

- If necessary, double-tap or double-click the My Documents folder in the navigation pane to expand the My Documents folder.

- If necessary, double-tap or double-click your class folder (CIS 101, in this case) in the navigation pane to expand the folder.

- Tap or click the PowerPoint folder in the navigation pane to display its contents in the file list.

- With the PowerPoint folder selected, press and hold or right-click an open area in the file list to display a shortcut menu.

- Tap or point to New on the shortcut menu to display the New submenu (Figure 77).

Figure 77

- Tap or click 'Microsoft PowerPoint Presentation' on the New submenu to display an icon and text box for a new file in the current folder window with the file name, New Microsoft PowerPoint Presentation, selected (Figure 78).

Figure 78

- Type `Elephant Habitat Volunteers` in the text box and then press the ENTER key to assign a new name to the new file in the current folder (Figure 79).

Figure 79

TO CREATE A NEW BLANK DOCUMENT FROM WINDOWS EXPLORER USING WINDOWS 7

If you are using Windows 7, perform these steps to create a new blank Office document from Windows Explorer instead of the previous steps that use Windows 8.

1. If necessary, click the Windows Explorer button on the taskbar to make the folder window the active window.

2. If necessary, double-click the Documents library in the navigation pane to expand the Documents library.

3. If necessary, double-click the My Documents folder in the navigation pane to expand the My Documents folder.

4. If necessary, double-click your class folder (CIS 101, in this case) in the navigation pane to expand the folder.

5. Click the PowerPoint folder in the navigation pane to display its contents in the file list.

6. With the PowerPoint folder selected, right-click an open area in the file list to display a shortcut menu.

7. Point to New on the shortcut menu to display the New submenu.

8. Click 'Microsoft PowerPoint Presentation' on the New submenu to display an icon and text box for a new file in the current folder window with the name, New Microsoft PowerPoint Presentation, selected.

9. Type `Elephant Habitat Volunteers` in the text box and then press the ENTER key to assign a new name to the new file in the current folder.

To Run an App from File Explorer and Open a File

1 SIGN IN | 2 USE WINDOWS | 3 USE APPS | 4 FILE MANAGEMENT | 5 SWITCH APPS | 6 SAVE FILES
7 CHANGE SCREEN RESOLUTION | 8 EXIT APPS | 9 USE ADDITIONAL APP FEATURES | 10 USE HELP

Previously, you learned how to run PowerPoint using the Start screen and the Search charm. The steps on the next page, which assume Windows is running, use File Explorer to run PowerPoint based on a typical installation. *Why? Another way to run an Office app is to open an existing file from File Explorer, which causes the app in which the file was created to run and then open the selected file.* You may need to ask your instructor how to run PowerPoint for your computer. If you are using Windows 7, follow the steps in the yellow box that immediately follows these Windows 8 steps.

1

- If necessary, display the file to open in the folder window in File Explorer (shown in Figure 79 on the previous page).

- Press and hold or right-click the file icon or file name (Elephant Habitat Volunteers, in this case) to display a shortcut menu (Figure 80).

Figure 80

2

- Tap or click Open on the shortcut menu to open the selected file in the app used to create the file, PowerPoint in this case (Figure 81).

- If the PowerPoint window is not maximized, tap or click the Maximize button on the title bar to maximize the window.

- Click the slide to display Slide 1 with the Title Slide layout applied.

Figure 81

To Run an App from Windows Explorer and Open a File Using Windows 7

If you are using Windows 7, perform these steps to run an app from Windows Explorer and open a file instead of the previous steps that use Windows 8.

1. Display the file to open in the folder window in Windows Explorer.
2. Right-click the file icon or file name (Elephant Habitat Volunteers, in this case) to display a shortcut menu.
3. Click Open on the shortcut menu to open the selected file in the app used to create the file, PowerPoint in this case.
4. If the PowerPoint window is not maximized, click the Maximize button on the title bar to maximize the window.

To Enter Text in a Document

The next step is to enter text in this blank PowerPoint document. The following step enters a line of text.

 Type **Elephant Habitat Volunteers** in the title text placeholder (shown in Figure 82).

To Save an Existing File with the Same File Name

Saving frequently cannot be overemphasized. *Why? You have made modifications to the file (presentation) since you created it. Thus, you should save again. Similarly, you should continue saving files frequently so that you do not lose the changes you have made since the time you last saved the file.* You can use the same file name, such as Elephant Habitat Volunteers, to save the changes made to the document. The following step saves a file again with the same file name.

1

- Tap or click the Save button on the Quick Access Toolbar to overwrite the previously saved file (Elephant Habitat Volunteers, in this case) in the PowerPoint folder (Figure 82).

Figure 82

Other Ways

1. Press CTRL+S or press SHIFT+F12

To Save a File with a New File Name

You might want to save a file with a different name or to a different location. For example, you might start a homework assignment with a data file and then save it with a final file name for submission to your instructor, saving it to a location designated by your instructor. The following steps save a file with a different file name.

1 Tap or click the FILE tab to open the Backstage view.

2 Tap or click the Save As tab to display the Save As gallery.

3 If necessary, tap or click Computer to display options in the right pane related to saving on your computer.

4 Tap or click the Browse button in the right pane to display the Save As dialog box.

5 Type **Elephant Habitat Staff and Volunteers** in the File name box (Save As dialog box) to change the file name. Do not press the ENTER key after typing the file name because you do not want to close the dialog box at this time.

6 If necessary, navigate to the desired save location (in this case, the PowerPoint folder in the CIS 101 folder [or your class folder] in the My Documents folder in the Documents library). For specific instructions, perform the tasks in Steps 4a and 4b on pages OFF 30 and OFF 31.

7 Tap or click the Save button (Save As dialog box) to save the presentation in the selected folder on the selected drive with the entered file name.

To Exit an Office App

You are finished using PowerPoint. The following steps exit PowerPoint. You would use similar steps to exit other Office apps.

1 Because you have multiple PowerPoint documents open, press and hold or right-click the app button on the taskbar and then tap or click 'Close all windows' on the shortcut menu to close all open documents and exit PowerPoint.

2 If a dialog box appears, tap or click the Save button to save any changes made to the file since the last save.

Renaming, Moving, and Deleting Files

Earlier in this chapter, you learned how to organize files in folders, which is part of a process known as **file management**. The following sections cover additional file management topics including renaming, moving, and deleting files.

1 SIGN IN | 2 USE WINDOWS | 3 USE APPS | 4 FILE MANAGEMENT | 5 SWITCH APPS | 6 SAVE FILES
7 CHANGE SCREEN RESOLUTION | 8 EXIT APPS | 9 USE ADDITIONAL APP FEATURES | 10 USE HELP

To Rename a File

In some circumstances, you may want to change the name of, or rename, a file or a folder. *Why? You may want to distinguish a file in one folder or drive from a copy of a similar file, or you may decide to rename a file to better identify its contents.* The PowerPoint folder shown in Figure 66 on page OFF 40 contains the PowerPoint document, Craft Store. The following steps change the name of the Craft Store file in the PowerPoint folder to Craft Store Presentation. If you are using Windows 7, skip these steps and instead perform the steps in the yellow box that immediately follows these Windows 8 steps.

1

- If necessary, tap or click the File Explorer app button on the taskbar to make the folder window the active window.

- If necessary, navigate to the location of the file to be renamed (in this case, the PowerPoint folder in the CIS 101 [or your class folder] folder in the My Documents folder in the Documents library) to display the file(s) it contains in the file list.

- Press and hold or right-click the Craft Store icon or file name in the file list to select the Craft Store file and display a shortcut menu that presents a list of commands related to files (Figure 83).

Figure 83

2

- Tap or click Rename on the shortcut menu to place the current file name in a text box.

- Type **Craft Store Presentation** in the text box and then press the ENTER key (Figure 84).

 Are any risks involved in renaming files that are located on a hard disk?
If you inadvertently rename a file that is associated with certain apps, the apps may not be able to find the file and, therefore, may not run properly. Always use caution when renaming files.

Can I rename a file when it is open?
No, a file must be closed to change the file name.

Figure 84

Other Ways

1. Select file, press F2, type new file name, press ENTER   2. Select file, tap or click Rename (Home tab | Organize group), type new file name, press ENTER

TO RENAME A FILE USING WINDOWS 7

If you are using Windows 7, perform these steps to rename a file instead of the previous steps that use Windows 8.

1. If necessary, click the Windows Explorer app button on the taskbar to make the folder window the active window.

2. Navigate to the location of the file to be renamed (in this case, the PowerPoint folder in the CIS 101 [or your class folder] folder in the My Documents folder in the Documents library) to display the file(s) it contains in the file list.

3. Right-click the Craft Store icon or file name in the file list to select the Craft Store file and display a shortcut menu that presents a list of commands related to files.

4. Click Rename on the shortcut menu to place the current file name in a text box.

5. Type **Craft Store Presentation** in the text box and then press the ENTER key.

To Move a File

1 SIGN IN | 2 USE WINDOWS | 3 USE APPS | 4 FILE MANAGEMENT | 5 SWITCH APPS | 6 SAVE FILES
7 CHANGE SCREEN RESOLUTION | 8 EXIT APPS | 9 USE ADDITIONAL APP FEATURES | 10 USE HELP

Why? At some time, you may want to move a file from one folder, called the source folder, to another, called the destination folder. When you move a file, it no longer appears in the original folder. If the destination and the source folders are on the same media, you can move a file by dragging it. If the folders are on different media, then you will need to press and hold and then drag, or right-drag the file, and then click Move here on the shortcut menu. The following step moves the Elephant Habitat Volunteers file from the PowerPoint folder to the CIS 101 folder. If you are using Windows 7, skip these steps and instead perform the steps in the yellow box that immediately follows these Windows 8 steps.

1

- In File Explorer, if necessary, navigate to the location of the file to be moved (in this case, the PowerPoint folder in the CIS 101 folder [or your class folder] in the Documents library).

- If necessary, tap or click the PowerPoint folder in the navigation pane to display the files it contains in the right pane.

- Drag the Elephant Habitat Volunteers file in the right pane to the CIS 101 folder in the navigation pane and notice the ScreenTip as you drag the mouse (Figure 85).

Figure 85

 Experiment

- Tap or click the CIS 101 folder in the navigation pane to verify that the file was moved.

Other Ways

1. Press and hold or right-click file to move, tap or click Cut on shortcut menu, press and hold or right-click destination folder, tap or click Paste on shortcut menu

2. Select file to move, press CTRL+X, select destination folder, press CTRL+V

To Move a File Using Windows 7

If you are using Windows 7, perform these steps to move a file instead of the previous steps that use Windows 8.

1. In Windows Explorer, navigate to the location of the file to be moved (in this case, the PowerPoint folder in the CIS 101 folder [or your class folder] in the Documents library).

2. Click the PowerPoint folder in the navigation pane to display the files it contains in the right pane.

3. Drag the Elephant Habitat Volunteers file in the right pane to the CIS 101 folder in the navigation pane.

1 SIGN IN | 2 USE WINDOWS | 3 USE APPS | **4 FILE MANAGEMENT** | 5 SWITCH APPS | 6 SAVE FILES
7 CHANGE SCREEN RESOLUTION | 8 EXIT APPS | 9 USE ADDITIONAL APP FEATURES | **10 USE HELP**

To Delete a File

A final task you may want to perform is to delete a file. Exercise extreme caution when deleting a file or files. When you delete a file from a hard disk, the deleted file is stored in the Recycle Bin where you can recover it until you empty the Recycle Bin. If you delete a file from removable media, such as a USB flash drive, the file is deleted permanently. The next steps delete the Elephant Habitat Volunteers file from the CIS 101 folder. *Why? When a file no longer is needed, you can delete it to conserve space in your storage location.* If you are using Windows 7, skip these steps and instead perform the steps in the yellow box that immediately follows these Windows 8 steps.

- In File Explorer, navigate to the location of the file to be deleted (in this case, the CIS 101 folder [or your class folder] in the Documents library).

- Press and hold or right-click the Elephant Habitat Volunteers icon or file name in the right pane to select the file and display a shortcut menu (Figure 86).

- Tap or click Delete on the shortcut menu to delete the file.

- If a dialog box appears, tap or click the Yes button to delete the file.

Q&A
Can I use this same technique to delete a folder?
Yes. Right-click the folder and then click Delete on the shortcut menu. When you delete a folder, all of the files and folders contained in the folder you are deleting, together with any files and folders on lower hierarchical levels, are deleted as well.

Figure 86

Other Ways

1. Select icon, press DELETE

To Delete a File Using Windows 7

If you are using Windows 7, perform these steps to delete a file instead of the previous steps that use Windows 8.

1. In Windows Explorer, navigate to the location of the file to be deleted (in this case, the CIS 101 folder [or your class folder] in the Documents library).

2. Right-click the Elephant Habitat Volunteers icon or file name in the right pane to select the file and display a shortcut menu.

3. Click Delete on the shortcut menu to delete the file.

4. If a dialog box appears, click the Yes button to delete the file.

Microsoft Office and Windows Help

At any time while you are using one of the Office apps, such as PowerPoint, you can use Office Help to display information about all topics associated with the app. This section illustrates the use of PowerPoint Help. Help in other Office apps operates in a similar fashion.

In Office, Help is presented in a window that has browser-style navigation buttons. Each Office app has its own Help home page, which is the starting Help page that is displayed in the Help window. If your computer is connected to the Internet, the contents of the Help page reflect both the local help files installed on the computer and material from Microsoft's website.

To Open the Help Window in an Office App

1 SIGN IN | 2 USE WINDOWS | 3 USE APPS | 4 FILE MANAGEMENT | 5 SWITCH APPS | 6 SAVE FILES

7 CHANGE SCREEN RESOLUTION | 8 EXIT APPS | 9 USE ADDITIONAL APP FEATURES | **10 USE HELP**

The following step opens the PowerPoint Help window. *Why? You might not understand how certain commands or operations work in PowerPoint, so you can obtain the necessary information using help. The step to open a Help window in other Office programs is similar.*

- Run PowerPoint.

- Tap or click the Microsoft PowerPoint Help button near the upper-right corner of the app window to open the PowerPoint Help window (Figure 87).

Figure 87

Other Ways

1. Press F1

Moving and Resizing Windows

At times, it is useful, or even necessary, to have more than one window open and visible on the screen at the same time. You can resize and move these open windows so that you can view different areas of and elements in the window. In the case of the Help window, for example, it could be covering document text in the PowerPoint window that you need to see.

To Move a Window by Dragging

1 SIGN IN | **2 USE WINDOWS** | 3 USE APPS | 4 FILE MANAGEMENT | 5 SWITCH APPS | 6 SAVE FILES

7 CHANGE SCREEN RESOLUTION | 8 EXIT APPS | 9 USE ADDITIONAL APP FEATURES | 10 USE HELP

You can move any open window that is not maximized to another location on the desktop by dragging the title bar of the window. *Why? You might want to have a better view of what is behind the window or just want to move the window so that you can see it better.* The step on the next page drags the PowerPoint Help window to the upper-left corner of the desktop.

• Drag the window title bar (the PowerPoint Help window title bar, in this case) so that the window moves to the upper-left corner of the desktop, as shown in Figure 88.

Figure 88

To Resize a Window by Dragging

1 SIGN IN | **2 USE WINDOWS** | 3 USE APPS | 4 FILE MANAGEMENT | 5 SWITCH APPS | 6 SAVE FILES
7 CHANGE SCREEN RESOLUTION | 8 EXIT APPS | 9 USE ADDITIONAL APP FEATURES | 10 USE HELP

A method used to change the size of the window is to drag the window borders. The following step changes the size of the PowerPoint Help window by dragging its borders. *Why? Sometimes, information is not visible completely in a window, and you want to increase the size of the window.*

• If you are using a mouse, point to the lower-right corner of the window (the PowerPoint Help window, in this case) until the pointer changes to a two-headed arrow.

• Drag the bottom border downward to display more of the active window (Figure 89).

Q&A
Can I drag other borders on the window to enlarge or shrink the window?
Yes, you can drag the left, right, and top borders and any window corner to resize a window.

Will Windows remember the new size of the window after I close it?
Yes. When you reopen the window, Windows will display it at the same size it was when you closed it.

Figure 89

Using Office Help

Once an Office app's Help window is open, several methods exist for navigating Help. You can search for help by using any of the three following methods from the Help window:

1. Enter search text in the 'Search online help' text box.
2. Click the links in the Help window.
3. Use the Table of Contents.

To Obtain Help Using the 'Search online help' Text Box

1 SIGN IN | 2 USE WINDOWS | 3 USE APPS | 4 FILE MANAGEMENT | 5 SWITCH APPS | 6 SAVE FILES
7 CHANGE SCREEN RESOLUTION | 8 EXIT APPS | 9 USE ADDITIONAL APP FEATURES | 10 USE HELP

Assume for the following example that you want to know more about fonts. The following steps use the 'Search online help' text box to obtain useful information about fonts by entering the word, fonts, as search text. *Why? You may not know the exact help topic you are looking to find, so using keywords can help narrow your search.*

1

- Type **fonts** in the 'Search online help' text box at the top of the PowerPoint Help window to enter the search text.

- Tap or click the 'Search online help' button to display the search results (Figure 90).

Q&A

Why do my search results differ?
If you do not have an Internet connection, your results will reflect only the content of the Help files on your computer. When searching for help online, results also can change as material is added, deleted, and updated on the online Help webpages maintained by Microsoft.

Why were my search results not very helpful?
When initiating a search, be sure to check the spelling of the search text; also, keep your search specific to return the most accurate results.

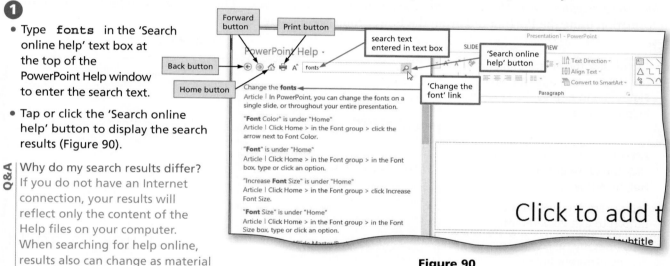

Figure 90

2

- Tap or click the 'Change the fonts' link to display the Help information associated with the selected topic (Figure 91).

Figure 91

• Tap or click the Home button in the Help window to clear the search results and redisplay the Help home page (Figure 92).

Figure 92

To Obtain Help Using Help Links

1 SIGN IN | 2 USE WINDOWS | 3 USE APPS | 4 FILE MANAGEMENT | 5 SWITCH APPS | 6 SAVE FILES
7 CHANGE SCREEN RESOLUTION | 8 EXIT APPS | 9 USE ADDITIONAL APP FEATURES | **10 USE HELP**

If your topic of interest is listed in the Help window, you can click the link to begin browsing the Help categories instead of entering search text. *Why? You browse Help just as you would browse a website. If you know which category contains your Help information, you may wish to use these links.* The following step finds the Portrait information using the Portrait link from the PowerPoint Help home page.

• Tap or click the Portrait link on the Help home page (shown in Figure 92) to display the Portrait help links (Figure 93).

• After reviewing the page, tap or click the Close button to close the Help window.

• Tap or click PowerPoint's Close button to exit PowerPoint.

Q&A Why does my Help window display different links?
The content of your Help window may differ because Microsoft continually updates its Help information.

Figure 93

Obtaining Help while Working in an Office App

Help in the Office apps, such as PowerPoint, provides you with the ability to obtain help directly, without opening the Help window and initiating a search. For example, you may be unsure about how a particular command works, or you may be presented with a dialog box that you are not sure how to use.

Figure 94 shows one option for obtaining help while working in an Office app. If you want to learn more about a command, point to its button and wait for the ScreenTip to appear. If the Help icon appears in the ScreenTip, press the F1 key while pointing to the button to open the Help window associated with that command.

Figure 95 shows a dialog box that contains a Help button. Pressing the F1 key while the dialog box is displayed opens a Help window. The Help

Figure 94

window contains help about that dialog box, if available. If no help file is available for that particular dialog box, then the main Help window opens.

Using Windows Help and Support

One of the more powerful Windows features is Windows Help and Support. **Windows Help and Support** is available when using Windows or when using any Microsoft app running in Windows. The same methods used for searching Microsoft Office Help can be used in Windows Help and Support. The difference is that Windows Help and Support displays help for Windows, instead of for Microsoft Office.

Figure 95

To Use Windows Help and Support

1 SIGN IN | 2 USE WINDOWS | 3 USE APPS | 4 FILE MANAGEMENT | 5 SWITCH APPS | 6 SAVE FILES
7 CHANGE SCREEN RESOLUTION | 8 EXIT APPS | 9 USE ADDITIONAL APP FEATURES | 10 USE HELP

The following steps use Windows Help and Support and open the Windows Help and Support window, which contains links to more information about Windows. *Why? This feature is designed to assist you in using Windows or the various apps.* If you are using Windows 7, skip these steps and instead perform the steps in the yellow box that immediately follows these Windows 8 steps.

- Swipe in from the right edge of the screen or point to the upper-right corner of the screen to display the Charms bar (Figure 96).

Figure 96

• Tap or click the Settings charm on the Charms bar to display the Settings menu (Figure 97).

Figure 97

• Tap or click Help to open the Windows Help and Support window (Figure 98).

• After reviewing the Windows Help and Support window, tap or click the Close button to close the Windows Help and Support window.

Figure 98

Other Ways

1. Press WINDOWS + F1

BTW

Certification
The Microsoft Office Specialist (MOS) program provides an opportunity for you to obtain a valuable industry credential — proof that you have the Microsoft Office 2013 skills required by employers. For more information, visit the Certification resource on the Student Companion Site located on www.cengagebrain.com. For detailed instructions about accessing available resources, visit www.cengage .com/ct/studentdownload or contact your instructor for information about accessing the required files.

BTW

Quick Reference
For a table that lists how to complete the tasks covered in this book using touch gestures, the mouse, ribbon, shortcut menu, and keyboard, see the Quick Reference Summary at the back of this book, or visit the Quick Reference resource on the Student Companion Site located on www.cengagebrain.com. For detailed instructions about accessing available resources, visit www.cengage .com/ct/studentdownload or contact your instructor for information about accessing the required files.

TO USE WINDOWS HELP AND SUPPORT WITH WINDOWS 7

If you are using Windows 7, perform these steps to start Windows Help and Support instead of the previous steps that use Windows 8.

1. Click the Start button on the taskbar to display the Start menu.

2. Click Help and Support on the Start menu to open the Windows Help and Support window.

3. After reviewing the Windows Help and Support window, click the Close button to exit Windows Help and Support.

Chapter Summary

In this chapter, you learned how to use the Windows interface, several touch screen and mouse operations, and file and folder management. You also learned some basic features of PowerPoint and discovered the common elements that exist among Microsoft Office apps. The items listed below include all of the new Windows and PowerPoint skills you have learned in this chapter, with the tasks grouped by activity.

CONSIDER THIS: PLAN AHEAD

What guidelines should you follow to plan your projects?

The process of communicating specific information is a learned, rational skill. Computers and software, especially Microsoft Office 2013, can help you develop ideas and present detailed information to a particular audience and minimize much of the laborious work of drafting and revising projects. No matter what method you use to plan a project, it is beneficial to follow some specific guidelines from the onset to arrive at a final product that is informative, relevant, and effective. Use some aspects of these guidelines every time you undertake a project, and others as needed in specific instances.

1. Determine the project's purpose.
   a) Clearly define why you are undertaking this assignment.
   b) Begin to draft ideas of how best to communicate information by handwriting ideas on paper; composing directly on a laptop, tablet, or mobile device; or developing a strategy that fits your particular thinking and writing style.

2. Analyze your audience.
   a) Learn about the people who will read, analyze, or view your work.
   b) Determine their interests and needs so that you can present the information they need to know and omit the information they already possess.
   c) Form a mental picture of these people or find photos of people who fit this profile so that you can develop a project with the audience in mind.

3. Gather possible content.
   a) Locate existing information that may reside in spreadsheets, databases, or other files.
   b) Conduct a web search to find relevant websites.
   c) Read pamphlets, magazine and newspaper articles, and books to gain insights of how others have approached your topic.
   d) Conduct personal interviews to obtain perspectives not available by any other means.
   e) Consider video and audio clips as potential sources for material that might complement or support the factual data you uncover.

4. Determine what content to present to your audience.

    a) Write three or four major ideas you want an audience member to remember after reading or viewing your project.

    b) Envision your project's endpoint, the key fact you wish to emphasize, so that all project elements lead to this final element.

    c) Determine relevant time factors, such as the length of time to develop the project, how long readers will spend reviewing your project, or the amount of time allocated for your speaking engagement.

    d) Decide whether a graph, photo, or artistic element can express or enhance a particular concept.

    e) Be mindful of the order in which you plan to present the content, and place the most important material at the top or bottom of the page, because readers and audience members generally remember the first and last pieces of information they see and hear.

CONSIDER THIS

How should you submit solutions to questions in the assignments identified with a symbol?
Every assignment in this book contains one or more questions identified with a ❈ symbol. These questions require you to think beyond the assigned file. Present your solutions to the questions in the format required by your instructor. Possible formats may include one or more of these options: write the answer; create a document that contains the answer; present your answer to the class; discuss your answer in a group; record the answer as audio or video using a webcam, smartphone, or portable media player; or post answers on a blog, wiki, or website.

Apply Your Knowledge

Reinforce the skills and apply the concepts you learned in this chapter.

Creating a Folder and a Presentation

Instructions: You will create a PowerPoint folder and then create a PowerPoint presentation and save it in the folder.

Perform the following tasks:

1. Open the File Explorer window and then double-tap or double-click to open the Documents library.

2. Tap or click the New folder button on the Quick Access Toolbar to display a new folder icon and text box for the folder name.

3. Type **PowerPoint** in the text box to name the folder. Press the ENTER key to create the folder in the Documents library.

4. Run PowerPoint.

5. Enter the text shown in Figure 99 in a new blank title slide.

6. If requested by your instructor, enter your name in the PowerPoint presentation.

Figure 99

7. Tap or click the Save button on the Quick Access Toolbar. Navigate to the PowerPoint folder in the Documents library and then save the document using the file name, Apply 1 Speech.

8. If your Quick Access Toolbar does not show the Quick Print button, add the Quick Print button to the Quick Access Toolbar. Print the document using the Quick Print button on the Quick Access Toolbar. When you are finished printing, remove the Quick Print button from the Quick Access Toolbar.

9. Submit the printout to your instructor.

10. Exit PowerPoint.

11. ❈ What other commands might you find useful to include on the Quick Access Toolbar?

Extend Your Knowledge

Extend the skills you learned in this chapter and experiment with new skills. You will use Help to complete the assignment.

Using Help

Instructions: Use PowerPoint Help to perform the following tasks.

Perform the following tasks:

1. Run PowerPoint.

2. Tap or click the Microsoft PowerPoint Help button to open the PowerPoint Help window (Figure 100).

3. Search PowerPoint Help to answer the following questions.

   a. What are three features new to PowerPoint 2013?
   b. What type of training courses are available through Help?
   c. What are the steps to add a new group to the ribbon?
   d. How do you add speaker notes to slides?
   e. How do you insert clip art?
   f. Where do you find templates that have complete formatting?
   g. How do Smart Guides help align slide content?
   h. What is a SmartArt graphic?
   i. What is cropping?
   j. How do you add sound to a presentation?

Figure 100

4. Type the answers from your searches in a new blank PowerPoint presentation. Save the document with a new file name and then submit it in the format specified by your instructor.

5. If requested by your instructor, enter your name in the PowerPoint document.

6. Exit PowerPoint.

7. ✳ What search text did you use to perform the searches above? Did it take multiple attempts to search and locate the exact information for which you were searching?

Analyze, Correct, Improve

Analyze a file structure, correct all errors, and improve the design.

Organizing Vacation Photos

Note: To complete this assignment, you will be required to use the Data Files for Students. Visit www.cengage.com/ct/student-download for detailed instructions or contact your instructor for information about accessing the required files.

Figure 101

Instructions: Traditionally, you have stored photos from past vacations together in one folder. The photos are becoming difficult to manage, and you now want to store them in appropriate folders. You will create the folder structure shown in Figure 101. You then will move the photos to the folders so that they will be organized properly.

1. Correct Create the folder structure in Figure 101 so that you are able to store the photos in an organized manner. If requested by your instructor, add another folder using your last name as the folder name.

2. Improve View each photo and drag it to the appropriate folder to improve the organization. Submit the assignment in the format specified by your instructor.

3. ✳ In which folder did you place each photo? Think about the files you have stored on your computer. What folder hierarchy would be best to manage your files?

In the Labs

Use the guidelines, concepts, and skills presented in this chapter to increase your knowledge of Windows 8 and PowerPoint 2013. Labs 1 and 2, which increase in difficulty, require you to create solutions based on what you learned in the chapter; Lab 3 requires you to create a solution, which uses cloud and web technologies, by learning and investigating on your own from general guidance.

Lab 1: Creating Folders for a Video Store

Problem: Your friend works for Ebaird Video. He would like to organize his files in relation to the types of videos available in the store. He has six main categories: drama, action, romance, foreign, biographical, and comedy. You are to create a folder structure similar to Figure 102.

Instructions: Perform the following tasks:

1. Insert a USB flash drive in an available USB port and then open the USB flash drive window.

2. Create the main folder for Ebaird Video.

3. Navigate to the Ebaird Video folder.

4. Within the Ebaird Video folder, create a folder for each of the following: Drama, Action, Romance, Foreign, Biographical, and Comedy.

5. Within the Action folder, create two additional folders, one for Science Fiction and the second for Western.

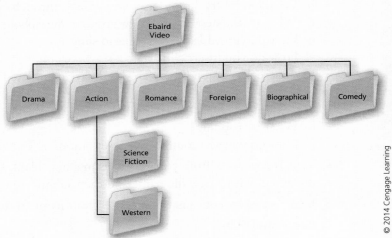

Figure 102

© 2014 Cengage Learning

6. If requested by your instructor, add another folder using your last name as the folder name.

7. Submit the assignment in the format specified by your instructor.

8. ✳ Think about how you use your computer for various tasks (consider personal, professional, and academic reasons). What folders do you think will be required on your computer to store the files you save?

Lab 2: Saving Files in Folders

Problem: You are taking a class that requires you to complete three PowerPoint chapters. You will save the work completed in each chapter in a different folder (Figure 103).

Instructions: Create the folders shown in Figure 103. Then, using PowerPoint, create three small files to save in each folder.

1. Create a PowerPoint document containing the text, First PowerPoint Chapter.

2. In the Backstage view, tap or click Save As and then tap or click Computer.

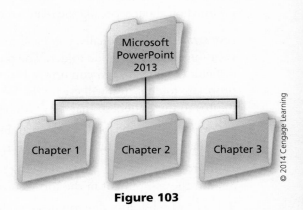

Figure 103

© 2014 Cengage Learning

3. Tap or click the Browse button to display the Save As dialog box.

4. Tap or click Documents to open the Documents library. Next, create the folder structure shown in Figure 103 using the New folder button.

5. Navigate to the Chapter 1 folder and then save the file in the Chapter 1 folder using the file name, PowerPoint Chapter 1 Document.

6. Create another PowerPoint document containing the text, Second PowerPoint Chapter, and then save it in the Chapter 2 folder using the file name, PowerPoint Chapter 2 Document.

7. Create a third PowerPoint document containing the text, Third PowerPoint Chapter, and then save it in the Chapter 3 folder using the file name, PowerPoint Chapter 3 Document.

8. If requested by your instructor, add your name to each of the three PowerPoint files.

9. Submit the assignment in the format specified by your instructor.

10. ✸ Based on your current knowledge of Windows and PowerPoint how will you organize folders for assignments in this class? Why?

Lab 3: Expand Your World: Cloud and Web Technologies
Creating Folders on SkyDrive and Using the PowerPoint Web App

Problem: You are taking a class that requires you to create folders on SkyDrive, use the PowerPoint Web App to create a document, and then save the document in a folder on SkyDrive (Figure 104).

Instructions: Perform the following tasks:

1. Sign in to SkyDrive in your browser.

2. Use the Create button to create the folder structure shown in Figure 104.

3. In the Notes folder, use the Create button to create a PowerPoint document with the file name, Notes, and containing the text, Important Test on Tuesday, on Slide 1.

4. If requested by your instructor, add your name to the PowerPoint document.

5. Save the document in the Notes folder and then exit the app.

6. Submit the assignment in the format specified by your instructor.

7. ✸ Based on your current knowledge of SkyDrive, do you think you will use it? What about the PowerPoint Web App?

Figure 104

© 2014 Cengage Learning

✸ Consider This: Your Turn

Apply your creative thinking and problem solving skills to design and implement a solution.

1: Creating Beginning Files for Classes

Personal

Part 1:   You are taking the following classes: Introduction to Sociology, Chemistry, Calculus, and Marketing. Create folders for each of the classes. Create a folder structure that will store the documents for each of these classes. Use PowerPoint to create a separate PowerPoint presentation for each class. Each document should contain the name of each class and the class meeting locations and times: Introduction to Sociology meets on Mondays and Wednesdays from 8:00 a.m. to 10:00 a.m.; Chemistry meets on Tuesdays and Thursdays from 11:00 a.m. to 1:00 p.m.; Calculus

Continued >

Consider This: Your Turn *continued*

meets on Mondays, Wednesdays, and Fridays from 1:30 p.m. to 3:00 p.m.; and Marketing meets on Tuesdays from 5:00 to 8:00 p.m. If requested by your instructor, add your name to each of the PowerPoint documents. Use the concepts and techniques presented in this chapter to create the folders and files, and store the files in their respective locations. Submit your assignment in the format specified by your instructor.

Part 2:   You made several decisions while determining the folder structure in this assignment. What was the rationale behind these decisions? Are there any other decisions that also might have worked?

2: Creating Folders
Professional

Part 1:   Your boss at the media store where you work part-time has asked for help with organizing his files. After looking through the files, you decided upon a file structure for her to use, including the following folders: CDs, DVDs, and general merchandise. Use PowerPoint to create separate PowerPoint presentations that list examples in each category. For example, CDs include music [blues, rock, country, new age, pop, and soundtracks], blank discs, books, and games; DVDs include movies [action, documentary, music videos, mystery, and drama], television series, and blank discs; and general merchandise includes clothing, portable media players, cases, earbuds, chargers, and cables. If requested by your instructor, add your name to each of the PowerPoint documents. Use the concepts and techniques presented in this chapter to create the folders. Submit your assignment in the format specified by your instructor.

Part 2:   You made several decisions while determining the folder structure in this assignment. What was the rationale behind these decisions? Justify why you feel this folder structure will help your boss organize her files.

3: Using Help
Research and Collaboration

Part 1:   You have just installed a new computer with the Windows operating system and want to be sure that it is protected from the threat of viruses. You ask two of your friends to help research computer viruses, virus prevention, and virus removal. In a team of three people, each person should choose a topic (computer viruses, virus prevention, and virus removal) to research. Use the concepts and techniques presented in this chapter to use Help to find information regarding these topics. Create a PowerPoint document that contains steps to properly safeguard a computer from viruses, ways to prevent viruses, as well as the different ways to remove a virus should your computer become infected. Submit your assignment in the format specified by your instructor.

Part 2:   You made several decisions while searching Windows Help and Support for this assignment. What decisions did you make? What was the rationale behind these decisions? How did you locate the required information about viruses in help?

Learn Online

Reinforce what you learned in this chapter with games, exercises, training, and many other online activities and resources.

Student Companion Site   Reinforcement activities and resources are available at no additional cost on www.cengagebrain.com. Visit www.cengage.com/ct/studentdownload for detailed instructions about accessing the resources available at the Student Companion Site.

SAM   Put your skills into practice with SAM Projects! If you have a SAM account, go to www.cengage.com/sam2013 to access SAM assignments for this chapter.

Office 365 Essentials

Microsoft product screen shots used with permission from Microsoft Corporation.

Objectives

You will have mastered the material in this chapter when you can:

- Describe the components of Office 365

- Compare Office 2013 to Office 365 subscription plans

- Understand the productivity tools of Office 365

- Sync multiple devices using Office 365

- Describe how business teams collaborate using SharePoint

- Describe how to use a SharePoint template to design a public website

- Describe how to conduct an online meeting with Lync

Explore Office 365

Introduction to Office 365

Microsoft Office 365 uses the cloud to deliver a subscription-based service offering the newest Office suite and much more. The Microsoft cloud provides Office software and information stored on remote servers all over the world. Your documents are located online or on the cloud, which provides you access to your information anywhere using a PC, Mac, tablet, mobile phone, or other device with an Internet connection. For businesses and students alike, Office 365 offers significant cost savings compared to the traditional cost of purchasing Microsoft Office 2013. In addition to the core desktop Office suite, Office 365 provides access to email, calendars, conferencing, file sharing, and website design, which sync across multiple devices.

Cloud Computing

Cloud computing refers to a collection of computer servers that house resources users access through the Internet (Figure 1). These resources include email messages, schedules, music, photos, videos, games, websites, programs, apps, servers, storage, and more. Instead of accessing these resources on your computer or mobile device, you access them on the cloud.

© iStockphoto / Petar Chernaev; © iStockphoto / cotesebastien; © Cengage Learning; © iStockphoto / Jill Fromer; © Cengage Learning; © iStockphoto / 123 render; © Cengage Learning; © Pablo Eder / Shutterstock.com; © Peter Gudella / Shutterstock.com; © Mr.Reborn55 / Shutterstock.com; Courtesy of LG Electronics USA Inc.; © Cengage Learning

Figure 1

Cloud computing can help businesses be more efficient and save them money by shifting usage and the consumption of resources, such as servers and programs, from a local environment to the Internet. For example, an employee working during the day in California could use computing resources located in an office in London that is closed for the evening. When the company in California uses the computing resources, it pays a fee that is based on the amount of computing time and other resources it consumes, much in the same way that consumers pay utility companies for the amount of electricity they use.

Cloud computing is changing how users access and pay for software applications. Fading fast are the days when software packages were sold in boxes at a physical store location with a one-time purchase software license fee. Instead, the new pricing structure is a subscription-based model, where users pay a monthly or annual fee for the software that you can use on multiple devices. The cloud-based Office 365 offers the Office suite with added features that allow you to communicate and collaborate with others in real time.

When you create a free Microsoft account, do you get free cloud storage space?
Yes, when you create a free Microsoft account at Outlook.com, you have access to 7 GB of cloud storage for any type of files.

CONSIDER THIS

What Is Office 365?

Office 365 (Office365.com) is a collection of programs and services, which includes the Microsoft Office 2013 suite, file storage, online collaboration, and file synchronization, as shown in Figure 2 on the next page. You can access these services using your computer, browser, or supported mobile device. For example, a business has two options for providing Office to their employees. A business could purchase Office 2013 and install the software on company computers and servers; however, this traditional Office 2013 package with perpetual licensing does not include the communication and collaboration tools. Employees could not access the Office software if they were not using their work computers. In contrast, if the business purchases a monthly subscription to Office 365, each employee has access to the Office suite on up to five different computers, whether at home or work; company-wide email; web conferencing; website creation capabilities; cloud storage; and shared files. For a lower price, Office 365 provides many more features. In addition, a business may prefer a subscription plan with predictable monthly costs and no up-front infrastructure costs.

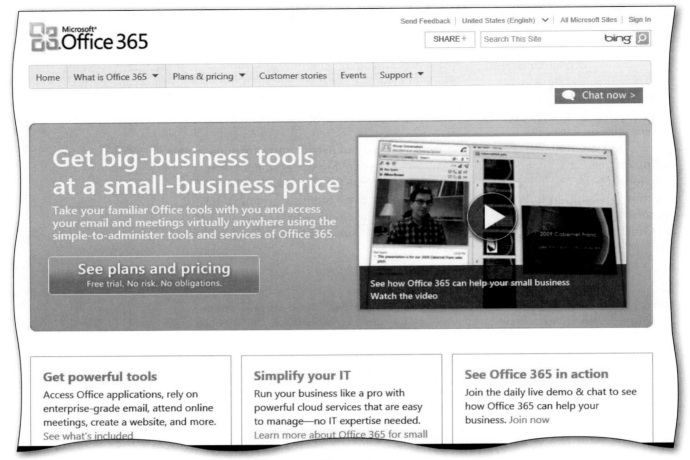

Figure 2

Office 2013 and Office 365 Features Comparison

Office 2013 is the name of the perpetual software package that includes individual applications that can be installed on a single computer. An Office 365 subscription comes with a license to install the software on multiple PCs or Macs at the same time, giving you more flexibility to use your Office products in your home, school, or workplace, whether on a computer or a mobile device. Office 365 provides the Office 2013 programs as part of a subscription service that includes online storage, sharing, and syncing via Microsoft cloud services as shown in Table 1.

Office 365 is available in business, consumer, education, and government editions. Office 365 combines the full version of the Microsoft Office desktop suite with cloud-based versions of Microsoft's communications and collaboration services. The subscription package includes:

- Microsoft Exchange online for shared email and calendars
- Microsoft SharePoint Online for shared file access and public website creation
- Microsoft Office Web apps for browser viewing
- Microsoft Lync Online for communication services

Table 1 Office 2013 and Office 365 Feature Comparison

Office 2013 Professional (Installed on a single device)	Office 365 Subscription (Installed on 2 to 5 devices)
Microsoft Word	Microsoft Word
Microsoft Excel	Microsoft Excel
Microsoft PowerPoint	Microsoft PowerPoint
Microsoft Access	Microsoft Access
Microsoft Outlook	Microsoft Outlook
Microsoft Publisher	Microsoft Publisher
Microsoft OneNote	Microsoft OneNote
	email and calendars (Exchange Online)
	file sharing (SharePoint Online)
	public website design and publishing (SharePoint Online)
	browser-based Office Web Apps
	instant messaging (Lync Online)
	audio and video web conferencing (Lync Online)
	screen sharing with shared control (Lync Online)
	technical support

© 2014 Cengage Learning

Subscription-Based Office 365 Plans

Microsoft provides various subscription plans for Office 365 with different benefits for each individual or organization. Subscription plans include Office 365 Home Premium for home users, Office 365 University for students, Office 365 Small Business, Office 365 Small Business Premium, Office 365 Midsize Business, and Office 365 Enterprise and Government. During the Office 365 sign-up process, you create a Microsoft email address and password to use on your multiple devices. A single subscription to an Office 365 Home Premium account can cover an entire household. The Office 365 Home Premium subscription allows up to five concurrent installations by using the same email address and password combination. This means that your mother could be on the main family computer while you use your tablet and smartphone at the same time. You each can sign in with your individual Microsoft accounts using your settings and accessing your own documents using a single Office 365 subscription.

The Office 365 University subscription plan is designed for higher-education full-time and part-time students, faculty, and staff. By submitting the proper credentials, such as a school email address, students and faculty can purchase Office 365 University, including Word, PowerPoint, Excel, Access, Outlook, Publisher, and OneNote. A one-time payment covers a four-year subscription. In addition, Office 365 University provides users with 27 GB of SkyDrive cloud storage rather than the free 7 GB provided by a Microsoft account, and 60 Skype world minutes per month for videoconferencing. Students have the option of renewing for another four years, for a total of eight years. The Office 365 University edition is limited to two computers (PC or Mac).

The Microsoft Office 365 Business Plans can provide full support for employees to work from any location, whether they are in their traditional business office, commuting to and from work across the country, or working from a home office. Office 365 small business plans (Small Business and Small Business Premium) are best for companies with up to 10 employees, but can accommodate up to 25 users. Office 365 Midsize Business accommodates from 11 to 300 users. Office 365 Enterprise Plan fits organizations ranging in size from a single employee to 50,000-plus users. Each employee can install Microsoft Office 365 on five different computers.

First Look at Office 365

Microsoft Office 365 subscription plans offer all the same applications that are available in the Microsoft Office Professional 2013 suite in addition to multiple communication and collaboration tools. With Office 365 you can retrieve, edit, and save Office documents on the Office 365 cloud, coauthor documents in real time with others, and quickly initiate computer-based calls, instant messages, and web conferences with others.

Productivity Tools

Whether you are inserting audio and video into a Word document to create a high-impact business plan proposal or utilizing the visualization tools in Excel to chart the return on investment of a new mobile marketing program, Office 365 premium plans deliver the full Office product with the same features as the latest version of Microsoft Office. Office 365 uses a quick-start installation technology, called **Click-to-Run**, that downloads and installs the basics within minutes, so that users are able to start working almost immediately. It also includes **Office on Demand**, which streams Office to Windows 7- and Windows 8-based PCs for work performed on public computers. The single-use copy that is installed temporarily on the Windows computer does not count toward the device limit. No installation is necessary when using Office on Demand, and the applications disappear from the computer once you are finished using them. If you have a document on a USB drive or on SkyDrive that you need to edit on another PC, you can use Office on Demand to get the full version of Word in just a few minutes.

In effect, the Office 365 subscription provides access to the full Office applications wherever you are working. When you access your Office 365 account management panel, three choices are listed: 32- and 64-bit versions of Office 2013, and Office for Mac. Selecting the third option will initiate a download of an installer that must be run in the standard OS X fashion. When you install Office 365 on a Mac, the most current Mac version of Office is installed.

CONSIDER THIS

Unlike Google, which offers online documents, spreadsheets, and presentations called Google Docs, Microsoft Office 365 installs locally on your computer in addition to being available online. Google Docs is entirely browser based, which means if you are not connected to the Internet, you cannot access your Google Docs files.

Email and Calendars

In business, sharing information is essential to meeting the needs of your customers and staff. Office 365 offers shared access to business email, calendars, and contacts using **Exchange Online** from a computer, tablet, phone, and browser. The cloud-based Exchange Online enables business people to access Outlook information from anywhere at any time, while eliminating the cost of purchasing and maintaining servers to store data. If you need to meet with a colleague about a new project, you can compare calendars to view availability, confirm conference room availability, share project contacts, search email messages related to the project, and send email invitations to the project meeting. Exchange Online also allows you to search and access your company's address list.

Online Meetings

When you are working with a team on a project that requires interaction, email and text communications can slow the communications process. Microsoft Lync connects you with others by facilitating real-time, interactive presentations and meetings over the Internet using both video and audio calling. As shown in Figure 3, you can conduct an online meeting with a team member or customer that includes an instant messaging conversation, audio, high-definition video, virtual whiteboards, and screen sharing. If the customer does not have an Office 365 subscription, they still can join the meeting through the invitation link, which runs the Lync Web App.

Skype is another tool in the Office 365 subscription, which enables users to place video calls to computers and smartphones and voice calls to landlines. Skype also supports instant message and file sharing to computers and mobile devices. While Skype may be adequate for simple communication, Lync provides for more robust, comprehensive communications. These robust features include high-definition (HD) videoconferencing capabilities, a whiteboard, and a larger audience. Using Lync, meeting attendees simultaneously can view up to five participants' video, identify the active speaker, and associate names with faces. Lync supports up to 250 attendees per meeting. Unlike Skype, Lync meetings can be recorded for replaying at a later time. This enables businesses and schools to schedule meetings or organize online classes using Lync capabilities.

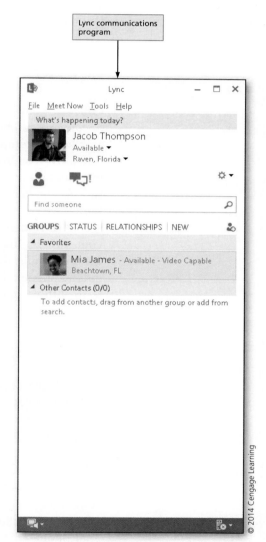

Figure 3

File Sharing

Office 365 includes a team site, which is a password-protected portal that supports sharing of large, difficult-to-email files and provides a single location for the latest versions of documents. In business, for example, colleagues working on common projects can save valuable time by being able to access instantly the latest master copy of each document. Security can be managed through different levels of user access so that users see only what they are supposed to see. Office 365 provides access to shared files using the cloud, making writing, editing, and sharing documents easier. If a construction company creates a commercial bid for a building project, the customers can be invited to view an Excel spreadsheet bid, construction timetable with a shared calendar, and an Access database of all the materials needed using the file sharing feature online.

Website Creation

Office 365 business plan subscriptions include a built-in hosted public website, where customers and clients can find an online storefront of a company. This public website, called the Website, can be customized to market a company by using various templates within the Office 365 cloud. The website creation tools include those for adding a theme, graphics, fonts, maps, directions, blogs, stock tickers, slide shows, PayPal, weather, and videos to interact with the website's visitors.

Synchronization

Office 365 subscription plans provide a central place to store and access your documents and business information. A feature of Office 365 ensures the original and backup computer files in two or more locations are identical through a process called **Active Directory Synchronization**. For example, if you open a PowerPoint presentation on your smartphone while you are riding a city bus and then add a new slide as you head to school, the PowerPoint presentation automatically is synced with Office 365. When you arrive on campus and open the PowerPoint presentation on a school computer, your new slide already is part of the finished slide show. By storing your files in Office 365, you can access your files on another computer if your home computer fails, with no loss of time or important information. When using your mobile phone's data plan, you do not need to search for a Wi-Fi hot spot to connect to the Office 365 cloud. Computer labs in schools can be configured to synchronize automatically all student files to Office 365 online.

Multiple Device Access to Office 365

With a single sign-in process, Office 365 provides access to multiple computers and mobile devices, including Android smartphones and tablets, Apple iPhones and iPads, Windows phones, and Blackberry phones. After you configure your devices' email settings, you can view your Microsoft account calendar, contacts, and email. Your personalized settings, preferences, and documents can be synchronized among all the different devices included in your Office 365 premium subscription. With the mobility of Office 365, students and employees can work anywhere, accessing information and responding to email requests immediately. If you lose your phone, Office 365 includes a feature that allows you to remotely wipe your phone clean of any data. By wiping your phone's data, you can prevent any unauthorized access to sensitive information, such as your banking information, passwords, and contacts, as well as discourage identity theft. Because your phone contacts and other information are stored on the Microsoft cloud, damaged or lost equipment is never a problem.

A thief can be quite resourceful if he or she steals your phone. Before you can alert your parents or spouse to the theft, they might receive a text from "you" asking for your ATM or credit card PIN number. Your parents or spouse might then reply with the PIN number. Your bank account could be emptied in minutes.

Teams Using Office 365 in Business

In the business world, rarely does an employee work in isolation. Companies need their employees to collaborate, whether they work in the same office or in locations around the world. Telecommuters working from home can communicate as if they were on-site by using a common team website and conferencing software. SharePoint Online and Lync Online provide seamless communication.

Small business subscription plans as low as $6.00 per user per month allow employees to create and store Word documents, Excel spreadsheets, and PowerPoint presentations online and communicate with one another via email, instant messaging, or video chat as they work on projects together. As shown in Figure 4, a team portal page is shown when you subscribe at https://portal.microsoftonline.com. Larger companies and those requiring more features can take advantage of the Office 365 business premium package, which, in addition to the features listed above, provides access to the Office 365 portal website and eliminates the effort and cost of the users maintaining their own costly computer servers.

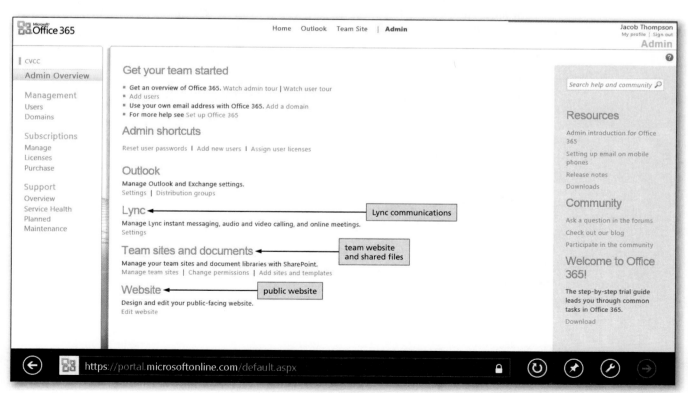

Figure 4

Email Communication Using Exchange

Office 365 includes Exchange Online, an email-based collaborative communications server for business. Exchange enables employees to be more productive by effectively managing email across multiple devices and facilitating teamwork.

Collaboration Using SharePoint

SharePoint Online, a part of Office 365 subscription plans, allows employees to collaborate with one another, share documents, post announcements, and track tasks, as shown in Table 2.

Table 2 Office 365 SharePoint Features	
Team Site Feature	**Description**
Calendar	Track important dates
Shared Document Library	Store related documents according to topic; picture, report, and slide libraries often are included
Task List	Track team tasks according to who is responsible for completion
Team Discussion Board	Discuss the topics at hand in an open forum
Contacts List	Share contact lists of employees, customers, contractors, and suppliers

© 2014 Cengage Learning

Office 365 provides the tools to plan meetings. Users can share calendars side by side, view availability, and suggest meeting times from shared calendars. Typically, a SharePoint team administrator or website owner establishes a folder structure to share and manage documents. The team website is fully searchable online, making locating and sharing data more efficient than using a local server. With a team website, everyone on the team has a central location to store and find all the information for a project, client, or department, as shown in Figure 5.

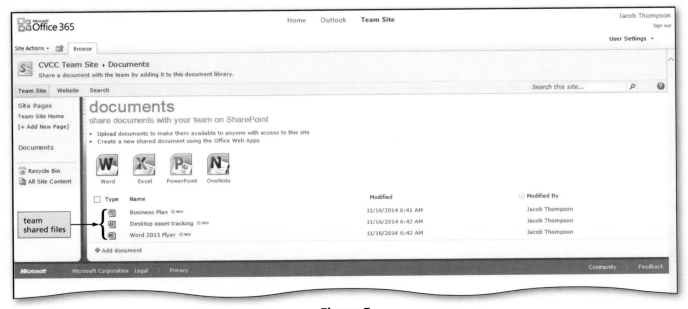

Figure 5

Website Design Using SharePoint

SharePoint provides templates to create a professional looking, public website for an online presence to market your business. As shown in Figure 6, a local pet sitting business is setting up a business website by customizing a SharePoint template. SharePoint Public Website includes features within the Design Manager that you use to customize and design your website by adding your own images, forms, style sheets, maps, themes, and social networking tools. When you finish customizing your business site, you can apply your own domain name to the site. A **domain** is a unique web address that identifies where your website can be found. Office 365 SharePoint hosts your website as part of your subscription. Your customers easily can find your business online and learn about your services.

BTW

Creating SharePoint Intranet Sites
A SharePoint website also can be customized to serve as an internal company website for private communications within the company.

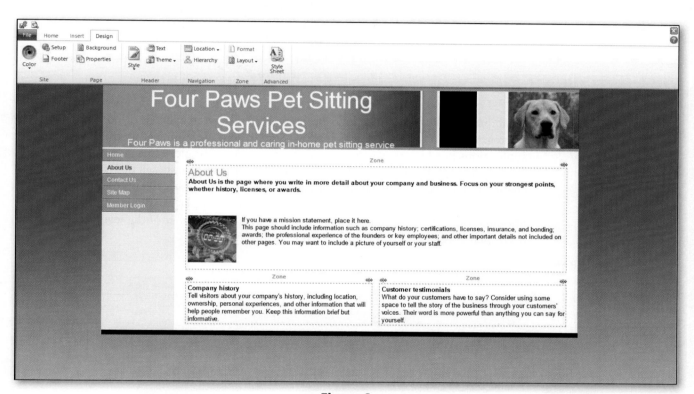

Figure 6

Real-Time Communications Using Lync

Lync Online is Microsoft's server platform for online team communications and comes bundled with Office 365 business subscriptions. As shown in Figure 7, Lync connects in real time to allow instant messaging, videoconferencing, and voice communications; it also integrates with email and Microsoft Office applications.

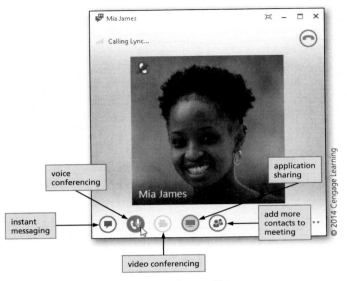

Figure 7

Lync allows you to connect with staff at remote locations using instant messaging capabilities, desktop sharing, videoconferencing, and shared agendas or documents. Lync is integrated into Office 365, which allows staff to start communicating from within the applications in which they currently are working. For example, while an employee is creating a PowerPoint presentation for a new product line, as shown in Figure 8, Lync enables him or her to collaborate with the entire team about the details of the product presentation. The team can view the presenter's screen displaying the PowerPoint presentation. The presenter can share control with any member of the team and can share his or her screen at any time during the Lync meeting.

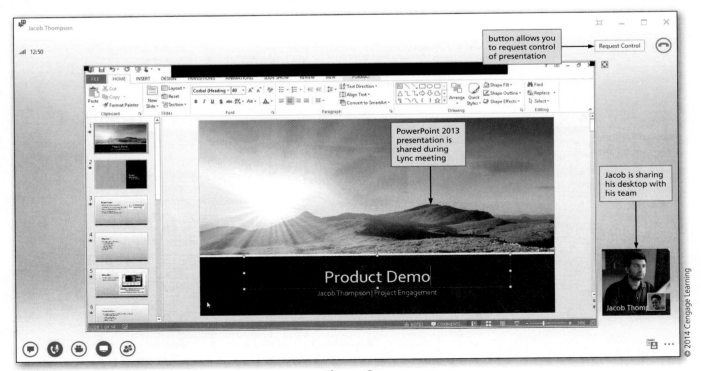

Figure 8

Users can send a Lync meeting request to schedule a team meeting, or an impromptu conversation can be started immediately using the Meet Now feature. Participants receive a Lync meeting request link via an email message, and when they click the meeting request link, Lync automatically connects them to the online conference. If the participant does not have Lync installed, the Lync Web App automatically connects to the Lync meeting through the user's PC or Mac OS X browser. If a participant is away from his or her computer, he or she still can participate using the Lync Mobile apps for Windows Phone, iOS, and Android. As shown in Figure 9, Lync utilizes **instant messaging** (IM), allowing two or more people to share text messages. They can communicate in real time, similar to a voice conversation. In addition to a simple instant message, Lync provides a feature called **persistent chat**, which allows end-users to participate in a working session of instant messages that is persistent or sustained over a specified amount of time in a moderated chat room. Consider having an instant messaging session with a group of colleagues in different parts of your organization, regardless of geographic region, where you all are working on the same project. Over the course of the project, different people post questions and concerns, and others are able to respond to all those who have subscribed to your topic or been admitted to the chat room. Instead of a long trail of email messages, a team can keep information in a controlled environment with a full history of the discussion in one location.

Figure 9

Lync also delivers support for full high-definition (HD) videoconferencing, so that a team can have a clear view of the participants, products, and demos. Before you join the video feed, you can preview your video feed to make sure your video camera is at the correct angle, your image is centered within the video frame, and that your room lighting provides for a clear image. The Lync preview option is important in creating a positive first impression over video. Your audio devices can be tested for clarity to make sure your headset, microphone, and speakers are functioning properly.

Lync provides a polling feature that presenters can use to ask the participants' opinions during a meeting (Figure 10). The poll question can consist of up to seven possible choices. The presenter has the option to view the results privately or share the results with the entire group.

Figure 10

Finally, by enabling the recording feature, Lync meetings and conversations can be captured for viewing at a later time. For instance, you can capture the audio, video, instant messaging (IM), screen sharing, Microsoft PowerPoint presentations, whiteboard, and polling portions of the Lync session and then play them back just as they transpired during the live Lync event. The meeting recordings can be made available to others so that they can view all or part of the Lync event. Instructors can record Lync online class sessions for students who were unable to attend the original presentation. The recording starts in Microsoft Lync; recordings then can be viewed within the Recording Manager feature.

Chapter Summary

In this chapter, you have learned how to subscribe to Office 365, which provides local and online access to Office applications, email, document sharing, web conferencing, and business websites. You also learned how a business can utilize Office 365 features on the cloud to facilitate teamwork. Finally, you learned about the features of SharePoint and Lync, which provide collaboration and communications for business teams using Office 365.

✳ Consider This: Your Turn

Apply your creative thinking and problem solving skills to design and implement a solution.

1: Comparing Office 365 Personal Plans

Personal

Part 1: You are a freshman in college living at home with your family. You are considering if it would be a better value to subscribe to Office 365 University or Office 365 Home Premium. Write a one-page document comparing the pros and cons of the two subscription plans. Research the different subscriptions in detail at Office365.com. Submit your assignment in the format specified by your instructor.

Part 2: ✳ Which type of computer and/or devices would you use with your Office 365 subscription? If you are at a friend's home that does not have Office 365, how could you access your Office files if you do not have your computer or mobile device with you?

2: Upgrading a Local Business to Office 365

Professional

Part 1: You are an employee at Impact Digital Marketing, a small marketing firm with 12 employees. The firm is setting up an Office 365 Small Business subscription next week, and you need to compose an email message with multiple paragraphs to explain the features of this new subscription plan to the members of your firm. Research the Office 365 Small Business subscription plan in detail at Office365.com, and compile your findings in an email message. Submit your assignment in the format specified by your instructor.

Part 2: ✳ Give three examples of how a marketing firm could use Lync. How could a marketing firm use the SharePoint Websites feature?

3: Conducting a Lync Meeting

Research and Collaboration

* Students need an Office 365 subscription to complete the following assignment.

Part 1: Using your Office 365 subscription, conduct a meeting using Lync. Working with a partner, use your Office 365 subscription to research how to use Lync. Then, conduct a 15-minute Lync meeting, including instant messaging, to discuss the features of Lync. Use the concepts and techniques presented in this chapter to create the Lync meeting. Submit your assignment in the format specified by your instructor.

Part 2: ✳ When using Lync in business, when would the video feature best be utilized?

1 | Creating and Editing a Presentation with Pictures

Microsoft product screenshots used with permission from Microsoft Corporation.

Objectives

You will have mastered the material in this chapter when you can:

- Select and change a document theme and variant

- Create a title slide and a text slide with a multilevel bulleted list

- Add new slides and change slide layouts

- Insert photos and illustrations into slides with and without content placeholders

- Move and resize photos and illustrations

- Change font size and color

- Bold and italicize text

- Duplicate a slide

- Arrange slides

- Select slide transitions

- View a presentation in Slide Show view

- Print a presentation

1 | Creating and Editing a Presentation with Pictures

Introduction

A PowerPoint **presentation,** also called a **slide show,** can help you deliver a dynamic, professional-looking message to an audience. PowerPoint allows you to produce slides to use in an academic, business, or other environment. The collection of slides in a presentation is called a **deck,** resembling a deck of cards that are stacked on top of each other. A common use of slide decks is to enhance an oral presentation. A speaker might desire to convey information, such as urging students to volunteer at a fund-raising event, explaining changes in employee compensation packages, or describing a new laboratory procedure. The PowerPoint slides should reinforce the speaker's message and help the audience retain the information presented. Custom slides can fit your specific needs and contain diagrams, charts, tables, pictures, shapes, video, sound, and animation effects to make your presentation more effective. An accompanying handout gives audience members reference notes and review material for your presentation.

Project — Presentation with a Bulleted List, Photos, and an Illustration

In this chapter's project, you will follow proper design guidelines and learn to use PowerPoint to create, save, and print the slides shown in Figures 1–1a through 1–1e. The objective is to produce a presentation, titled Keeping Hydrated, to help athletes understand the need to drink water before, during, and after a workout. This slide show has a variety of pictures and visual elements to add interest and give facts about proper hydration. Some of the text has formatting and color enhancements. Transitions help one slide flow gracefully into the next during a slide show. In addition, you will print a handout of your slides to distribute to audience members.

(a) Slide 1 (Title Slide with Photo)

(b) Slide 2 (Multilevel Bulleted List with Photo)

(c) Slide 3 (Title and Illustration)

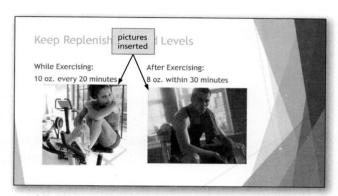

(d) Slide 4 (Comparison Layout and Photos)

(e) Slide 5 (Closing Slide)

Figure 1–1

For an introduction to Windows and instruction about how to perform basic Windows tasks, read the Office and Windows chapter at the beginning of this book, where you can learn how to resize windows, change screen resolution, create folders, move and rename files, use Windows Help, and much more.

Roadmap

In this chapter, you will learn how to create the slides shown in Figure 1–1 on the previous page. The following roadmap identifies general activities you will perform as you progress through this chapter:

1. INSERT the four PRESENTATION SLIDES, using various layouts.
2. ENTER the TEXT for the slides.
3. FORMAT the TEXT on each slide.
4. INSERT GRAPHICAL ELEMENTS, including photos and an illustration.
5. SIZE AND POSITION the graphical elements.
6. ENHANCE the SLIDE SHOW by adding a closing slide and transition.
7. DISPLAY AND PRINT the SLIDES and a handout.

At the beginning of step instructions throughout the chapter, you will see an abbreviated form of this roadmap. The abbreviated roadmap uses colors to indicate chapter progress: gray means the chapter is beyond that activity; blue means the task being shown is covered in that activity, and black means that activity is yet to be covered. For example, the following abbreviated roadmap indicates the chapter would be showing a task in the 5 Size & Position activity.

1 INSERT PRESENTATION SLIDES | 2 ENTER TEXT | 3 FORMAT TEXT | 4 INSERT GRAPHICAL ELEMENTS

5 SIZE & POSITION | 6 ENHANCE SLIDE SHOW | 7 DISPLAY & PRINT SLIDES

Use the abbreviated roadmap as a progress guide while you read or step through the instructions in this chapter.

To Run PowerPoint

One of the few differences between Windows 7 and Windows 8 occurs in the steps to run PowerPoint. If you are using Windows 7, click the Start button, type **PowerPoint** in the 'Search programs and files' box, click PowerPoint 2013, and then, if necessary, maximize the PowerPoint window. For detailed steps to run PowerPoint in Windows 7, refer to the Office and Windows chapter at the beginning of this book. For a summary of the steps, refer to the Quick Reference located at the back of this book.

If you are using a computer to step through the project in this chapter and you want your screens to match the figures in this book, you should change your screen's resolution to 1366 × 768. For information about how to change a computer's resolution, refer to the Office and Windows chapter at the beginning of this book.

The following steps, which assume Windows 8 is running, use the Start screen or the search box to run PowerPoint based on a typical installation. You may need to ask your instructor how to run PowerPoint on your computer. For a detailed example of the procedure summarized below, refer to the Office and Windows chapter.

1 Scroll the Start screen for a PowerPoint 2013 tile. If your Start screen contains a PowerPoint 2013 tile, tap or click it to run PowerPoint and then proceed to Step 5; if the Start screen does not contain the PowerPoint 2013 tile, proceed to the next step to search for the PowerPoint app.

2 Swipe in from the right edge of the screen or point to the upper-right corner of the screen to display the Charms bar and then tap or click the Search charm on the Charms bar to display the Search menu.

3 Type **PowerPoint** as the search text in the Search box and watch the search results appear in the Apps list.

4 Tap or click PowerPoint 2013 in the search results to run PowerPoint.

5 If the PowerPoint window is not maximized, tap or click the Maximize button on its title bar to maximize the window.

Choosing a Document Theme and Variant

You easily can give the slides in a presentation a professional and integrated appearance by using a theme. A document **theme** is a specific design with coordinating colors, fonts, and special effects such as shadows and reflections. Several themes are available when you run PowerPoint, each with a specific name. Using one of the formatted themes makes creating a professional-looking presentation easier and quicker than using the Blank Presentation template, where you would need to make all design decisions.

Each theme has a set of four alternate designs, called **variants.** Each variant has the same overall composition, but the colors, fonts, and design elements differ. Once you select a theme, you then can select a variation that best fits your overall design needs. If you later decide that another theme or variant would better fit the presentation's general theme, you can change these elements while you are developing slides.

To Choose a Document Theme and Variant

1 INSERT PRESENTATION SLIDES | 2 ENTER TEXT | 3 FORMAT TEXT | 4 INSERT GRAPHICAL ELEMENTS
5 SIZE & POSITION | 6 ENHANCE SLIDE SHOW | 7 DISPLAY & PRINT SLIDES

When you begin creating a new PowerPoint presentation, you need to select a theme. You either can start with no design elements by using the Blank Presentation, or you select one of the available professionally designed themes. The following steps apply the Ion theme and then change the variant. *Why? The title slide will have text and a photo, so you want to select a theme, like Ion, with an uncluttered background. The presentation discusses the importance of drinking water while exercising, and blue is the color commonly associated with water in lakes and oceans. The default Ion theme is predominantly green and white, but one of its variants is blue and is an appropriate choice to relate to the water concept.*

- Press and hold or point to the Ion theme on the New screen (Figure 1–2).

Q&A | Why are my theme images, called thumbnails, displaying in a different order?
PowerPoint places the themes you have used recently in the first rows. You may need to scroll down to locate the Ion theme.

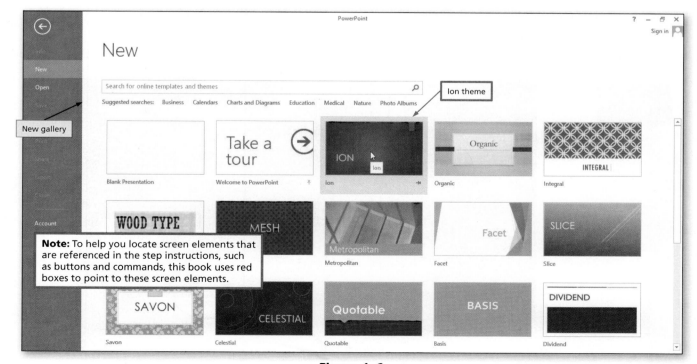

Figure 1–2

2

- Tap or click the Ion theme to display a theme preview dialog box with a thumbnail view of the theme and its variants (Figure 1–3).

Q&A Can I see previews of other themes?

Yes. Tap or click the right or left arrows on the sides of the theme preview dialog box.

Figure 1–3

3

- Tap or click the upper-right (blue) variant to view previews of that style applied to the thumbnail.

Q&A Can I see previews of the Ion theme and blue variant applied to layouts other than the title slide?

Yes. Tap or click the right or left arrows beside the words, More Images, below the thumbnail. Three other layouts will be displayed: Title and Content, Two Content, and Photo.

- Tap or click the Create button to apply the Ion theme and blue variant to the presentation and to display Slide 1 (Figure 1–4).

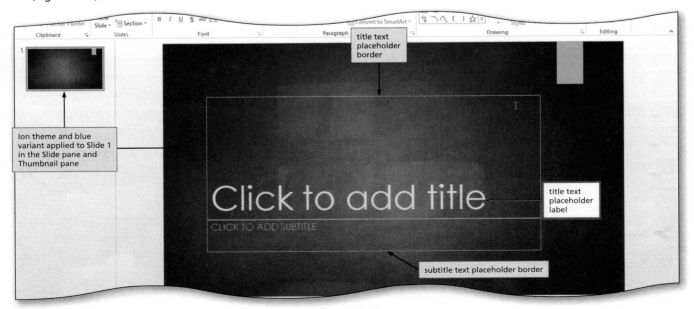

Figure 1–4

Creating a Title Slide

When you open a new presentation, the default **Title Slide** layout appears. The purpose of this layout is to introduce the presentation to the audience. PowerPoint includes other standard layouts for each of the themes. The slide layouts are set up in **landscape orientation**, where the slide width is greater than its height. In landscape orientation, the slide size is preset to 10 inches wide and 7.5 inches high when printed on a standard sheet of paper measuring 11 inches wide and 8.5 inches high.

    Placeholders are boxes with dotted or hatch-marked borders that are displayed when you create a new slide. Most layouts have both a title text placeholder and at least one content placeholder. Depending on the particular slide layout selected, title and subtitle placeholders are displayed for the slide title and subtitle; a content text placeholder is displayed for text, art, or a table, chart, picture, graphic, or movie. The title slide has two text placeholders where you can type the main heading, or title, of a new slide and the subtitle.

    With the exception of the Blank slide layout, PowerPoint assumes every new slide has a title. To make creating a presentation easier, any text you type after a new slide appears becomes title text in the title text placeholder. The following steps create the title slide for this presentation.

Choose the words for the slide.
All presentations should follow the 7 × 7 rule, which states that each slide should have a maximum of seven lines, and each line should have a maximum of seven words. PowerPoint designers must choose their words carefully and, in turn, help viewers read the slides easily.

Avoid line wraps. Your audience's eyes want to stop at the end of a line. Thus, you must plan your words carefully or adjust the font size so that each point displays on only one line.

To Enter the Presentation Title

1 INSERT PRESENTATION SLIDES | 2 ENTER TEXT | 3 FORMAT TEXT | 4 INSERT GRAPHICAL ELEMENTS
5 SIZE & POSITION | 6 ENHANCE SLIDE SHOW | 7 DISPLAY & PRINT SLIDES

    The presentation title for Project 1 is Healthy Hydration. **Why?** *The presentation discusses the importance of drinking water while exercising, and blue is the color associated with water.* The following step creates the slide show's title.

- Tap or click the label, 'Tap to add title', or, 'Click to add title', located inside the title text placeholder to select the placeholder (Figure 1–5).

Figure 1–5

2

- Type **Healthy Hydration** in the title text placeholder. Do not press the ENTER key (Figure 1–6).

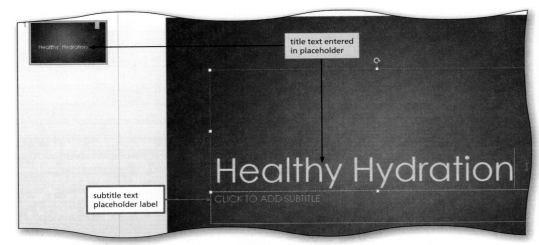

Figure 1–6

Correcting a Mistake When Typing

If you type the wrong letter, press the BACKSPACE key to erase all the characters back to and including the one that is incorrect. If you mistakenly press the ENTER key after typing the title and the insertion point is on the new line, simply press the BACKSPACE key to return the insertion point to the right of the letter in the word, Water.

When you install PowerPoint, the default setting allows you to reverse up to the last 20 changes by tapping or clicking the Undo button on the Quick Access Toolbar. The ScreenTip that appears when you point to the Undo button changes to indicate the type of change just made. For example, if you type text in the title text placeholder and then point to the Undo button, the ScreenTip that appears is Undo Typing. For clarity, when referencing the Undo button in this project, the name displaying in the ScreenTip is referenced. You can reapply a change that you reversed with the Undo button by tapping or clicking the Redo button on the Quick Access Toolbar. Tapping or clicking the Redo button reverses the last undo action. The ScreenTip name reflects the type of reversal last performed.

Paragraphs

Text in the subtitle text placeholder supports the title text. It can appear on one or more lines in the placeholder. To create more than one subtitle line, you press the ENTER key after typing some words. PowerPoint creates a new line, which is the second paragraph in the placeholder. A **paragraph** is a segment of text with the same format that begins when you press the ENTER key and ends when you press the ENTER key again. This new paragraph is the same level as the previous paragraph. A **level** is a position within a structure, such as an outline, that indicates the magnitude of importance. PowerPoint allows for five paragraph levels.

How do you use the touch keyboard with a touch screen?
To display the on-screen touch keyboard, tap the Touch Keyboard button on the Windows taskbar. When finished using the touch keyboard, tap the X button on the touch keyboard to close the keyboard.

To Enter the Presentation Subtitle Paragraph

1 INSERT PRESENTATION SLIDES | 2 ENTER TEXT | 3 FORMAT TEXT | 4 INSERT GRAPHICAL ELEMENTS
5 SIZE & POSITION | 6 ENHANCE SLIDE SHOW | 7 DISPLAY & PRINT SLIDES

The first subtitle paragraph links to the title. *Why? The subtitle gives additional detail that the presentation will focus on water consumption while exercising.* The following steps enter the presentation subtitle.

- Tap or click the label, 'Tap to add subtitle', or, 'Click to add subtitle', located inside the subtitle text placeholder to select the placeholder (Figure 1–7).

Figure 1–7

- Type **Drinking Water While Exercising** but do not press the ENTER key (Figure 1–8).

Q&A Why does the text display with capital letters despite the fact I am typing uppercase and lowercase letters? The Ion theme uses the All Caps effect for the subtitle text. This effect converts lowercase letters to uppercase letters.

Figure 1–8

To Zoom a Slide

You will be modifying the text and other slide components as you create the presentation, so you can enlarge the slide on the screen. *Why? Zooming the slide can help you see slide elements more clearly so that you can position them precisely where desired.* The following step changes the zoom to 80 percent.

1

Experiment

- Repeatedly tap or click the Zoom In and Zoom Out buttons on the status bar and watch the size of the slide change in the Slide pane.

- Tap or click the Zoom In or Zoom Out button as many times as necessary until the Zoom button on the status bar displays 80% on its face (Figure 1–9).

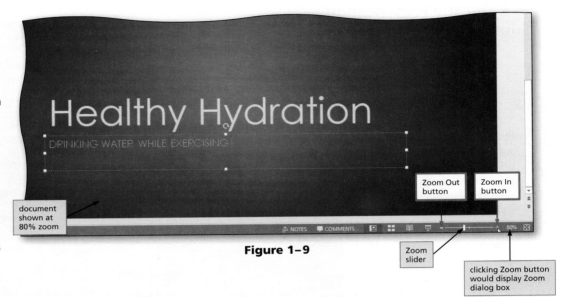

Figure 1–9

Q&A If I change the zoom percentage, will the slide display differently when I run the presentation?
No. Changing the zoom helps you develop the slide content and does not affect the slide show.

Other Ways

1. Drag Zoom slider on status bar	2. Tap or click Zoom level button on status bar, select desired zoom percent or type (Zoom dialog box), tap or click OK button	3. Tap or click Zoom button (VIEW tab | Zoom group), select desired zoom percent or type (Zoom dialog box), tap or click OK button	4. For touch screens: Pinch two fingers together in Slide pane (zoom out) or stretch two fingers apart (zoom in)

Formatting Characters in a Presentation

BTW
BTWs
For a complete list of the BTWs found in the margins of this book, visit the BTW resource on the Student Companion Site located on www.cengagebrain.com. For detailed instructions about accessing available resources, visit www.cengage.com/ct/studentdownload or see the inside back cover of this book.

Recall that each document theme determines the color scheme, font set, and layout of a presentation. You can use a specific document theme and then change the characters' formats any time before, during, or after you type the text.

Fonts and Font Styles

Characters that appear on the screen are a specific shape and size. Examples of how you can modify the appearance, or **format**, of these typed characters on the screen and in print include changing the font, style, size, and color. The **font**, or typeface, defines the appearance and shape of the letters, numbers, punctuation marks, and symbols. **Style** indicates how the characters are formatted. PowerPoint's text font styles include regular, italic, bold, and bold italic. **Size** specifies the height of the characters and is gauged by a measurement system that uses points. A **point** is 1/72 of an inch in height. Thus, a character with a font size of 36 is 36/72 (or 1/2) of an inch in height. **Color** defines the hue of the characters.

This presentation uses the Ion document theme, which has particular font styles and font sizes. The Ion document theme default title text font is named Century Gothic. It has no special effects, and its size is 54 point. The Ion default subtitle text font also is Century Gothic with a font size of 18 point.

To Select a Paragraph

1 INSERT PRESENTATION SLIDES | 2 ENTER TEXT | 3 FORMAT TEXT | 4 INSERT GRAPHICAL ELEMENTS
5 SIZE & POSITION | 6 ENHANCE SLIDE SHOW | 7 DISPLAY & PRINT SLIDES

You can use many techniques to format characters. When you want to apply the same formats to multiple words or paragraphs, it is helpful to select these words. **Why?** *It is efficient to select the desired text and then make the desired changes to all the characters simultaneously.* The first formatting change you will make will apply to the title slide subtitle. The following step selects this paragraph.

- If you are using a touch screen, tap to position the insertion point in the text to select, and then drag the selection handles as necessary to select the entire paragraph; if you are using a mouse, triple-click the paragraph, Drinking Water While Exercising, in the subtitle text placeholder to select the paragraph (Figure 1–10).

Figure 1–10

Q&A What is the selection handle?
When working on a touch screen, a **selection handle** (small circle) appears below the insertion point. Using a fingertip, you drag the selection handle to select text.

Other Ways

1. Position pointer to left of first paragraph and drag to end of line

To Italicize Text

1 INSERT PRESENTATION SLIDES | 2 ENTER TEXT | 3 FORMAT TEXT | 4 INSERT GRAPHICAL ELEMENTS
5 SIZE & POSITION | 6 ENHANCE SLIDE SHOW | 7 DISPLAY & PRINT SLIDES

Different font styles often are used on slides. **Why?** *These style changes make the words more appealing to the reader and emphasize particular text.* **Italicized** text has a slanted appearance. Used sparingly, it draws the readers' eyes to these characters. The following step adds emphasis to the line of the subtitle text by changing regular text to italic text.

- With the subtitle text still selected, tap or click the Italic button on the mini toolbar to italicize that text on the slide (Figure 1–11).

Q&A If I change my mind and decide not to italicize the text, how can I remove this style?
Tap or click the Italic button a second time, immediately tap or click the Undo button on the Quick Access Toolbar, or press CTRL+Z.

Figure 1–11

Other Ways

1. Tap 'Show Context Menu' button on mini toolbar or right-click selected text, tap or click Font on shortcut menu, tap or click Font tab (Font dialog box), tap or click Italic in Font style list, tap or click OK button

2. Select text, tap or click Italic button (HOME tab | Font group)

3. Tap or click Font dialog box launcher (HOME tab | Font group), tap or click Font tab (Font dialog box), tap or click Italic in Font style list, tap or click OK button

4. Select text, press CTRL+I

To Increase Font Size

Why? *To add emphasis, you increase the font size for the subtitle text.* The Increase Font Size button on the mini toolbar increases the font size in preset increments. The following step uses this button to increase the font size.

• Tap or click the 'Increase Font Size' button on the mini toolbar three times to increase the font size of the selected text from 20 to 32 point (Figure 1–12).

Figure 1–12

Other Ways

1. Tap or click Font Size arrow on mini toolbar, tap or click desired font size in Font Size gallery	2. Tap or click Increase Font Size button (HOME tab | Font group)	3. Tap or click Font Size arrow (HOME tab | Font group), tap or click desired font size in Font size gallery	4. Press CTRL+SHIFT+>

To Select a Word

PowerPoint designers use many techniques to emphasize words and characters on a slide. To accentuate the word, Water, on your slide, you want to increase the font size and change the font color to dark blue for the word, WATER, in the subtitle text. To make these changes, you should begin by selecting the word, WATER. *Why? You could perform these actions separately, but it is more efficient to select the word and then change the font attributes.* The following steps select a word.

• Position the pointer somewhere in the word to be selected (in this case, in the word, WATER) (Figure 1–13).

Figure 1–13

- Double-tap or double-click the word to select it (Figure 1–14).

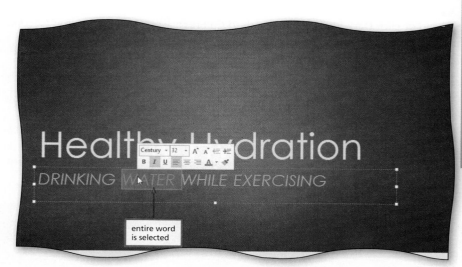

Figure 1–14

Other Ways

1. Position pointer before first character, press CTRL+SHIFT+RIGHT ARROW

To Change the Text Color

1 INSERT PRESENTATION SLIDES | 2 ENTER TEXT | 3 FORMAT TEXT | 4 INSERT GRAPHICAL ELEMENTS
5 SIZE & POSITION | 6 ENHANCE SLIDE SHOW | 7 DISPLAY & PRINT SLIDES

PowerPoint allows you to use one or more text colors in a presentation. You decide to change the color of the word you selected, WATER. *Why? The color, blue, is associated with water, and you want to add more emphasis, subtly, to that word in your subtitle slide text.* The following steps add emphasis to this word by changing the font color from green to blue.

- With the word, WATER, selected, tap or click the Font Color arrow on the mini toolbar to display the Font Color gallery, which includes Theme Colors and Standard Colors (Figure 1–15).

Q&A If the mini toolbar disappears from the screen, how can I display it once again?
Press and hold or right-click the text, and the mini toolbar should appear.

Experiment

- If you are using a mouse, point to various colors in the gallery and watch the word's font color change.

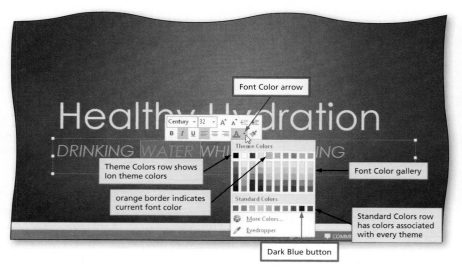

Figure 1–15

2

- Tap or click Dark Blue in the Standard Colors row on the mini toolbar (second color from right) to change the font color to Dark Blue (Figure 1–16).

Q&A

Why did I select the color Dark Blue?
Dark Blue is one of the 10 standard colors associated with every document theme, and it is a universal color representing the natural resource of water. The color will emphasize the fact that the presentation focuses on water.

What is the difference between the colors shown in the Theme Colors area and the Standard Colors?
The 10 colors in the top row of the Theme Colors area are two text, two background, and six accent colors in the Ion theme; the five colors in each column under the top row display different transparencies. The Standard Colors are available in every document theme.

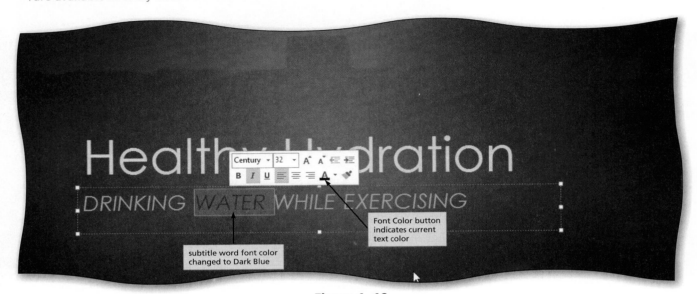

Figure 1–16

3

- Tap or click outside the selected area to deselect the word.

Other Ways
1. Tap 'Show Context Menu' button on mini toolbar or right-click selected text, tap or click Font on shortcut menu, tap or click Font Color button, tap or click Dark Blue in Standard Colors row   2. Tap or click Font Color arrow (HOME tab | Font group), tap or click Dark Blue in Standard Colors row

BTW

Organizing Files and Folders

You should organize and store files in folders so that you easily can find the files later. For example, if you are taking an introductory computer class called CIS 101, a good practice would be to save all PowerPoint files in a PowerPoint folder in a CIS 101 folder. For a discussion of folders and detailed examples of creating folders, refer to the Office and Windows chapter at the beginning of this book.

To Save a Presentation with a New File Name

You have performed many tasks while creating this presentation and do not want to risk losing work completed thus far. Accordingly, you should save the presentation on your hard disk, SkyDrive, or a location that is most appropriate to your situation.

The following steps assume you already have created folders for storing your files, for example, a CIS 101 folder (for your class) that contains a PowerPoint folder (for your assignments). Thus, these steps save the presentation in the PowerPoint folder in the CIS 101 folder on your desired save location. For a detailed example of the procedure for saving a file in a folder or saving a file on SkyDrive, refer to the Office and Windows chapter at the beginning of this book.

1 Tap or click the Save button on the Quick Access Toolbar, which depending on settings, will display either the Save As gallery in the Backstage view or the Save As dialog box.

2 To save on a hard disk or other storage media on your computer, proceed to Step 2a. To save on SkyDrive, proceed to Step 2b.

2a If your screen opens the Backstage view and you want to save on storage media on your computer, tap or click Computer in the left pane, if necessary, to display options in the right pane related to saving on your computer. If your screen already displays the Save As dialog box, proceed to Step 3.

2b If your screen opens the Backstage view and you want to save on SkyDrive, tap or click SkyDrive in the left pane to display SkyDrive saving options or a Sign In button. If your screen displays a Sign In button, tap or click it and then sign in to SkyDrive.

3 Tap or click the Browse button in the right pane to display the Save As dialog box associated with the selected save location (i.e., Computer or SkyDrive).

4 Type **Keeping Hydrated** in the File name box to change the file name. Do not press the ENTER key after typing the file name because you do not want to close the dialog box at this time.

5 Navigate to the desired save location (in this case, the PowerPoint folder in the CIS 101 folder [or your class folder] on your computer or SkyDrive).

6 Tap or click the Save button (Save As dialog box) to save the presentation in the selected folder on the selected save location with the entered file name.

BTW
The Ribbon and Screen Resolution
PowerPoint may change how the groups and buttons within the groups appear on the ribbon, depending on the computer's screen resolution. Thus, your ribbon may look different from the ones in this book if you are using a screen resolution other than 1366 × 768.

Adding a New Slide to a Presentation

With the text for the title slide for the presentation created, the next step is to add the first text slide immediately after the title slide. Usually, when you create a presentation, you add slides with text, pictures, graphics, or charts. Some placeholders allow you to double-tap or double-click the placeholder and then access other objects, such as videos, charts, diagrams, and organization charts. You can change the layout for a slide at any time during the creation of a presentation.

To Add a New Text Slide with a Bulleted List

1 INSERT PRESENTATION SLIDES | 2 ENTER TEXT | 3 FORMAT TEXT | 4 INSERT GRAPHICAL ELEMENTS
5 SIZE & POSITION | 6 ENHANCE SLIDE SHOW | 7 DISPLAY & PRINT SLIDES

When you add a new slide, PowerPoint uses the Title and Content slide layout. This layout provides a title placeholder and a content area for text, art, charts, and other graphics. A vertical scroll bar appears in the Slide pane when you add the second slide. *Why? The scroll bar allows you to move from slide to slide easily.* A small image of this slide also appears in the Thumbnail pane. The step on the next page adds a new slide with the Title and Content slide layout.

❶

- Tap or click the New Slide button (HOME tab | Slides group) to insert a new slide with the Title and Content layout (Figure 1–17).

Why does the bullet character display a green triangle?
The Ion document theme determines the bullet characters. Each paragraph level has an associated bullet character.

I clicked the New Slide arrow instead of the New Slide button. What should I do?
Tap or click the Title and Content slide thumbnail in the Ion layout gallery.

How do I know which slide number I am viewing?
The left edge of the status bar shows the current slide number followed by the total number of slides in the document. In addition, the slide number is displayed to the left of the slide thumbnail.

What are those six icons grouped in the middle of the Slide pane?
You can tap or click one of the icons to insert a specific type of content: table, chart, SmartArt graphic, pictures, online pictures, or video.

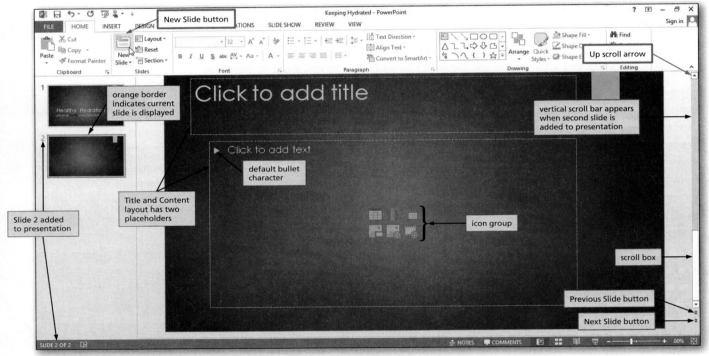

Figure 1–17

Other Ways

1. Press CTRL+M

Creating a Text Slide with a Multilevel Bulleted List

The information in the Slide 2 text placeholder is presented in a bulleted list with three levels. A **bulleted list** is a list of paragraphs, each of which may be preceded by a bullet character, such as a dot, arrow, or checkmark. Some themes, such as the Ion theme, do not display a bullet character at the start of a paragraph by default. A slide that consists of more than one level of bulleted text is called a **multilevel bulleted list slide**. In a multilevel bulleted list, a lower-level paragraph is a subset of a higher-level paragraph. It usually contains information that supports the topic in the paragraph immediately above it.

As you can see in Figure 1–1b on page PPT 3, two of the Slide 2 paragraphs appear at the same level, called the first level: Cushions and protects vital organs, and Regulates body temperature. Beginning with the second level, each paragraph indents to the right of the preceding level and is pushed down to a lower level. For example, if you increase the indent of a first-level paragraph, it becomes a second-level paragraph. The second, fourth, and fifth paragraphs on Slide 2 are second-level paragraphs. The last paragraph, Can cause muscle fatigue and heat stroke, is a third-level paragraph.

Creating a text slide with a multilevel bulleted list requires several steps. Initially, you enter a slide title in the title text placeholder. Next, you select the content text placeholder. Then, you type the text for the multilevel bulleted list, increasing and decreasing the indents as needed. The next several sections add a slide with a multilevel bulleted list.

BTW

Touch Screen Differences
The Office and Windows interfaces may vary if you are using a touch screen. For this reason, you might notice that the function or appearance of your touch screen differs slightly from this chapter's presentation.

To Enter a Slide Title

1 INSERT PRESENTATION SLIDES | 2 ENTER TEXT | 3 FORMAT TEXT | 4 INSERT GRAPHICAL ELEMENTS
5 SIZE & POSITION | 6 ENHANCE SLIDE SHOW | 7 DISPLAY & PRINT SLIDES

PowerPoint assumes every new slide has a title. ***Why?*** *The audience members read the title and then can begin to focus their attention on the information being presented on that slide.* The title for Slide 2 is Water: Your Essential Nutrient. The following step enters this title.

- Tap or click the label, 'Tap to add title', or, 'Click to add title', to select it and then type `Water: Your Essential Nutrient` in the title text placeholder. Do not press the ENTER key (Figure 1–18).

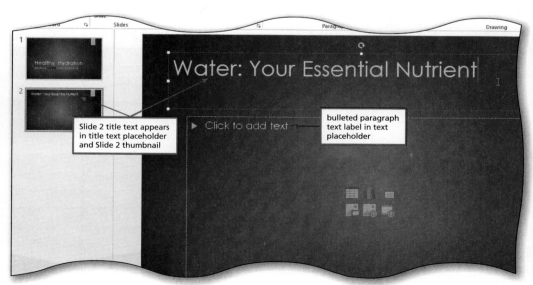

Figure 1–18

To Select a Text Placeholder

Why? Before you can type text into a content placeholder, you first must select it. The following step selects the text placeholder on Slide 2.

- Tap or click the label, 'Tap to add text', or 'Click to add text', to select the content placeholder (Figure 1–19).

Q&A Why does my pointer have a different shape?
If you move the pointer away from the bullet, it will change shape.

Figure 1–19

Other Ways

1. Press CTRL+ENTER

To Type a Multilevel Bulleted List

The content placeholder provides an area for the text characters. When you tap or click inside a placeholder, you then can type or paste text. As discussed previously, a bulleted list is a list of paragraphs, each of which is preceded by a bullet. A paragraph is a segment of text ended by pressing the ENTER key. The theme determines the bullets for each level. *Why? The bullet variations are determined by the specific paragraph levels, and they generally vary in size, shape, and color.*

The content text placeholder is selected, so the next step is to type the multilevel bulleted list that consists of six paragraphs, as shown in Figure 1–1b on page PPT 3. Creating a lower-level paragraph is called **demoting** text; creating a higher-level paragraph is called **promoting** text. The following steps create a multilevel bulleted list consisting of three levels.

- Type **Cushions and protects vital organs** and then press the ENTER key (Figure 1–20).

Figure 1–20

2

- Tap or click the 'Increase List Level' button (HOME tab | Paragraph group) to indent the second paragraph below the first and create a second-level paragraph (Figure 1–21).

 Why does the bullet for this paragraph have a different size? A different bullet is assigned to each paragraph level.

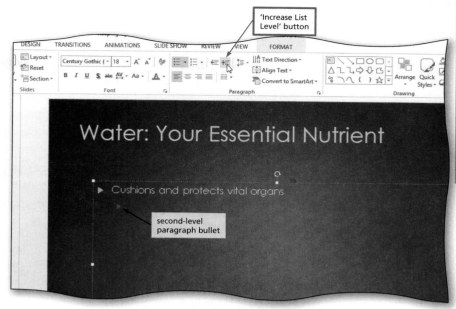

Figure 1–21

3

- Type **Transports nutrients and oxygen to cells** and then press the ENTER key (Figure 1–22).

Figure 1–22

4

- Tap or click the 'Decrease List Level' button (HOME tab | Paragraph group) so that the second-level paragraph becomes a first-level paragraph (Figure 1–23).

 Can I delete bullets on a slide? Yes. If you do not want bullets to display in a particular paragraph, tap or click the Bullets button (HOME tab | Paragraph group) or press and hold or right-click the paragraph and then tap or click the Bullets button on the shortcut menu.

Figure 1–23

Other Ways

1. Press TAB to promote paragraph; press SHIFT+TAB to demote paragraph

To Type the Remaining Text for Slide 2

The following steps complete the text for Slide 2.

1 Type `Regulates body temperature` and then press the ENTER key.

2 Tap or click the 'Increase List Level' button (HOME tab | Paragraph group) to demote the paragraph to the second level.

3 Type `Dehydrated body cannot cool itself` and then press the ENTER key to add a new paragraph at the same level as the previous paragraph.

4 Tap or click the 'Increase List Level' button (HOME tab | Paragraph group) to demote the paragraph to the third level.

5 Type `Can cause muscle fatigue and heat stroke` but do not press the ENTER key (Figure 1–24).

Q&A I pressed the ENTER key in error, and now a new bullet appears after the last entry on this slide. How can I remove this extra bullet?
Press the BACKSPACE key twice.

Figure 1–24

To Select a Group of Words

1 INSERT PRESENTATION SLIDES | 2 ENTER TEXT | 3 FORMAT TEXT | 4 INSERT GRAPHICAL ELEMENTS
5 SIZE & POSITION | 6 ENHANCE SLIDE SHOW | 7 DISPLAY & PRINT SLIDES

PowerPoint designers use many techniques to emphasize words and characters on a slide. To highlight your slide show's concept of the dangers of not drinking water while exercising, you want to bold and increase the font size of the words, cannot cool itself, in the body text. The following steps select three words. *Why? You could perform these actions separately, but it is more efficient to select the words and then change the font attributes.*

- Position the pointer immediately to the left of the first character of the text to be selected (in this case, the c in the word, cannot) (Figure 1–25).

Figure 1–25

2

- Drag the pointer through the last character of the text to be selected (in this case, the f in the word, itself) (Figure 1–26).

Figure 1–26

Other Ways

1. Press CTRL+SHIFT+RIGHT ARROW repeatedly until desired words are selected

To Bold Text

1 INSERT PRESENTATION SLIDES | 2 ENTER TEXT | 3 FORMAT TEXT | 4 INSERT GRAPHICAL ELEMENTS
5 SIZE & POSITION | 6 ENHANCE SLIDE SHOW | 7 DISPLAY & PRINT SLIDES

Why? Bold characters display somewhat thicker and darker than those that display in a regular font style. Tapping or clicking the Bold button on the mini toolbar is an efficient method of bolding text. To add more emphasis to the fact that the body needs water for cooling purposes, you want to bold the words, cannot cool itself. The following step bolds this text.

1

- With the words, cannot cool itself, selected, tap or click the Bold button on the mini toolbar to bold the three words (Figure 1–27).

Figure 1–27

Other Ways

1. Tap 'Show Context Menu' button on mini toolbar or right-click selected text, tap or click Font on shortcut menu, tap or click Font tab (Font dialog box), tap or click Bold in Font style list, tap or click OK button

2. Select text, tap or click Bold button (HOME tab | Font group)

3. Tap or click Font dialog box launcher (HOME tab | Font group), tap or click Font tab (Font dialog box), tap or click Bold in Font style list, tap or click OK button

4. Select text, press CTRL+B

To Increase Font Size

Why? To add emphasis, you increase the font size for the words, cannot cool itself. The following steps increase the font size from 16 to 18 point.

1 With the words, cannot cool itself, still selected, tap or click the 'Increase Font Size' button on the mini toolbar once (Figure 1–28).

2 Tap or click outside the selected area to deselect the three words.

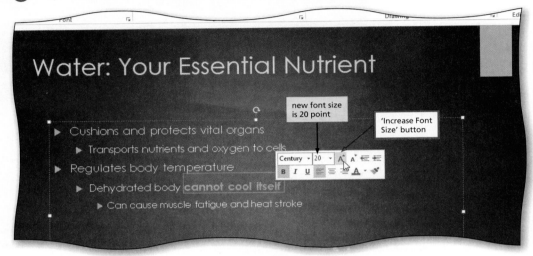

Figure 1–28

Adding New Slides, Changing Slide Layouts, and Changing the Theme

BTW
Customizing
a Slide Layout
PowerPoint provides a wide variety of slide layouts for each theme, but you can customize the layouts to make your deck unique. Display the VIEW tab, tap or click Slide Master (VIEW tab | Master Views group), select the thumbnail below the slide master in the left pane that you would like to customize, and then make the desired modifications.

Slide 3 in Figure 1–1c on page PPT 3 contains an illustration of a character drinking water and does not contain a bulleted list. When you add a new slide, PowerPoint applies the Title and Content layout. This layout, along with the Title Slide layout for Slide 1, are the default styles. A **layout** specifies the arrangement of placeholders on a slide. These placeholders are arranged in various configurations and can contain text, such as the slide title or a bulleted list, or they can contain content, such as SmartArt graphics, photos, charts, tables, and shapes. The placement of the text, in relationship to content, depends on the slide layout. You can specify a particular slide layout when you add a new slide to a presentation or after you have created the slide.

Using the **layout gallery**, you can choose a slide layout. The nine layouts in this gallery have a variety of placeholders to define text and content positioning and formatting. Three layouts are for text: Title Slide, Section Header, and Title Only. Five are for text and content: Title and Content, Two Content, Comparison, Content with Caption, and Picture with Caption. The Blank layout has no placeholders. If none of these standard layouts meets your design needs, you can create a **custom layout**. A custom layout specifies the number, size, and location of placeholders, background content, and optional slide and placeholder-level properties.

When you change the layout of a slide, PowerPoint retains the text and objects and repositions them into the appropriate placeholders. Using slide layouts eliminates the need to resize objects and the font size because PowerPoint automatically sizes the objects and text to fit the placeholders. At any time when creating the slide content, you can change the theme and variant to give the presentation a different look and feel.

To Add a Slide with the Title Only Layout

The following steps add Slide 3 to the presentation with the Title Only slide layout style. *Why? The only text on the slide is the title, and the majority of the slide content is the illustration.*

- If necessary, tap or click HOME on the ribbon to display the HOME tab.
- Tap or click the New Slide arrow (HOME tab | Slides group) to display the Ion layout gallery (Figure 1–29).

Figure 1–29

- Tap or click Title Only to add a new slide and apply that layout to Slide 3.
- If necessary, swipe up or click the Up scroll arrow several times until the title text placeholder is visible (Figure 1–30).

Figure 1–30

To Enter a Slide Title

The only text on Slide 3 is the title. The following step enters the title text for this slide.

1 Type **Begin Workout with Plenty of Water** as the title text but do not press the ENTER key (Figure 1–31).

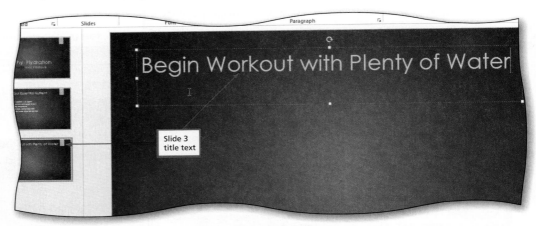

Figure 1–31

To Add a New Slide and Enter a Slide Title and Headings

1 INSERT PRESENTATION SLIDES | 2 ENTER TEXT | 3 FORMAT TEXT | 4 INSERT GRAPHICAL ELEMENTS
5 SIZE & POSITION | 6 ENHANCE SLIDE SHOW | 7 DISPLAY & PRINT SLIDES

The text on Slide 4 in Figure 1–1d on page PPT 3 consists of a title and two headings. The appropriate layout for this slide is named Comparison. ***Why?*** *The Comparison layout has two headings and two text placeholders adjacent to each other, so an audience member easily can compare and contrast the items shown side by side.* The following steps add Slide 4 to the presentation with the Comparison layout and then enter the title and heading text for this slide.

• Tap or click the New Slide arrow in the Slides group to display the Ion layout gallery (Figure 1–32).

Figure 1–32

- Tap or click Comparison to add Slide 4 and apply that layout (Figure 1–33).

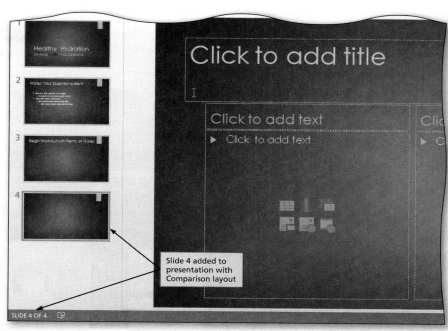

Figure 1–33

③

- Type **Keep Replenishing Fluid Levels** in the title text placeholder.

- Tap or click the left heading placeholder with the label, 'Tap to add text', or 'Click to add text', to select this placeholder (Figure 1–34).

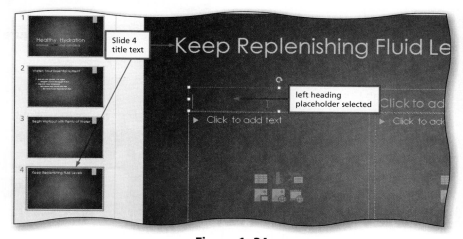

Figure 1–34

④

- Type **While Exercising:** and then press the ENTER key.

- Type **10 oz. every 20 minutes** but do not press the ENTER key.

- Select the right heading placeholder and then type **After Exercising:** and press the ENTER key.

- Type **8 oz. within 30 minutes** but do not press the ENTER key (Figure 1–35).

Figure 1–35

Q&A What is the white box with the arrow between the placeholders?

The text is too large to fit in the placeholder using the default font and paragraph attributes, so PowerPoint adjusts the text so it displays properly. That icon informs you that the font was altered.

To Change the Theme

A theme provides consistency in design and color throughout the entire presentation by setting the color scheme, font set, and layout of a presentation. This collection of formatting choices includes a set of colors (the Theme Colors group), a set of heading and content text fonts (the Theme Fonts group), and a set of lines and fill effects (the Theme Effects group). These groups allow you to choose and change the appearance of all the slides or individual slides in your presentation. *Why? At any time while creating the slide deck, you may decide to switch the theme so that the slides have a totally different appearance.* The following steps change the theme for this presentation from Ion to Facet.

- Tap or click DESIGN on the ribbon to display the DESIGN tab (Figure 1–36).

Figure 1–36

- Tap or click the More button (DESIGN tab | Themes group) to expand the gallery, which shows more theme gallery options (Figure 1–37).

Experiment

- If you are using a mouse, point to various document themes in the Themes gallery and watch the colors and fonts change on the title slide.

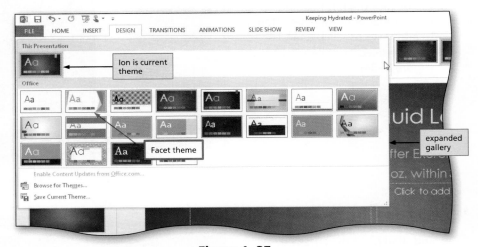

Figure 1–37

Q&A Are the themes displayed in a specific order?
They are listed in alphabetical order in two groups: Facet to Wisp beginning in the first row and Banded to Wood Type beginning in the second row. If you are using a mouse and point to a theme, a ScreenTip with the theme's name appears on the screen.

- Tap or click the Facet theme to apply this theme to all four slides (Figure 1–38).

Q&A The Facet theme is visible in the first row of the gallery, so why did I click the More button to expand the gallery?
While it is not necessary to view all the thumbnails, it sometimes is helpful to see all possible themes when deciding which one best fits the presentation.

If I decide at some future time that this design does not fit the theme of my presentation, can I apply a different design?
Yes. You can repeat these steps at any time while creating your presentation.

Figure 1–38

To Change the Variant

When you began creating this presentation, you selected the Ion theme and then chose a blue variant. You can change the color variation at any time for any theme. *Why? The new Facet theme has a default green color, but you want to emphasize the blue color associated with water, just like you initially did when you chose the blue variant for the Ion theme.* The following steps change the variant from green to blue.

- If you are using a mouse, point to the blue variation (DESIGN tab | Variants group) to see a preview of the blue variation on Slide 4 (Figure 1–39).

🔍 Experiment

- If you are using a mouse, point to the pink and black variants and watch the colors change on the slide.

Figure 1–39

2

- Tap or click the blue variant to apply this color to all four slides (Figure 1–40).

Q&A If I decide at some future time that this color variation does not fit the theme of my presentation, can I apply a different variant?

Yes. You can repeat these steps at any time while creating your presentation.

orange border indicates blue variant is applied

Figure 1–40

To Save an Existing Presentation with the Same File Name

You have made several modifications to the presentation since you last saved it. Thus, you should save it again. The following step saves the presentation again. For an example of the step listed below, refer to the Office and Windows chapter at the beginning of this book.

1 Tap or click the Save button on the Quick Access Toolbar to overwrite the previously saved file.

Break Point: If you wish to take a break, this is a good place to do so. You can exit PowerPoint now (refer to page PPT 55 for instructions). To resume at a later time, run PowerPoint (refer to page PPT 4 for instructions), open the file called Keeping Hydrated, and continue following the steps from this location forward.

BTW
Welcome Back!
If you are designing a slide in your deck other than Slide 1 and then save and close the document, PowerPoint's new Welcome back! feature allows you to continue where you left off at the last save when you open the document. You may need to adjust the zoom if you are working at a different level than the default setting.

PowerPoint Views

The PowerPoint window display varies depending on the view. A **view** is the mode in which the presentation appears on the screen. You will use some views when you are developing slides and others when you are delivering your presentation. When creating a presentation, you most likely will use Normal, Slide Sorter, Notes Page, and Outline views. When presenting your slides to an audience, you most likely will use Slide Sorter, Presenter, and Reading views.

The default view is **Normal view**, which is composed of three areas that allow you to work on various aspects of a presentation simultaneously. The large area in the middle, called the **Slide pane**, displays the slide you currently are developing and allows you to enter text, tables, charts, graphics, pictures, video, and other elements. As you create the slides, miniature views of the individual slides, called thumbnails, are displayed in the **Thumbnail pane**. You can rearrange the thumbnails in this pane. The **Notes pane**, by default, is hidden at the bottom of the window. If you want to type notes to yourself or remarks to share with your audience, you can click the Notes button in the status bar to open the Notes pane. After you have created at least two slides, a scroll bar containing **scroll arrows** and **scroll boxes** will appear on the right edge of the window.

To Move to Another Slide in Normal View

Why? *When creating or editing a presentation in Normal view (the view you are currently using), you often want to display a slide other than the current one.* Before continuing with developing this project, you want to display the title slide. If you are using a touch screen, you can tap the desired slide in the Thumbnail pane; if you are using a mouse, you can click the desired slide in the Thumbnail pane or drag the scroll box on the vertical scroll bar. When you drag the scroll box, the **slide indicator** shows the number and title of the slide you are about to display. Releasing shows the slide. The following steps move from Slide 4 to Slide 1 using the scroll box in the Slide pane.

- Position the pointer on the scroll box.

- Press and hold down the mouse button so that Slide: 4 of 4 Keep Replenishing Fluid Levels appears in the slide indicator (Figure 1–41).

Figure 1–41

2

- Drag the scroll box up the vertical scroll bar until Slide: 1 of 4 Healthy Hydration appears in the slide indicator (Figure 1–42).

Figure 1–42

- Release so that Slide 1 appears in the Slide pane and the Slide 1 thumbnail has an orange border in the Thumbnail pane (Figure 1–43).

Figure 1–43

Other Ways

1. Click Next Slide button or Previous Slide button to move forward or back one slide

2. Tap or click slide in Thumbnail pane

3. Press PAGE DOWN or PAGE UP to move forward or back one slide

Inserting Photos and Illustrations into Slides

A **clip** is a single media file, such as a photo, illustration, sound, or video. Adding a clip can help increase the visual and audio appeal of many slides and can offer a quick way to add professional-looking graphics and multimedia to a presentation without creating these files yourself. This material is contained in the **Office.com Clip Art** collection of drawings, photos, sounds, and other media files shared among Microsoft Office applications.

You also can add your own clips to slides. These images may include scanned photos, illustrations, and artwork from storage media, such as USB flash drives, hard disks, and memory cards. If you have a Microsoft account, you can add photos from other websites, including Flickr and SkyDrive.

You can add images from Office.com to your presentation in two ways. One way is by selecting one of the slide layouts that includes a content placeholder with an Online Pictures button. A second method is by tapping or clicking the Online Pictures button in the Images area on the INSERT tab. Tapping or clicking the Online Pictures button opens the Insert Pictures dialog box. The **Insert Pictures dialog box** allows you to search for clip art by using descriptive keywords. Clips have one or more keywords associated with various entities, activities, labels, and emotions.

If you have an active connection to the Internet, clips from the Microsoft Office.com website will display automatically as the result of your search. Microsoft constantly revises the content of Office.com, so you may not be able to locate the pictures used in this chapter. Contact your instructor if you need the photos and illustration used in the following steps.

How can you design a title slide that holds your audience's attention?

Develop a slide that reflects the content of your presentation but does so in a thought-provoking way. A title, at the very least, should prepare your audience for the material they are about to see and hear. Look for ways to focus attention on your theme and the method in which you plan to present this theme. A unique photograph or graphic can help generate interest. You may decide to introduce your topic with a startling fact, a rhetorical question, or a quotation. The device you choose depends upon your audience, the occasion, and the presentation's purpose.

To Insert a Picture from Office.com into the Title Slide

1 INSERT PRESENTATION SLIDES | 2 ENTER TEXT | 3 FORMAT TEXT | 4 INSERT GRAPHICAL ELEMENTS

5 SIZE & POSITION | 6 ENHANCE SLIDE SHOW | 7 DISPLAY & PRINT SLIDES

Slide 1 uses the Title Slide layout, which has two placeholders for text but none for graphical content. You desire to place a graphic on Slide 1. *Why? It is likely that your viewers will see an image on this slide before they read any text, so you want to include a photo to create interest in the presentation and introduce your audience to the topic. For this presentation,* you will locate a photo of a person holding a water bottle and then insert this photo in this slide. Later in this chapter, you will resize and position the photo in an appropriate location. The following steps add a photo to Slide 1.

- Tap or click INSERT on the ribbon to display the INSERT tab.

- Tap or click the Online Pictures button (INSERT tab | Images group) to display the Insert Pictures dialog box.

- With the insertion point in the Office.com Clip Art area, type **water bottle** in the search box (Figure 1–44).

Figure 1–44

2

- Tap or click the Search button (the magnifying glass) or press the ENTER key so that Office.com will search for and display all clips having the keywords, water bottle.

 Why does the x button display when I begin typing the search terms?

Clicking the x button deletes all letters in the box.

3

- If necessary, slide or scroll down the list to display the photo shown in Figure 1–45.

- Tap or click the photo to select it (Figure 1–45).

Q&A What if the water bottle image displayed in Figure1–45 is not shown in my Office.com Clip Art dialog box?

Select a similar photo. Microsoft updates the files in the Office.com Clip art collection, so the images change constantly.

What are the words and numbers in the lower-left corner of the dialog box?

The words are the keywords associated with this photo, and the figures are the number of pixels associated with the width and height of the clip.

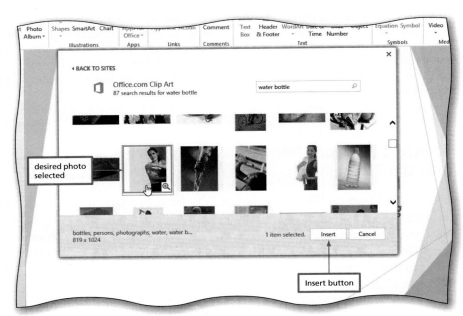

Figure 1–45

4

- Tap or click the Insert button to download the photo and insert it into the slide (Figure 1–46).

Q&A Can I double-tap or double-click the photo instead of selecting it and then tap or click the Insert button?

Yes. Either method downloads and inserts the photo.

Why is this photo displayed in this location on the slide?

The slide layout does not have a content placeholder, so PowerPoint inserts the file in the center of the slide.

Figure 1–46

To Insert a Picture from Office.com into a Slide without a Content Placeholder

The next step is to add a water bottle photo to Slide 2. This slide has a bulleted list in the text placeholder, so the icon group does not display in the center of the placeholder. Later in this chapter, you will resize the inserted photo. The following steps add one photo to Slide 2.

1 Tap or click the Slide 2 thumbnail in the Thumbnail pane to display Slide 2.

2 Tap or click INSERT on the ribbon to display the INSERT tab and then tap or click the Online Pictures button (INSERT tab | Images group) to display the Insert Pictures dialog box.

3 Type **water bottle** in the Office.com Clip Art search box and then tap or click the Search button.

4 If necessary, slide or scroll down the list to display the water bottle photo shown in Figure 1–47, tap or click the photo to select it, and then tap or click the Insert button to download and insert the photo into Slide 2 (Figure 1–47).

Q&A Why is my photo a different size from the one shown in Figure1–1b on page PPT 3? The clip was inserted into the slide and not into a content placeholder. You will resize the photo later in this chapter.

desired photo inserted into Slide 2

Figure 1–47

To Insert an Illustration from Office.com into a Slide without a Content Placeholder

Next, you will add an illustration to Slide 3. You will not insert this file into a content placeholder, so it will display in the center of the slide. Later in this chapter, you will resize this illustration. You locate and download illustrations in the same manner you used to locate and download photos. The following steps add an illustration to Slide 3.

1 Tap or click the Slide 3 thumbnail in the Thumbnail pane.

2 Display the INSERT tab, tap or click the Online Pictures button, type **drinking water** as the search text, and then tap or click the Search button.

3
If necessary, slide or scroll down the list to display the picture of a character drinking water shown in Figure 1–48 and then insert it into Slide 3 (Figure 1–48).

Figure 1–48

To Insert a Picture from Office.com into a Content Placeholder

1 INSERT PRESENTATION SLIDES | 2 ENTER TEXT | 3 FORMAT TEXT | 4 INSERT GRAPHICAL ELEMENTS
5 SIZE & POSITION | 6 ENHANCE SLIDE SHOW | 7 DISPLAY & PRINT SLIDES

Slide 4 uses the Comparison layout, which has a content placeholder below each of the two headings. You desire to insert photos into both content placeholders. **Why?** *You want to reinforce the concept that people should drink water during and after workouts.* The following steps insert photos of a female into the left content placeholder and a male into the right content placeholder on Slide 4.

1
• Tap or click the Slide 4 thumbnail in the Thumbnail pane to display Slide 4 (Figure 1–49).

Figure 1–49

- Tap or click the Online Pictures icon in the left content placeholder to select that placeholder and to open the Insert Pictures dialog box.

- Tap or click the search box, type **women bottled water** as the search text, and then press the ENTER key.

- If necessary, slide or scroll down the list to display the photo shown in Figure 1–50.

- Select the photo and then double-tap or double-click to download and insert it into the left content placeholder (Figure 1–50).

Figure 1–50

- Tap or click the Online Pictures icon in the right content placeholder to select that placeholder and to open the Insert Pictures dialog box.

- Tap or click the search box, type **men exercises hydration** as the search text, and press or tap the ENTER key.

- If necessary, slide or scroll down the list to display the photo shown in Figure 1–51.

- Insert the photo into the right content placeholder (Figure 1–51).

Figure 1–51

Break Point: If you wish to take a break, this is a good place to do so. You can save your presentation and then exit PowerPoint now. To resume at a later time, run PowerPoint, open the file called Keeping Hydrated, and continue following the steps from this location forward.

Resizing Photos and Illustrations

Sometimes it is necessary to change the size of photos and illustrations. **Resizing** includes enlarging or reducing the size of a graphic. You can resize these images using a variety of techniques. One method involves changing the size of a picture by specifying exact dimensions in a dialog box. Another method involves sliding or dragging one of the graphic's sizing handles to the desired location. A selected graphic appears surrounded by a **selection rectangle**, which has small squares and circles, called **sizing handles** or move handles, at each corner and middle location.

To Proportionally Resize Pictures

Why? On Slides 1, 2, and 3, the photo and illustration sizes are either too small or too large to display aesthetically on the slides. The photo and illustration on Slides 1 and 3 are too small, and the photo on Slide 2 is too large. The photo on Slide 1 is of a person, so it generally is important to maintain the proportions. To change the size of a photo and keep the width and height in proportion to each other, drag the corner sizing handles to view how the image will look on the slide. Using these corner handles maintains the graphic's original proportions. If, however, the proportions do not need to be maintained, as with the water bottle on Slide 2, drag the square sizing handles to alter the proportions so that the graphic's height and width become larger or smaller. The following steps proportionally increase the size of the Slide 1 photo using a corner sizing handle.

1

- Click the Slide 1 thumbnail in the Thumbnail pane to display Slide 1.

- Tap or click the photo to select it and display the selection rectangle.

- Point to the upper-right corner sizing handle on the illustration so that the pointer changes to a two-headed arrow (Figure 1–52).

Q&A I am using a touch screen and do not see a two-headed arrow when I press and hold the upper-right sizing handle. Why?
Touch screens may not display pointers; you can just press and slide sizing handles to resize.

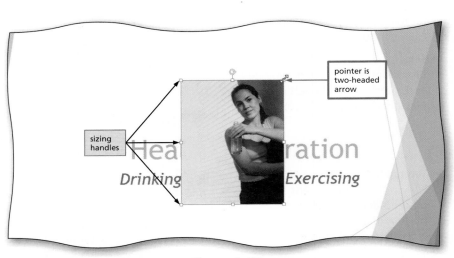

Figure 1–52

2

- Drag the sizing handle diagonally toward the upper-right corner of the slide until the upper-right sizing handle or the crosshair is positioned approximately as shown in Figure 1–53.

Q&A What if the illustration is not the same size as the one shown in Figure 1–53?
Repeat Steps 1 and 2.

Figure 1–53

- Release to resize the illustration.

- Tap or click outside the illustration to deselect it (Figure 1–54).

Q&A What happened to the PICTURE TOOLS FORMAT tab?
When you tap or click outside the illustration, PowerPoint deselects the illustration and removes the PICTURE TOOLS FORMAT tab from the screen.

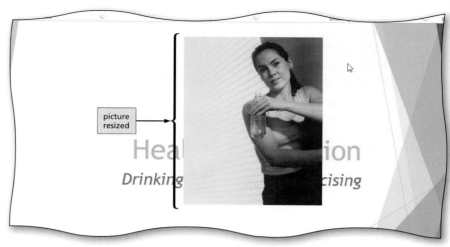

Figure 1–54

To Nonproportionally Resize the Photograph on Slide 2

1 INSERT PRESENTATION SLIDES | 2 ENTER TEXT | 3 FORMAT TEXT | 4 INSERT GRAPHICAL ELEMENTS
5 SIZE & POSITION | 6 ENHANCE SLIDE SHOW | 7 DISPLAY & PRINT SLIDES

Why? *The height of the water bottle photo in Slide 2 extends from the top to the bottom of the slide. The width, however, will cover some of the text when the photo is positioned on the right side of the slide.* The width of this photo can be decreased slightly without negatively distorting the original image. You can decrease the width of a photo by sliding or dragging one of the square sizing handles on the sides of the image. The following steps resize the width of the water bottle photo using a sizing handle along the side of the image.

- Display Slide 2 and then tap or click the water bottle photo to select it and display the selection rectangle.

- Tap or click the Zoom Out button as many times as necessary until the Zoom level is 60%.

- Press or point to the sizing handle on the left side of the photo so that the pointer changes to a two-headed arrow (Figure 1–55).

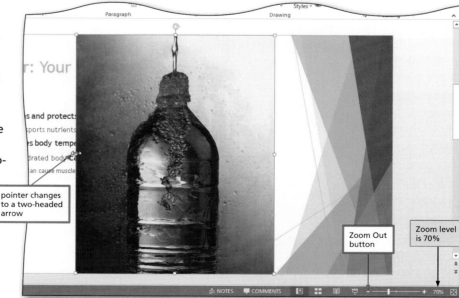

Figure 1–55

2

- Drag the sizing handle toward the right side of the slide until the sizing handle or crosshair is positioned approximately as shown in Figure 1–56.

Q&A What if the illustration is not the same size as the one shown in Figure 1–56?
Repeat Steps 1 and 2.

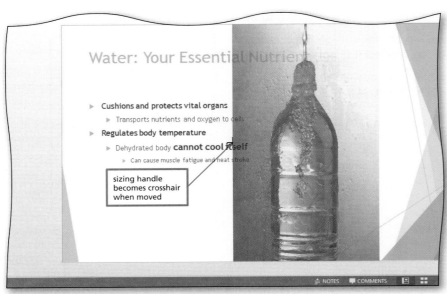

Figure 1–56

3

- Release to resize the photo.
- Tap or click outside the photo to deselect it (Figure 1–57).

Q&A What if I want to return the photo to its original size and start again?
With the photo selected, tap or click the Reset Picture arrow (PICTURE TOOLS FORMAT tab | Adjust group) and then click Reset Picture & Size in the Reset Picture gallery.

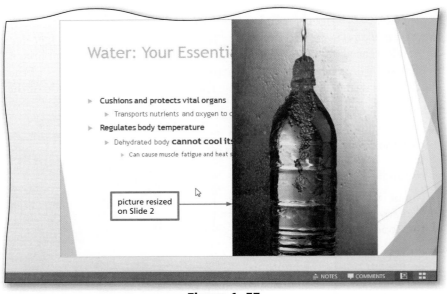

Figure 1–57

To Resize the Illustration on Slide 3

The illustration on Slide 3 can be reduced slightly to fit entirely on the slide. You resize an illustration in the same manner that you resize a photo. You want to maintain the proportions of the character and water in this illustration, so you will drag one of the corner sizing handles. The following steps resize this illustration using a corner sizing handle.

1 Display Slide 3 and then tap or click the character drinking water illustration to select it.

2 Drag the lower-left corner sizing handle on the illustration diagonally outward until the illustration is resized approximately as shown in Figure 1–58.

Figure 1–58

To Move Pictures

1 INSERT PRESENTATION SLIDES | 2 ENTER TEXT | 3 FORMAT TEXT | 4 INSERT GRAPHICAL ELEMENTS
5 SIZE & POSITION | 6 ENHANCE SLIDE SHOW | 7 DISPLAY & PRINT SLIDES

Why? After you insert a photo or an illustration on a slide, you might want to reposition it. The female athlete photo on Slide 1 could be moved to the left side of the slide, the water bottle on Slide 2 could be moved to the right side of the slide, and the illustration on Slide 3 could be positioned in the center of the slide. PowerPoint displays **Smart Guides** automatically when a photo, illustration, shape, or other object is close to lining up with another slide element. For example, a Smart Guide will display to help you align the right or left edge of a picture in relation to a text placeholder or to another picture. The following steps move the photos on Slides 1 and 2 and center the illustration on Slide 3.

1

- If necessary, tap or click the character illustration on Slide 3 to select it.

- Drag the illustration upward until the horizontal Smart Guide is displayed under the title text placeholder and the vertical Smart Guide is displayed through the center of the slide, as shown in Figure 1–59, and then release.

- If necessary, select the photo and then use the ARROW keys to position it precisely as shown in Figure 1–59.

Q&A The illustration still is not located exactly where I want it to display. What can I do to align the image?
Press the CTRL key while you press the ARROW keys. This key combination moves the illustration in smaller increments than when you press only an ARROW key.

Figure 1–59

2

- Display Slide 2 and then tap or click the water bottle photo to select it.

- Drag the photo to align with the right edge of the slide (Figure 1–60).

Q&A

My water bottle photo is covering some of the title text on the slide. What should I do?

Either resize the photo to make it narrower or move the photo to the right so that it is hanging slightly off the side of the slide.

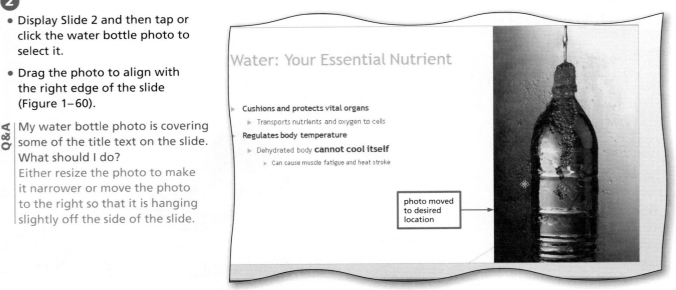

Figure 1–60

3

- Display Slide 1 and then tap or click the athlete photo to select it.

- Drag the photo to the left and either upward or downward until the horizontal center Smart Guide is displayed, as shown in Figure 1–61, and then release.

4

- Tap or click outside the photo to deselect it.

Figure 1–61

Q&A

The athlete photo is too wide and is covering some of the text on the slide. What should I do?

Changing the width of a photo showing a person generally is not advisable because the altered proportions make the person appear tall and thin or short and overweight. In this case, move the photo to the left so that it is hanging slightly off the side of the slide, as shown in Figure1–61.

Ending a Slide Show with a Closing Slide

All the text for the slides in the Healthy Hydration slide show has been entered. This presentation thus far consists of a title slide, one text slide with a multilevel bulleted list, a third slide for a photo, and a fourth slide with a Comparison layout. A closing slide that resembles the title slide is the final slide to create.

CONSIDER THIS

What factors should you consider when developing a closing slide for the presentation?

After the last slide appears during a slide show, the default PowerPoint setting is to end the presentation with a **black slide**. This black slide appears only when the slide show is running and concludes the slide show, so your audience never sees the PowerPoint window. It is a good idea, however, to end your presentation with a final closing slide to display at the end of the presentation. This slide ends the presentation gracefully and should be an exact copy, or a very similar copy, of your title slide. The audience will recognize that the presentation is drawing to a close when this slide appears. It can remain on the screen when the audience asks questions, approaches the speaker for further information, or exits the room.

To Duplicate a Slide

Why? *When two slides contain similar information and have the same format, duplicating one slide and then making minor modifications to the new slide saves time and increases consistency.*

Slide 5 will have the same layout and design as Slide 1. The most expedient method of creating this slide is to copy Slide 1 and then make minor modifications to the new slide. The following steps duplicate the title slide.

1

• With Slide 1 selected, tap or click the New Slide arrow (HOME tab | Slides group) to display the Facet layout gallery (Figure 1–62).

Figure 1–62

2

• Tap or click 'Duplicate Selected Slides' in the Facet layout gallery to create a new Slide 2, which is a duplicate of Slide 1 (Figure 1–63).

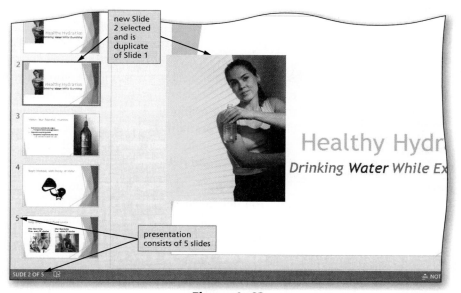

Figure 1–63

Break Point: If you wish to take a break, this is a good place to do so. Be sure to save the Keeping Hydrated file again and then you can exit PowerPoint. To resume at a later time, run PowerPoint, open the file called Keeping Hydrated, and continue following the steps from this location forward.

To Arrange a Slide

The new Slide 2 was inserted directly below Slide 1 because Slide 1 was the selected slide. This duplicate slide needs to display at the end of the presentation directly after the final title and content slide. ***Why?*** *It is a closing slide that reinforces the concept presented in Slide 1 and indicates to your audiences that your presentation is ending.*

Changing slide order is an easy process and is best performed in the Thumbnail pane. When you tap or click the thumbnail and begin to drag it to a new location, the remaining thumbnails realign to show the new sequence. When you release, the slide drops into the desired location. Hence, this process of sliding or dragging and then dropping the thumbnail in a new location is called **drag and drop**. You can use the drag-and-drop method to move any selected item, including text and graphics. The following step moves the new Slide 2 to the end of the presentation so that it becomes a closing slide.

- With Slide 2 selected, drag the Slide 2 slide thumbnail below the last slide in the Thumbnail pane (Figure 1–64).

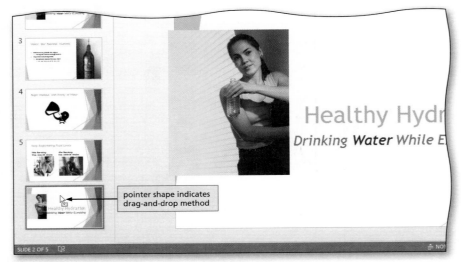

pointer shape indicates drag-and-drop method

Figure 1–64

Other Ways

1. Tap or click Slide Sorter button on status bar, drag thumbnail to new location

2. Tap or click Slide Sorter button (VIEW tab | Presentation Views group), tap or click slide thumbnail, drag thumbnail to new location

Making Changes to Slide Text Content

After creating slides in a presentation, you may find that you want to make changes to the text. Changes may be required because a slide contains an error, the scope of the presentation shifts, or the style is inconsistent. This section explains the types of changes that commonly occur when creating a presentation.

You generally make three types of changes to text in a presentation: additions, replacements, and deletions.

- Additions are necessary when you omit text from a slide and need to add it later. You may need to insert text in the form of a sentence, word, or single character. For example, you may want to add the presenter's middle name on the title slide.

- Replacements are needed when you want to revise the text in a presentation. For example, you may want to substitute the word, *their*, for the word, *there*.

- Deletions are required when text on a slide is incorrect or no longer is relevant to the presentation. For example, a slide may look cluttered. Therefore, you may want to remove one of the bulleted paragraphs to add more space.

Editing text in PowerPoint basically is the same as editing text in a word processing program. The following sections illustrate the most common changes made to text in a presentation.

Replacing Text in an Existing Slide

When you need to correct a word or phrase, you can replace the text by selecting the text to be replaced and then typing the new text. As soon as you press any key on the keyboard, the selected text is deleted and the new text is displayed.

PowerPoint inserts text to the left of the insertion point. The text to the right of the insertion point moves to the right (and shifts downward if necessary) to accommodate the added text.

Deleting Text

You can delete text using one of many methods. One is to use the BACKSPACE key to remove text just typed. The second is to position the insertion point to the left of the text you want to delete and then press the DELETE key. The third method is to drag through the text you want to delete and then tap or click the Cut button on the mini toolbar, press DELETE or BACKSPACE key, or press CTRL + X. Use the third method when deleting large sections of text.

To Delete Text in a Placeholder

1 INSERT PRESENTATION SLIDES | 2 ENTER TEXT | **3 FORMAT TEXT** | 4 INSERT GRAPHICAL ELEMENTS
5 SIZE & POSITION | 6 ENHANCE SLIDE SHOW | **7 DISPLAY & PRINT SLIDES**

Why? *To keep the ending slide clean and simple, you want to delete a few words in the slide title and subtitle text.* The following steps change Healthy Hydration to Be Healthy and then change Drinking Water While Exercising to Drink Water.

- With Slide 5 selected, position the pointer immediately to the right of the last character of the text to be selected in the title text placeholder (in this case, the n in the word, Hydration).

- Drag the pointer through the first character of the text to be selected (in this case, the space after the word, Healthy) (Figure 1–65).

Q&A I am having difficulty selecting the required text. Can I drag from left to right or right to left?
Yes. You may need several attempts to select the correct characters.

Could I also have selected the word, Hydration, by double-tapping or double-clicking it?
Yes. Either method works to select a word.

Figure 1–65

2

- Tap or click the Cut button (HOME tab | Clipboard group) to delete the selected text and space.

- Position the pointer to the left of the word, Healthy, and then type **Be** and press the SPACEBAR as the first word in the title text placeholder (Figure 1–66).

- If requested by your instructor, add your mother's first name after the word, Healthy, in the title text placeholder.

Figure 1–66

3

- Position the pointer immediately to the right of the last character of the text to be selected in the subtitle text placeholder (in this case, the g in the word, Exercising).

- Drag the pointer to the left through the last character of the text to be selected (in this case, the space after the word, Water) (Figure 1–67).

Figure 1–67

- Tap or click the Cut button.

- Select the letters, ing, in the word, Drinking.

- Tap or click the Cut button (Figure 1–68).

Figure 1–68

Other Ways

1. Tap 'Show Context Menu' button on mini toolbar or right-click selected text, tap or click Cut on shortcut menu
2. Select text, press DELETE or BACKSPACE key
3. Select text, press CTRL+X

Adding a Transition

PowerPoint includes a wide variety of visual and sound effects that can be applied to text or content. A **slide transition** is a special effect used to progress from one slide to the next in a slide show. You can control the speed of the transition effect and add a sound.

To Add a Transition between Slides

1 INSERT PRESENTATION SLIDES | 2 ENTER TEXT | 3 FORMAT TEXT | 4 INSERT GRAPHICAL ELEMENTS
5 SIZE & POSITION | 6 ENHANCE SLIDE SHOW | 7 DISPLAY & PRINT SLIDES

Why? Transitions add interest when you advance the slides in a presentation and make a slide show presentation look *professional.* In this presentation, you apply the Switch transition in the Exciting category to all slides and change the transition speed from 1.25 seconds to 2 seconds. The following steps apply this transition to the presentation.

- Tap or click the TRANSITIONS tab on the ribbon and then point to the More button (TRANSITIONS tab | Transition to This Slide group) in the Transition to This Slide gallery (Figure 1–69).

Figure 1–69

Q&A

Is a transition applied now?

No. None, the first slide icon in the Transition to This Slide group, is selected, which indicates no transition has been applied.

- Tap or click the More button to expand the Transitions gallery.
- Point to the Switch transition in the Exciting category in the Transitions gallery (Figure 1–70).

Figure 1–70

- Tap or click Switch in the Exciting category in the Transitions gallery to apply this transition to the closing slide.

◄ | Why does a star appear next to Slide 5 in the Thumbnail pane?
Q&A | The star indicates that a transition animation effect is applied to that slide.

- Tap or click the Duration up arrow (TRANSITIONS tab | Timing group) seven times to change the transition speed from 01.25 seconds to 03.00 seconds (Figure 1–71).

◄ | Why did the time change from the default 2.00 to 1.25?
Q&A | Each transition has a default duration time. The default Switch transition time is 01.25 seconds.

Figure 1–71

- Tap or click the Preview Transitions button (TRANSITIONS tab | Preview area) to view the transition and the new transition time (Figure 1–72).

Q&A Can I adjust the duration time I just set?

Yes. Tap or click the Duration up or down arrows or type a speed in the Duration box and preview the transition until you find the time that best fits your presentation.

Figure 1–72

- Tap or click the 'Apply To All' button (TRANSITIONS tab | Timing group) to apply the Switch transition and the increased transition time to Slides 1 through 4 in the presentation (Figure 1–73).

Q&A What if I want to apply a different transition and duration to each slide in the presentation?

Repeat Steps 2 and 3 for each slide individually.

Figure 1–73

Document Properties

PowerPoint helps you organize and identify your files by using **document properties**, which are the details about a file such as the project author, title, and subject. For example, a class name or presentation topic can describe the file's purpose or content.

CONSIDER THIS

Why would you want to assign document properties to a presentation?
Document properties are valuable for a variety of reasons:

- Users can save time locating a particular file because they can view a file's document properties without opening the presentation.
- By creating consistent properties for files having similar content, users can better organize their presentations.
- Some organizations require PowerPoint users to add document properties so that other employees can view details about these files.

The more common document properties are standard and automatically updated properties. **Standard properties** are associated with all Microsoft Office files and include author, title, and subject. **Automatically updated properties** include file system properties, such as the date you create or change a file, and statistics, such as the file size.

TO CHANGE DOCUMENT PROPERTIES

BTW
Printing Document Properties
PowerPoint 2013 does not allow you to print document properties. This feature, however, is available in other Office 2013 apps, including Word and Excel.

To change document properties, you would follow these steps.

1. Tap or click FILE on the ribbon to open the Backstage view and then, if necessary, tap or click the Info tab in the Backstage view to display the Info gallery.

2. If the property you wish to change is displayed in the Properties list in the right pane of the Info gallery, try to tap or click to the right of the property. If a box appears to the right of the property, type the text for the property in the box, and then tap or click the Back button in the upper-left corner of the Backstage view to return to the PowerPoint window. Skip the remaining steps.

3. If the property you wish to change is not displayed in the Properties list in the right pane of the Info gallery or you cannot change it in the Info gallery, tap or click the Properties button in the right pane to display the Properties menu, and then tap or click 'Show Document Panel' on the Properties menu to close the Backstage view and display the Document Information Panel in the PowerPoint presentation window.

Q&A Why are some of the document properties in my Document Information Panel already filled in?
The person who installed Office 2013 on your computer or network may have set or customized the properties.

4. Type the desired text in the appropriate property boxes.

Q&A What if the property I want to change is not displayed in the Document Information Panel?
Tap or click the Document Properties button in the Document Information Panel and then tap or click Advanced Properties on the menu to display the Properties dialog box. If necessary, tap or click the Summary tab (Properties dialog box) to display the Summary sheet, fill in the appropriate boxes, and then tap or click the OK button.

5. Tap or click the 'Close the Document Information Panel' button at the right edge of the Document Information Panel so that the panel no longer appears in the PowerPoint presentation window.

Viewing the Presentation in Slide Show View

The Start From Beginning button, located in the Quick Access Toolbar, allows you to show a presentation using a computer. As the name implies, the first slide to be displayed always will be Slide 1. You also can run a presentation starting with the slide currently displaying when you tap or click the Slide Show button on the status bar. In either case, PowerPoint displays the slides on the full screen without any of the PowerPoint window objects, such as the ribbon. The full-screen slide hides the toolbars, menus, and other PowerPoint window elements.

To Start Slide Show View

1 INSERT PRESENTATION SLIDES | 2 ENTER TEXT | 3 FORMAT TEXT | 4 INSERT GRAPHICAL ELEMENTS
5 SIZE & POSITION | 6 ENHANCE SLIDE SHOW | 7 DISPLAY & PRINT SLIDES

Why? *You run a presentation in for your audience so they can see the slides in their entirety and view any transitions or other effects added to the slides.* When making a presentation, you use **Slide Show view.** You can start Slide Show view from Normal view or Slide Sorter view. Slide Show view begins when you tap or click the Start From Beginning button or the Slide Show button. The following steps start Slide Show view starting with Slide 1.

- If you are using a touch screen, proceed to Step 2. If you are using a mouse, point to the Start From Beginning button (Figure 1–74).

Q&A | What would have displayed if I had tapped or clicked the Slide Show button instead of the Start From Beginning button?
When you tap or click the Slide Show button to start the presentation, PowerPoint begins the show with the currently displayed slide, which in this case is Slide 5. Only Slide 5 would display during the slide show.

Figure 1–74

2

● Tap or click the Start From Beginning button to display the title slide (Figure 1–75).

Q&A Where is the PowerPoint window?
When you run a slide show, the PowerPoint window is hidden. It will reappear once you end your slide show.

title slide in Slide Show view

Figure 1–75

Other Ways
1. Display Slide 1, tap or click Slide Show button on status bar	2. Tap or click Start From Beginning button (SLIDE SHOW tab | Start Slide Show group)	3. Press F5

To Move Manually through Slides in a Slide Show

1 INSERT PRESENTATION SLIDES | 2 ENTER TEXT | 3 FORMAT TEXT | 4 INSERT GRAPHICAL ELEMENTS

5 SIZE & POSITION | 6 ENHANCE SLIDE SHOW | **7 DISPLAY & PRINT SLIDES**

After you begin Slide Show view, you can move forward or backward through the slides. PowerPoint allows you to advance through the slides manually or automatically. During a slide show, each slide in the presentation shows on the screen, one slide at a time. Each time you tap or click, the next slide appears. The following steps move manually through the slides. *Why? You can control the length of time each slide is displayed and change the preset order if you need to review a slide already shown or jump ahead to another slide designed to display later in the presentation.*

1

- Swipe forward on or click each slide until Slide 5 (Be Healthy) is displayed (Figure 1–76).

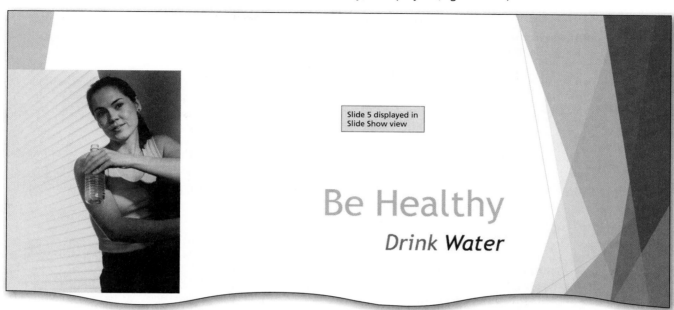

Figure 1–76

2

- Swipe forward on or click Slide 5 so that the black slide appears with a message announcing the end of the slide show (Figure 1–77).

◁ | I see a small toolbar in the lower-left corner of my slide. What is this toolbar?
Q&A | The Slide Show toolbar appears when you begin running a slide show and then tap a slide or move the pointer. The buttons on this toolbar allow you to navigate to the next slide, the previous slide, to mark up the current slide, or to change the current display.

Figure 1–77

- Swipe forward on or click the black slide to return to Normal view in the PowerPoint window.

Other Ways

1. Press PAGE DOWN to advance one slide at a time, or press PAGE UP to go back one slide at a time

2. Press RIGHT ARROW or DOWN ARROW to advance one slide at a time, or press LEFT ARROW or UP ARROW to go back one slide at a time

3. If Slide Show toolbar is displayed, tap or click Next Slide or Previous Slide button on toolbar

Printing a Presentation

After creating a presentation, you may want to print it. Printing a presentation enables you to distribute it to others in a form that can be read or viewed but typically not edited. It is a good practice to save a presentation before printing it, in the event you experience difficulties printing.

CONSIDER THIS

What is the best method for distributing a presentation?

The traditional method of distributing a presentation uses a printer to produce a hard copy. A **hard copy** or **printout** is information that exists on a physical medium such as paper. Hard copies can be useful for the following reasons:

- Some people prefer proofreading a hard copy of a presentation rather than viewing it on the screen to check for errors and readability.

- Hard copies can serve as a backup reference if your storage medium is lost or becomes corrupted and you need to recreate the presentation.

Instead of distributing a hard copy of a presentation, users can distribute the presentation as an electronic image that mirrors the original presentation's appearance. The electronic image of the presentation can be sent as an email attachment, posted on a website, or copied to a portable storage medium such as a USB flash drive. Two popular electronic image formats, sometimes called fixed formats, are PDF by Adobe Systems and XPS by Microsoft. In PowerPoint, you can create electronic image files through the Save As dialog box and the Export, Share, and Print tabs in the Backstage view. Electronic images of presentations, such as PDF and XPS, can be useful for the following reasons:

- Users can view electronic images of presentations without the software that created the original presentation (e.g., PowerPoint). Specifically, to view a PDF file, you use a program called Adobe Reader, which can be downloaded free from Adobe's website. Similarly, to view an XPS file, you use a program called XPS Viewer, which is included in the latest versions of Windows and Internet Explorer.

- Sending electronic presentations saves paper and printer supplies. Society encourages users to contribute to **green computing**, which involves reducing the electricity consumed and environmental waste generated when using computers, mobile devices, and related technologies.

To Print a Presentation

1 INSERT PRESENTATION SLIDES | 2 ENTER TEXT | 3 FORMAT TEXT | 4 INSERT GRAPHICAL ELEMENTS | 5 SIZE & POSITION | 6 ENHANCE SLIDE SHOW | **7 DISPLAY & PRINT SLIDES**

With the completed presentation saved, you may want to print it. *Why? You could distribute a handout of the slides to your audience members, or you might want to keep a printed copy as a backup in the event you experience technical difficulties before or during your speech. You, therefore, will print a hard copy on a printer.* The following steps print a hard copy of the contents of the saved Keeping Hydrated presentation.

1

- Tap or click FILE on the ribbon to open the Backstage view.

- Tap or click the Print tab in the Backstage view to display the Print gallery (Figure 1–78).

Q&A How do I preview Slides 2 through 5?
Tap or click the Next Page button in the Print gallery to scroll forward through pages in the document; similarly, tap or click the Previous Page button to scroll backward through pages.

How can I print multiple copies of my presentation?
Increase the number in the Copies box in the Print gallery.

What if I decide not to print the presentation at this time?
Tap or click the Back button in the upper-left corner of the Backstage view to return to the presentation window.

2

- Verify that the printer listed on the Printer Status button will print a hard copy of the presentation. If necessary, click the Printer Status button to display a list of available printer options and then click the desired printer to change the currently selected printer.

Q&A The selected printer is a black-and-white laser printer, so the preview is grayscale and shows varying shades of gray. If I change the currently selected printer to a color printer, will the preview display in color?
Yes, the preview will match the printer output.

BTW

Conserving Ink and Toner
If you want to conserve ink or toner, you can instruct PowerPoint to print draft quality documents by tapping or clicking FILE on the ribbon to open the Backstage view, tapping or clicking Options in the Backstage view to display the PowerPoint Options dialog box, tapping or clicking Advanced in the left pane (PowerPoint Options dialog box), sliding or scrolling to the Print area in the right pane, not placing a check mark in the High quality check box, and then tapping or clicking the OK button. Then, use the Backstage view to print the document as usual.

Figure 1–78

- Tap or click the Print button in the Print gallery to print the presentation on the currently selected printer.

- When the printer stops, retrieve the hard copy (Figure 1–79).

Q&A

Do I have to wait until my presentation is complete to print it?
No, you can follow these steps to print a presentation at any time while you are creating it.

What if I want to print an electronic image of a presentation instead of a hard copy?
You would click the Printer Status button in the Print gallery and then select the desired electronic image option, such as Microsoft XPS Document Writer, which would create an XPS file.

(a) Slide 1

(b) Slide 2

(c) Slide 3

(d) Slide 4

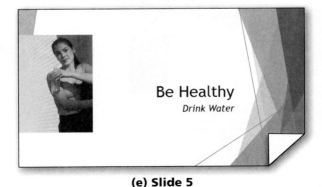

(e) Slide 5

Figure 1–79   (Handouts printed using a black-and-white printer)

Other Ways

1. Press CTRL+P, press ENTER

To Sign Out of a Microsoft Account

If you are signed in to a Microsoft account and are using a public computer or otherwise wish to sign out of your Microsoft account, you should sign out of the account from the Accounts gallery in the Backstage view before exiting PowerPoint. Signing out of the account is the safest way to make sure that nobody else can access SkyDrive files or settings stored in your Microsoft account. The following steps sign out of a Microsoft account from PowerPoint. For a detailed example of the procedure summarized below, refer to the Office and Windows chapter at the beginning of this book.

1 If you wish to sign out of your Microsoft account, tap or click FILE on the ribbon to open the Backstage view and then tap or click the Account tab to display the Account gallery.

2 Tap or click the Sign out link, which displays the Remove Account dialog box. If a Can't remove Windows accounts dialog box appears instead of the Remove Account dialog box, click the OK button and skip the remaining steps.

Q&A Why does a Can't remove Windows accounts dialog box appear?
If you signed in to Windows using your Microsoft account, then you also must sign out from Windows, rather than signing out from within PowerPoint. When you are finished using Windows, be sure to sign out at that time.

3 Tap or click the Yes button (Remove Account dialog box) to sign out of your Microsoft account on this computer.

Q&A Should I sign out of Windows after signing out of my Microsoft account?
When you are finished using the computer, you should sign out of your account for maximum security.

4 Tap or click the Back button in the upper-left corner of the Backstage view to return to the presentation.

To Exit PowerPoint

This project now is complete. The following steps exit PowerPoint. For a detailed example of the procedure summarized below, refer to the Office and Windows chapter at the beginning of this book.

1a If you have one PowerPoint presentation open, tap or click the Close button on the right side of the title bar to close the open document and exit PowerPoint.

1b If you have multiple PowerPoint presentations open, press and hold or right-click the PowerPoint app button on the taskbar and then tap or click 'Close all windows' on the shortcut menu, or press ALT+F4 to close all open presentations and exit PowerPoint.

Q&A Could I press and hold or repeatedly click the Close button to close all open documents and exit PowerPoint?
Yes.

2 If a Microsoft PowerPoint dialog box appears, tap or click the Save button to save any changes made to the presentation since the last save.

BTW
Certification
The Microsoft Office Specialist (MOS) program provides an opportunity for you to obtain a valuable industry credential — proof that you have the PowerPoint 2013 skills required by employers. For more information, visit the Certification resource on the Student Companion Site located on www.cengagebrain.com. For detailed instructions about accessing available resources, visit www.cengage.com/ct/studentdownload or see the inside back cover of this book.

BTW
Quick Reference
For a table that lists how to complete the tasks covered in this book using touch gestures, the mouse, ribbon, shortcut menu, and keyboard, see the Quick Reference Summary at the back of this book, or visit the Quick Reference resource on the Student Companion Site located on www.cengagebrain.com. For detailed instructions about accessing available resources, visit www.cengage.com/ct/studentdownload or see the inside back cover of this book.

Chapter Summary

In this chapter you have learned how to apply and change a document theme and variant, create a title slide and text slides with a bulleted list, insert photos and an illustration and then resize and move them on a slide, format and edit text, add a slide transition, view the presentation in Slide Show view, and print slides as handouts. The items listed below include all the new PowerPoint skills you have learned in this chapter, with the tasks grouped by activity.

Enter and Edit Text
Enter the Presentation Title (PPT 7)
Enter the Presentation Subtitle Paragraph (PPT 9)
Zoom a Slide (PPT 10)
Add a New Text Slide with a Bulleted List (PPT 15)
Enter a Slide Title (PPT 17)
Type a Multilevel Bulleted List (PPT 18)
Add a Slide with the Title Only Layout (PPT 23)
Add a New Slide and Enter a Slide Title and Headings (PPT 24)
Move to Another Slide in Normal View (PPT 29)
Duplicate a Slide (PPT 41)
Arrange a Slide (PPT 42)
Delete Text in a Placeholder (PPT 43)

Format a Slide
Choose a Document Theme and Variant (PPT 5)
Change the Theme (PPT 26)
Change the Variant (PPT 27)

Format Text
Italicize Text (PPT 11)
Increase Font Size (PPT 12, 22)

Change the Text Color (PPT 13)
Bold Text (PPT 21)

Enhance Slides with Pictures and a Transition
Insert a Picture from Office.com into the Title Slide (PPT 31)
Insert a Picture from Office.com into a Content Placeholder (PPT 34)
Proportionally Resize Pictures (PPT 36)
Move Pictures (PPT 39)
Add a Transition between Slides (PPT 45)

Run and Print a Slide Show
Change Document Properties (PPT 48)
Start Slide Show View (PPT 49)
Move Manually through Slides in a Slide Show (PPT 50)
Print a Presentation (PPT 52)

Select Text and Slide Elements
Select a Paragraph (PPT 11)
Select a Word (PPT 12)
Select a Text Placeholder (PPT 18)
Select a Group of Words (PPT 20)

CONSIDER THIS

What decisions will you need to make when creating your next presentation?
Use these guidelines as you complete the assignments in this chapter and create your own slide show decks outside of this class.

1. Determine the content you want to include on your slides.

2. Determine which theme and variant are appropriate.

3. Identify the slide layouts that best communicate your message.

4. Format various text elements to emphasize important points.

    a) Select appropriate font sizes.

    b) Emphasize important words with bold or italic type and color.

5. Locate graphical elements, such as photos and illustrations, that reinforce your message.

    a) Size and position them aesthetically on slides.

6. Determine a storage location for the presentation.

7. Determine the best method for distributing the presentation.

How should you submit solutions to questions in the assignments identified with a ✳ symbol?

CONSIDER THIS

Apply Your Knowledge

Reinforce the skills and apply the concepts you learned in this chapter.

Modifying Character Formats and Paragraph Levels and Moving an Illustration

Note: To complete this assignment, you will be required to use the Data Files for Students. Visit www.cengage.com/ct/studentdownload for detailed instructions or contact your instructor for information about accessing the required files.

Instructions: Run PowerPoint. Open the presentation, Apply 1-1 Effective Writing, from the Data Files for Students.

The two slides in the presentation discuss steps to follow when writing a persuasive essay. The document you open is an unformatted presentation. You are to modify the document theme, indent the paragraphs, resize and move the photo, and format the text so the slides look like Figure 1–80 on this page and the next page.

Perform the following tasks:

1. Change the document theme to Ion.

2. On the title slide, use your name in place of Student Name and bold and italicize your name.

3. If requested by your instructor, change your first name to your grandmother's first name on the title slide.

4. Increase the title text font size to 60 point. Size and position the photo using the Smart Guides to align the image with the bottom of the title placeholder, as shown in Figure 1–80a.

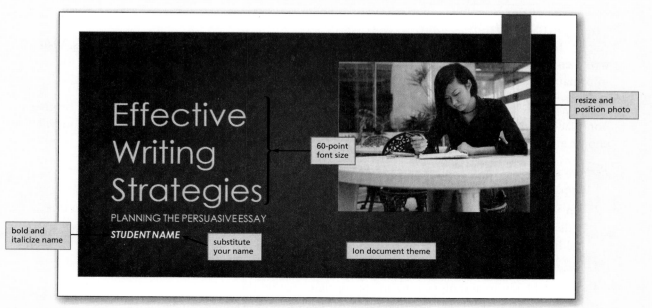

(a) Slide 1 (Title Slide with a Picture)
Figure 1–80

Continued >

Apply Your Knowledge *continued*

5. On Slide 2, increase the indent of the third and fourth paragraphs to second-level paragraphs. Then combine paragraphs six and seven (To change readers' minds? and To confirm opinions?) to read, To change readers' minds or confirm opinions?, as shown in Figure 1–80b. Increase the indent of this paragraph to second level.

6. Save the presentation using the file name, Apply 1-1 Effective Writing Strategies.

7. Submit the revised document in the format specified by your instructor.

8. ✴ In Step 5 you combined two paragraphs. How did this action improve the slide content?

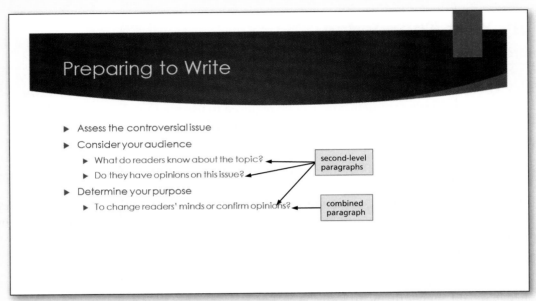

(b) Slide 2 (Multilevel Bulleted List)
Figure 1–80 (Continued)

Extend Your Knowledge

Extend the skills you learned in this chapter and experiment with new skills. You may need to use Help to complete the assignment.

Changing Slide Theme, Layout, and Text
Note: To complete this assignment, you will be required to use the Data Files for Students. Visit www.cengage.com/ct/studentdownload for detailed instructions or contact your instructor for information about accessing the required files.

Instructions: Run PowerPoint. Open the presentation that you are going to prepare for your brother's horseback riding business, Extend 1-1 Horseback Riding, from the Data Files for Students. You will choose a theme, format slides, and create a closing slide.

Perform the following tasks:

1. Apply an appropriate document theme.

2. On Slide 1 (Figure 1–81), use your name in place of Student Name. Format the text on this slide using techniques you learned in this chapter, such as changing the font size and color and bolding and italicizing words.

3. Delete the bullets in the subtitle text.

4. Resize the photo and move it to an appropriate area on the slide.

5. On Slide 2, add bullets to the paragraphs in the Beginners and Advanced boxes, and then change the look of the default bullets.

6. On Slide 3, create paragraphs and adjust the paragraph levels to create a bulleted list. Edit the text so that the slide meets the 7 × 7 rule, which states that each line should have a maximum of seven words, and each slide should have a maximum of seven lines.

7. Create an appropriate closing slide using the title slide as a guide. Change the title text to, See you at the Trails!

8. The slides contain a variety of pictures downloaded from Office.com. Size and move them when necessary.

9. Apply an appropriate transition to all slides.

10. Save the presentation using the file name, Extend 1-1 Horseback Riding Lessons.

11. Submit the revised document in the format specified by your instructor.

12. If requested by your instructor, replace the word, you, with your mother's first name on the closing slide.

13. ✳ In this assignment, you changed the bullet style on Slide 2. Which bullet style did you select and why?

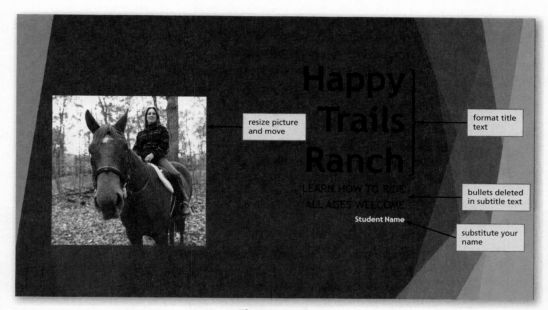

Figure 1–81

Analyze, Correct, Improve

Analyze a presentation, correct all errors, and improve it.

Correcting Formatting and List Levels

Note: To complete this assignment, you will be required to use the Data Files for Students. Visit www.cengage.com/ct/studentdownload for detailed instructions or contact your instructor for information about accessing the required files.

Instructions: Run PowerPoint. Open the presentation, Analyze 1-1 Math Tutor, from the Data Files for Students. As a part-time job while attending college, you decide to tutor students who are struggling with math. You decide to create a presentation promoting your service and begin with this document. Modify the slides by making the indicated corrections and improvements.

Continued >

Analyze, Correct, Improve *continued*

1. Correct

    a. Change the document theme from Office Theme Dark, shown in Figure 1–82, to Organic with the rightmost color variant.

    b. If requested by your instructor, change the Southtown Library Room number, 201, to your birth year on Slide 2.

    c. Correct the spelling errors on Slides 2 and 3.

    d. Use your name in place of Student Name on Slide 1.

2. Improve

    a. Adjust the size of the picture on Slide 1 and move it to the left of the subtitle text.

    b. Move Slide 2 to the end of the presentation so that it becomes the new Slide 3.

    c. On Slide 2, increase the font size of the Slide 2 title text, A Math Tutor Is Your Answer, to 54 point. Increase the size of the picture and move it to fill the white space on the right of the bulleted list. Align the picture using the right and bottom Smart Guides.

    d. On Slide 3, increase the font size of the title text, Schedule, to 60 point. Decrease the indent level for both bulleted lists to first level. Adjust the size of the picture and move it to the upper-right corner of the slide so that the upper edge of the image is aligned with the top edge of the title text placeholder.

    e. Apply the same transition and duration to all slides.

    f. Save the presentation using the file name, Analyze 1-1 – Math Tutor Info.

    g. Submit the revised document in the format specified by your instructor.

3. ✸ Which errors existed in the starting file? How did decreasing the indent level of the bulleted lists on Slide 3 and increasing the title text on Slides 2 and 3 enhance the presentation? When you adjusted the pictures, how did you determine their final sizes?

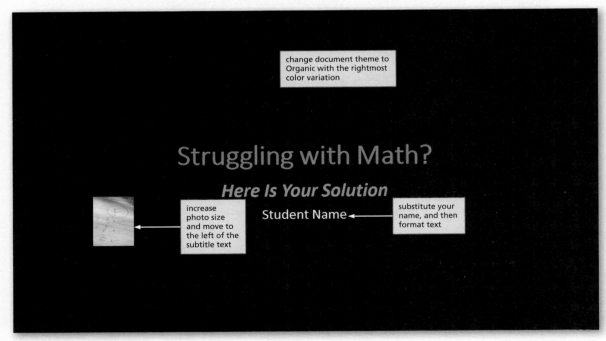

Figure 1–82

In the Labs

Design and/or create a presentation using the guidelines, concepts, and skills presented in this chapter. Labs 1 and 2, which increase in difficulty, require you to create solutions based on what you learned in the chapter; Lab 3 requires you to create a solution, which uses cloud and web technologies, by learning and investigating on your own from general guidance.

Lab 1: Creating a Presentation with Bulleted Lists, a Closing Slide, and Pictures

Problem: You are majoring in accounting and work part-time at a tax-filing service. Your clients have asked you numerous times what documents they should keep at home to support their tax returns. You decide to put together a presentation that would offer some basic guidelines about how to organize personal documents. You develop the outline shown in Figure 1–83 and then prepare the PowerPoint presentation shown in Figures 1–84a through 1–84e on pages PPT 62–64.

Files or Piles
>   Document Storage and Retention at Home

Store and Retain
>   **In Home Office Safe**
>> Tax records for six years
>> Pay stubs until W2 arrives
>> Credit card statements
>> Canceled checks
>> Utility bills
>   **In Bank Safe Deposit Box**
>> Wills, deeds, and titles
>> Birth and death certificates
>> Passports
>> Military records

Keep Indefinitely
>   Personal health records
>   Medical history
>   Retirement benefit statements

General Rules
>   Shred documents showing personal information
>   Organize and store chronologically
>   Keep list of important documents
>> State their location
>> Share with relative or friend

Figure 1–83

Continued >

In the Labs *continued*

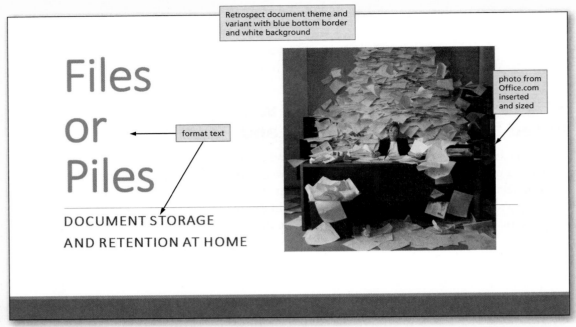

(a) Slide 1 (Title Slide)

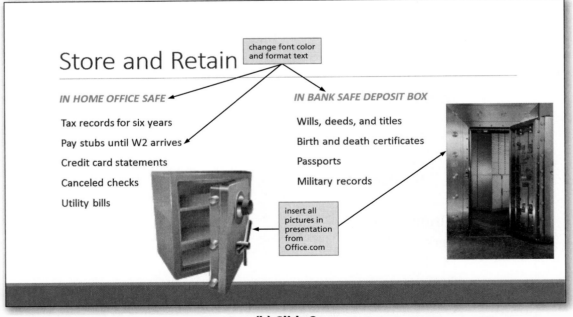

(b) Slide 2

Figure 1–84

(c) Slide 3

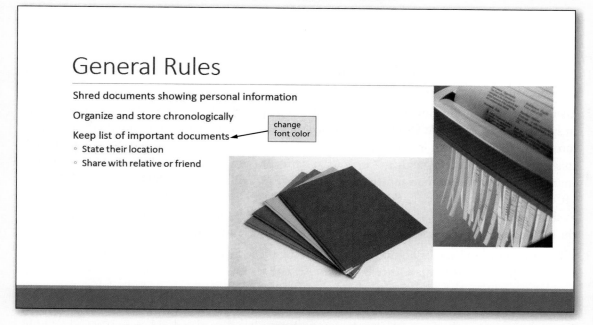

(d) Slide 4

Figure 1–84 (Continued)

Continued >

In the Labs *continued*

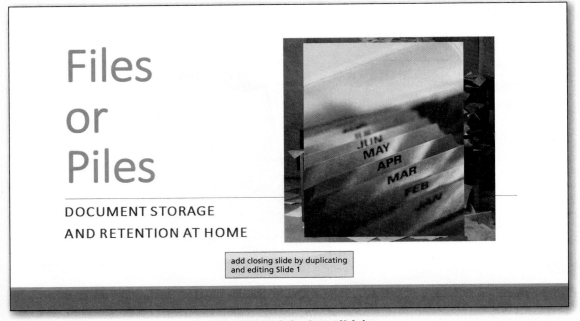

add closing slide by duplicating and editing Slide 1

(e) Slide 5 (Closing Slide)
Figure 1–84 (Continued)

Instructions: Perform the following tasks:

1. Create a new presentation using the Retrospect document theme and select the variant with the blue bottom border and white background.

2. Using the typed outline illustrated in Figure 1–83 on page PPT 61, create the title slide shown in Figure 1–84a. Press the ENTER key to place each word on a separate line and divide the title into three lines, as shown in the figure. Increase the font size of the title text to 88 point and bold this text. Change the font color to Green (the sixth color from left in the Standard Colors row). Increase the font size of the subtitle text, DOCUMENT STORAGE AND RETENTION AT HOME, to 28 point and bold this text. Press the ENTER key to divide the subtitle into two lines, as shown in the figure. Find and insert the picture from the Office.com Clip Art collection. Size the picture and use the Smart Guides to position it as shown in the figure.

3. Using the typed outline in Figure 1–83, create the three text slides with lists and find and insert the pictures from the Office.com Clip Art collection. Size the pictures and use the Smart Guides to position these images, as shown in Figures 1–84b, 1–84c, and 1–84d. You may want to zoom the slides to help you align these graphic elements.

4. On Slide 2, change the font color in the left and right heading placeholders to Green and bold and italicize this text.

5. On Slides 2, 3 and 4, change the font color of the lists to Dark Blue (second color from right in the Standard Colors row).

6. Create a closing slide by duplicating Slide 1 and adding the photo using the Smart Guides to center it on top of the existing photo.

7. If requested by your instructor, use your father's first name in place of the word, Piles, and replace the word, or, with the word, for, on Slide 5.

8. Apply the Shred transition in the Exciting category to all slides. Change the duration to 4.5 seconds.

9. Tap or click the Start From Beginning button to start the show from the first slide. Then swipe or click to display each slide.

10. Save the presentation using the file name, Lab 1-1 Document Storage at Home.

11. Submit the document in the format specified by your instructor.

12. ✳ What is the significance of placing the neat file folders photo on top of the messy desk photo on the closing slide? Why did you change the font color on Slides 2, 3, and 4 to Dark Blue?

Lab 2: **Creating a Presentation with Bulleted Lists and Pictures**

Problem: The number of reported West Nile Virus (WNV) cases across the continental United States has been growing steadily. After a discussion in your biology class, your instructor assigned everyone in the class to research WNV and to outline the facts that were discussed. You use your class notes to create the outline shown in Figure 1–85 and then create the presentation shown in Figures 1–86a through 1–86d on pages PPT 66–68.

West Nile Virus (WNV)
Facts, Signs, and Prevention
Student Name

What Is WNV?
  Transmitted by mosquitoes that bit infected birds
  First identified in eastern Africa in 1937
    Now worldwide in tropical and temperate climates
  Appeared in United States in 1999
    Now reported in 48 states
  At risk: People with weak immune systems

What Are the Symptoms?
  Most commonly resemble the flu
    High fever
    Headache
    Body aches
    Nausea / vomiting
    Vision problems

How Can I Avoid WNV?
  Protect against mosquito bites
    Wear repellent with EPA-recommended ingredients
    Avoid being outdoors at dawn and dusk
    Wear clothes that cover skin
  Remove standing water from yard vessels
  Repair damaged window and door screens

Figure 1–85

Continued >

In the Labs *continued*

Instructions: Perform the following tasks:

1. Create a new presentation using the Facet document theme.

2. Using the outline illustrated in Figure 1–85 on the previous page, create the title slide shown in Figure 1–86a, using your name in place of Student Name.

3. If requested by your instructor, substitute the name of your hometown in place of your last name.

4. On Slide 1, bold the text, West Nile Virus (WNV). Decrease the font size of the text, Facts, Signs, and Prevention, to 44 point. Change the font color of all the title text to Red, Accent 5 (second color from right in the Theme Colors row).

5. Using the outline in Figure 1–85, create the three text slides with bulleted lists shown in Figures 1–86b, 1–86c, and 1–86d. Change the color of the title text on these three text slides to Red, Accent 5.

6. Add the pictures shown in Figures 1–86a through 1–86d from Office.com. Zoom the slide and then resize the pictures when necessary.

7. Apply the Page Curl transition in the Exciting category to all slides. Change the duration to 2.25 seconds.

8. Tap or click the Start From Beginning button to start the slide show and then display each slide.

9. Save the presentation using the file name, Lab 1–2 West Nile Virus.

10. Submit the revised document in the format specified by your instructor.

11. ✱ How does changing the font color to red help reinforce the West Nile Virus prevention concept? What is the significance of adding a mosquito illustration to every slide?

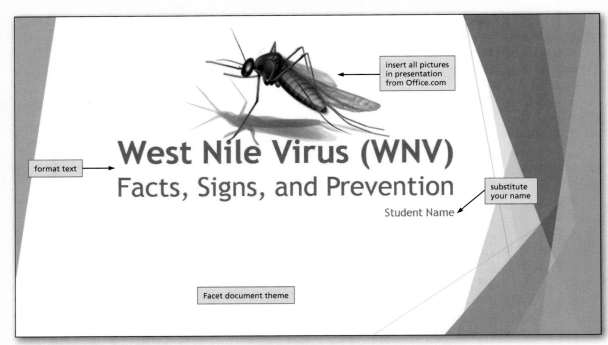

(a) Slide 1 (Title Slide)

Figure 1–86

(b) Slide 2

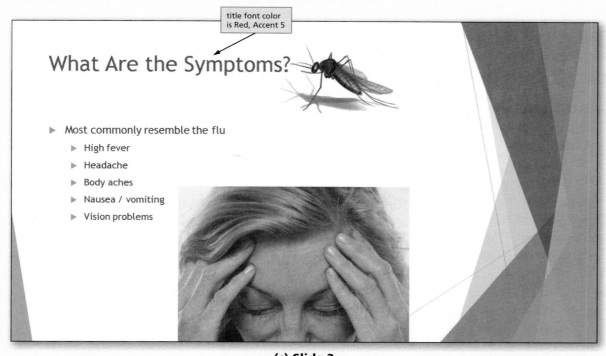

(c) Slide 3
Figure 1–86 (Continued)

Continued >

In the Labs *continued*

(d) Slide 4

Figure 1–86 (Continued)

Lab 3: Expand Your World: Cloud and Web Technologies
Modifying and Exporting a Presentation

Problem: Your local library is planning events to celebrate Hispanic Heritage Month, and you are part of a committee to publicize the event. You want to share the title slide of your preliminary PowerPoint presentation with fellow committee members, so you have decided to store the file on SkyDrive. You are going to modify the slide you have created thus far shown in Figure 1–87 and save it to SkyDrive.

Note: To complete this assignment, you will be required to use the Data Files for Students. Visit www.cengage.com/ct/studentdownload for detailed instructions or contact your instructor for information about accessing the required files.

Instructions:
1. Open the Lab 1–3 Hispanic Heritage file.
2. Insert another picture on the title slide in the area indicated in Figure 1–87.
3. If requested to do so by your instructor, change the city to the town where you were born.
4. Save the presentation using the file name, Lab 1–3 Heritage Month.
5. Export the file to your SkyDrive in the Chapter 01 folder in the PowerPoint folder.
6. Submit the assignment in the format specified by your instructor.
7. ✹ When would you save one of your files for school or your job to SkyDrive? Do you think using SkyDrive enhances collaboration efforts? Why?

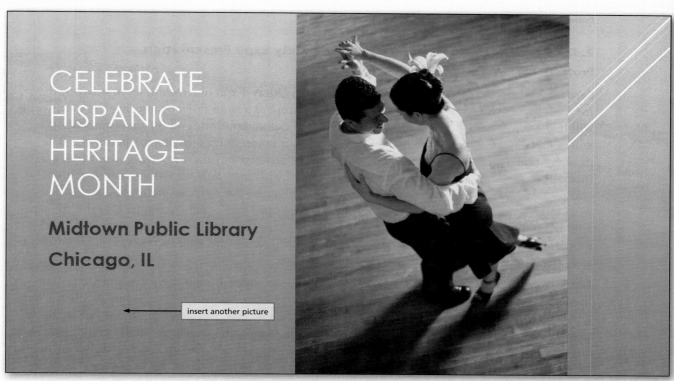

Figure 1–87 Slide 1 (Title Slide)

✳ Consider This: Your Turn

Apply your creative thinking and problem-solving skills to design and implement a solution.

1. Design and Create a Presentation about Mars Exploration

Personal

Part 1: Your astronomy class is studying the solar system, and you have been assigned the topic of the Mars Curiosity rover and its exploration of that planet. You have learned that the rover was launched from Cape Canaveral, Florida, on November 26, 2011, and landed in the Gale Crater on Mars on August 6, 2012. The mission was scheduled to last two years and had the major goal of assessing whether Mars was or is capable of supporting life. The Curiosity rover is the size of a car and has a MastCam equipped with two camera systems to take photos of the landscape as it maneuvers around the rocky surface. The rover also can scoop up samples of the Martian soil, fire a laser at rocks as far away as nine feet (2.7 meters), and make weather station readings. Use the concepts and techniques you learned in the chapter to create a PowerPoint presentation with a suitable theme, a title slide, and three text slides with bulleted lists. Add pictures from Office.com and apply a transition. Submit your assignment in the format specified by your instructor.

Part 2: ✳ You made several decisions while creating the presentation in this assignment: what theme to use, where to place text, how to format the text (font, font size, paragraph alignment, bulleted paragraphs, italics, bold, color). You also decided which graphical images to use, where to position the graphical images, if a closing slide would be useful, and which transition would be most effective. What was the rationale behind each of these decisions? When you proofed the document, what further revisions did you make and why? Where would you recommend showing this slide show?

Continued >

Consider This: Your Turn *continued*

2. Design and Create a Fire Department Safety Expo Presentation
Professional

Part 1: Your local fire department is sponsoring a Safety Expo one month from today at the local hardware store. The chief has asked you to prepare a slide show promoting the event, which will be held from noon to 5 p.m. A wide variety of demonstrations and informational booths will be present. They include: firefighters from your community's fire department, who will discuss home emergency planning, proper car seat installation, and fire extinguisher use; a local insurance agent, who will distribute tote bags filled with materials regarding adequate home and rental insurance coverage and also a nine-volt battery for a smoke alarm; and a children's workshop, where participants under 10 years of age can build a picture frame. Use the concepts and techniques presented in this chapter to develop and format this slide show with at least four slides with bulleted lists. Add pictures from Office.com and apply a transition. Submit your assignment in the format specified by your instructor.

Part 2: ✳ You made several decisions while creating the presentation in this assignment: what theme to use, where to place text, how to format the text (font, font size, paragraph alignment, bulleted paragraphs, italics, bold, color). You also decided which graphical images to use, where to position the graphical images, if a closing slide would be useful, and which transition would be most effective. What was the rationale behind each of these decisions? When you proofed the document, what further revisions did you make and why? Where would you recommend showing this slide show?

3. Design and Create a Presentation about Commemorative Postage Stamps
Research and Collaboration

Part 1: Stamp collecting is one of the world's more popular indoor hobbies. Collectors often seek postage stamps pertaining to a particular interest, such as birds, flowers, famous people, or ships. Have each member of your team gather information on these topics: stamp collecting equipment, popular commemorative stamps issued, current commemorative stamps for sale at your local post office, and rare stamps. After coordinating these facts, use the concepts and techniques presented in this chapter to prepare a presentation with a minimum of four slides that explore the subject of stamp collection. Select a suitable theme and include a title slide, bulleted lists, and a closing slide. Add pictures from Office.com and apply a transition. Submit your assignment in the format specified by your instructor.

Part 2: ✳ You made several decisions while creating the presentation in this assignment: what theme to use, where to place text, how to format the text (font, font size, paragraph alignment, bulleted paragraphs, italics, bold, color). You also decided which graphical images to use, where to position the graphical images, if a closing slide would be useful, and which transition would be most effective. What was the rationale behind each of these decisions? When you proofed the document, what further revisions did you make and why? Where would you recommend showing this slide show?

Learn Online

Reinforce what you learned in this chapter with games, exercises, training, and many other online activities and resources.

Student Companion Site Reinforcement activities and resources are available at no additional cost on www.cengagebrain.com. Visit www.cengage.com/ct/studentdownload for detailed instructions about accessing the resources available at the Student Companion Site.

 SAM Put your skills into practice with SAM! If you have a SAM account, go to www.cengage.com/sam2013 to access SAM assignments for this chapter.

2 Enhancing a Presentation with Pictures, Shapes, and WordArt

Microsoft product screenshots used with permission from Microsoft Corporation.

Objectives

You will have mastered the material in this chapter when you can:

- Search for and download an online theme
- Insert and format pictures
- Insert and size a shape
- Apply effects to a shape
- Add text to a shape
- Change the text font

- Insert and format WordArt
- Insert a picture to create a background
- Format slide backgrounds
- Find and replace text and check spelling
- Add and print speaker notes

2 | Enhancing a Presentation with Pictures, Shapes, and WordArt

Introduction

In our visually oriented culture, audience members enjoy viewing effective graphics. Whether reading a document or viewing a PowerPoint presentation, people increasingly want to see photographs, artwork, graphics, and a variety of typefaces. Researchers have known for decades that documents with visual elements are more effective than those that consist of only text because the illustrations motivate audiences to study the material. People remember at least one-third more information when the document they are seeing or reading contains visual elements. These graphics help clarify and emphasize details, so they appeal to audience members with differing backgrounds, reading levels, attention spans, and motivations.

Project — Presentation with Pictures, Shapes, and WordArt

The project in this chapter focuses on helping families plan for emergencies. Children need to prepare for the unexpected by collecting supplies to make an emergency supply kit, developing a communication plan, and realizing the need to be ready for any unexpected situation that may arise. The presentation shown in Figure 2–1 follows graphical guidelines and has a variety of illustrations and visual elements that are colorful and appealing to children. For example, the pictures have particular shapes and effects. The enhanced type has a style that blends well with the formatted background and illustrations. Pictures and type are formatted using picture styles and WordArt, which give the presentation a professional look. You plan to present the material during community safety open houses at fire stations and local hardware stores, so you want to add notes explaining concepts you will be discussing during the meeting.

BTW

BTWs

For a complete list of the BTWs found in the margins of this book, visit the BTW resource on the Student Companion Site located on www.cengagebrain.com. For detailed instructions about accessing available resources, visit www.cengage.com/ct/studentdownload or see the inside back cover of this book.

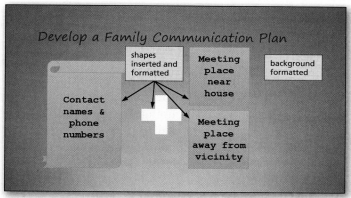

(a) Slide 1 (Title Slide)

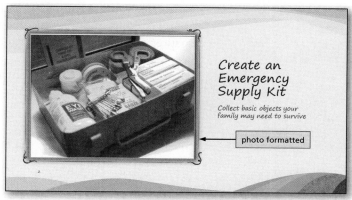

(b) Slide 2 (Formatted Picture)

(c) Slide 3 (Shapes Inserted and Formatted)

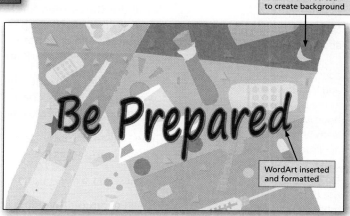

(d) Slide 4 (Picture Background)

Figure 2–1

For an introduction to Windows and instruction about how to perform basic Windows tasks, read the Office and Windows chapter at the beginning of this book, where you can learn how to resize windows, change screen resolution, create folders, move and rename files, use Windows Help, and much more.

One of the few differences between Windows 7 and Windows 8 occurs in the steps to run PowerPoint. If you are using Windows 7, click the Start button, type **PowerPoint** in the 'Search programs and files' box, click PowerPoint 2013, and then, if necessary, maximize the PowerPoint window. For detailed steps to run PowerPoint in Windows 7, refer to the Office and Windows chapter at the beginning of this book. For a summary of the steps, refer to the Quick Reference located at the back of this book.

For an introduction to Office and instruction about how to perform basic tasks in Office apps, read the Office and Windows chapter at the beginning of this book, where you can learn how to run an application, use the ribbon, save a file, open a file, exit an application, use Help, and much more.

Roadmap

In this chapter, you will learn how to create the slides shown in Figure 2 – 1 on the previous page. The following roadmap identifies general activities you will perform as you progress through this chapter:

1. DOWNLOAD a theme and SELECT SLIDES for the presentation.
2. INSERT and FORMAT PICTURES for the slides.
3. INSERT and FORMAT SHAPES on one slide.
4. INSERT and FORMAT WORDART by changing the shape, fill, and outline.
5. FORMAT SLIDE BACKGROUNDS with a gradient, texture, and picture fill.
6. REVIEW and REVISE SLIDES by finding a synonym and checking spelling.

At the beginning of step instructions throughout the chapter, you will see an abbreviated form of this roadmap. The abbreviated roadmap uses colors to indicate chapter progress: gray means the chapter is beyond that activity; blue means the task being shown is covered in that activity, and black means that activity is yet to be covered. For example, the following abbreviated roadmap indicates the chapter would be showing a task in the 5 FORMAT SLIDE BACKGROUNDS activity.

1 DOWNLOAD & SELECT SLIDES | 2 INSERT & FORMAT PICTURES | 3 INSERT & FORMAT SHAPES
4 INSERT & FORMAT WORDART | **5 FORMAT SLIDE BACKGROUNDS** | 6 REVIEW & REVISE SLIDES

Use the abbreviated roadmap as a progress guide while you read or step through the instructions in this chapter.

To Run PowerPoint

If you are using a computer to step through the project in this chapter and you want your screens to match the figures in this book, you should change your screen's resolution to 1366×768. For information about how to change a computer's resolution, refer to the Office and Windows chapter at the beginning of this book.

The following steps, which assume Windows 8 is running, use the Start screen or the search box to run PowerPoint based on a typical installation. You may need to ask your instructor how to run PowerPoint on your computer. For a detailed example of the procedure summarized below, refer to the Office and Windows chapter.

1 Scroll the Start screen for a PowerPoint 2013 tile. If your Start screen contains a PowerPoint 2013 tile, tap or click it to run PowerPoint and then proceed to Step 5; if the Start screen does not contain the PowerPoint 2013 tile, proceed to the next step to search for the PowerPoint app.

2 Swipe in from the right edge of the screen or point to the upper-right corner of the screen to display the Charms bar and then tap or click the Search charm on the Charms bar to display the Search menu.

3 Type **PowerPoint** as the search text in the Search box and watch the search results appear in the Apps list.

4 Tap or click PowerPoint 2013 in the search results to run PowerPoint.

5 If the PowerPoint window is not maximized, tap or click the Maximize button on its title bar to maximize the window.

Downloading a Theme and Editing Slides

In Chapter 1, you selected a theme and then typed the content for the title and text slides. In this chapter, you will type the slide content for the title and text slides, select a background, insert and format pictures and shapes, and then insert and format WordArt. To begin creating the four slides in this presentation, you will download a theme, delete unneeded slides in this downloaded presentation, and then enter text in three of the four slides.

To Search for and Download an Online Theme

1 DOWNLOAD & SELECT SLIDES | 2 INSERT & FORMAT PICTURES | 3 INSERT & FORMAT SHAPES
4 INSERT & FORMAT WORDART | 5 FORMAT SLIDE BACKGROUNDS | 6 REVIEW & REVISE SLIDES

PowerPoint displays many themes that are varied and appealing and give you an excellent start at designing a presentation. At times, however, you may have a specific topic and design concept and could use some assistance in starting to develop the presentation. Microsoft offers hundreds of predesigned themes and templates that could provide you with an excellent starting point. *Why? You can search for one of these ready-made presentations, or you can browse one of the predefined categories, such as business, medical, education, and nature. The themes and templates can save you time and help you develop content.* The following steps search for a theme that has an educational concept and is oriented toward children.

- Press and hold or point to Education in the Suggested searches list (Figure 2–2).

Q&A Why does a Recent Presentation list display on the left side of my screen?
You can specify the number of recent presentations to display in the Advanced tab of the PowerPoint Options dialog box.

Figure 2–2

②

- Tap or click Education to search for themes with an academic subject.

Q&A Can I also use keywords to search for themes?
Yes. Tap or click the 'Search for online templates and themes' search box, type terms that relate to the topic of your presentation, and then click the Start searching button (the magnifying glass) or press the ENTER key so that Office.com will search for and display all themes with your keywords.

③

- Slide or scroll down about halfway through the theme thumbnails until the 'Colorful nature presentation, illustrated landscape design (widescreen)' theme, shown in Figure 2–3, is displayed.

Q&A Why are my theme thumbnails displaying in a different order?
Microsoft adds and modifies the themes, so the order may change.

④

- Tap or click the 'Colorful nature presentation, illustrated landscape design (widescreen)' theme to display a theme preview dialog box with a thumbnail view of the theme (Figure 2–3).

Q&A Can I see previews of the slides in this theme?
Yes. Click the right or left arrows beside the words, More Images, below the thumbnail. On some devices, a preview of all slides starts automatically after you tap the theme.

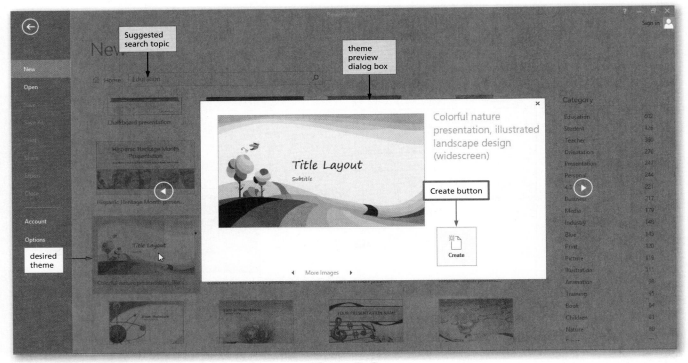

Figure 2–3

⑤

- Tap or click the Create button to download the theme and open a presentation with that theme in PowerPoint.

BTW
Additional Theme Information
You may see additional information regarding the theme in the theme preview dialog box if you are downloading the file for the first time. This information includes the provider (in this case, Microsoft Corporation), a description of the theme content and the intended audience, the file size (in this case, 2190 KB), and a rating.

To Delete a Slide

The downloaded theme has 13 slides with a variety of layouts. You will use four different layouts in your Be Prepared presentation, so you can delete the slides you downloaded that you will not need. *Why? Deleting the extra slides now helps reduce clutter and helps you focus on the layouts you will use.* The following steps delete the extra slides.

1

- If necessary, tap or click the Slide 1 thumbnail in the Thumbnail pane to select this slide.

- Swipe horizontally across each of the Slide 2, 3, and 4 thumbnails, or press and hold the SHIFT key and then click the thumbnail for Slide 4 to select slides 1 through 4 (Figure 2–4).

Q&A Why would I select Slide 1, the Title Slide layout, for deletion if I need a title slide for my presentation?
Slide 9 also will work well to format as the title slide (Slide 1) in this presentation.

Figure 2–4

2

- Press and hold or right-click any selected slide to display the shortcut menu (Figure 2–5).

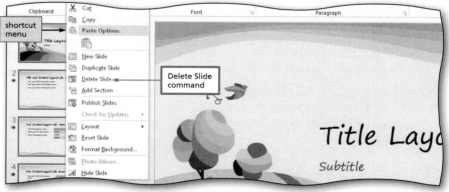

Figure 2–5

3

- Tap Delete or click Delete Slide to delete the selected slides from the presentation (Figure 2–6).

Q&A How would I delete several slides simultaneously if they are not sequential?
Repeat this procedure except make a short swipe across each slide thumbnail you want to delete to select it, or press and hold the CTRL key while you tap or click each slide you want to delete.

Figure 2–6

- Select the new Slides 2, 3, and 4, display the shortcut menu, and then delete these slides (Figure 2–7).

Q&A Why am I selecting and then deleting these slides?
You want to use the current slides 1 and 5 in your presentation, so you need to delete the slides between these two slides.

Figure 2–7

- Tap or click the Slide 3 thumbnail to select this slide.

- Scroll down and then swipe the Slide 6 thumbnail or press and hold the CTRL key and then click the thumbnail for Slide 6 to select both slides 3 and 6 (Figure 2–8).

Q&A Why did I press and hold down the CTRL key instead of the SHIFT key?
Holding down the CTRL key selects only the slides you tap or click, whereas holding the SHIFT key selects consecutive slides between the first and last selected slides.

Figure 2–8

Why am I selecting and then deleting these slides?
You want to use the current slides 4 and 5 in your presentation, so you need to delete slides 3 and 6.

- Display the shortcut menu and then delete slides 3 and 6 (Figure 2–9).

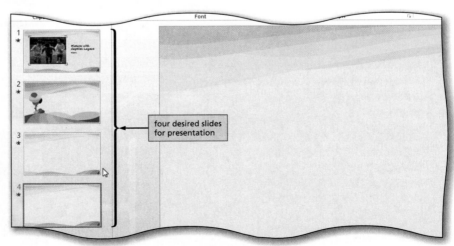

Figure 2–9

Other Ways

1. Select slide(s), press DELETE

To Create a Title Slide

Recall from Chapter 1 that the title slide introduces the presentation to the audience. In addition to introducing the presentation, this project uses the title slide to capture the audience's attention by using title text and an illustration. *Why? The presentation focuses on families and their need to work together to develop an emergency plan. The illustration of a fire truck and firefighter help introduce the concept.* The following steps rearrange Slide 1 and Slide 2 and then create the slide show's title slide.

1 Move Slide 2 in the Thumbnail pane above Slide 1 so that it becomes the first slide in the deck.

2 Type `Prepare` as the first text paragraph in the title text placeholder.

3 Press the ENTER key and then type `for the Unexpected` as the second paragraph in the title text placeholder.

4 Tap or click the subtitle text placeholder and then type `Plan for a Disaster` as the subtitle text (Figure 2–10).

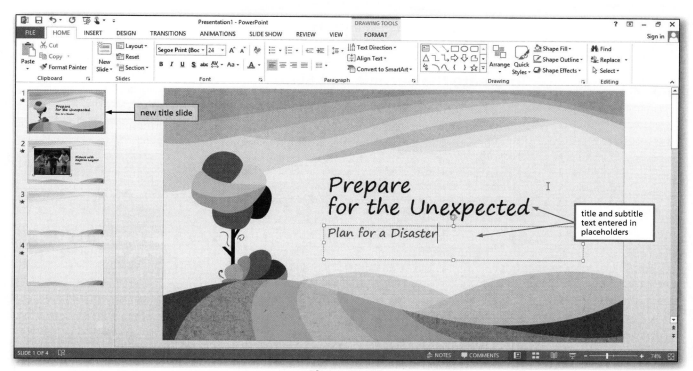

Figure 2–10

To Create the First Text Slide

The first text slide you create in Chapter 2 emphasizes the need to make an emergency supply kit that contains supplies and other necessities for survival. The following steps create the Slide 2 text slide using the Picture with Caption layout.

1 Display Slide 2, select the text in the title text placeholder, and then type `Create a Disaster Supply Kit` in the placeholder.

2 Tap or click the caption placeholder and then type `Collect basic objects your family may need to stay alive` in this placeholder (Figure 2–11).

BTW

Q&As

For a complete list of the Q&As found in many of the step-by-step sequences in this book, visit the Q&A resource on the Student Companion Site located on www.cengagebrain.com. For detailed instructions about accessing available resources, visit www.cengage.com/ct/studentdownload or see the inside back cover of this book.

Figure 2-11

To Create the Second Text Slide

The second text slide you create shows two components of the family communication plan: carrying a contact list and arranging meeting places. The following step adds a title to Slide 3, which uses the Title Only layout.

Note: In the following step, the word, Communication, has been misspelled intentionally as Comunication to illustrate the use of PowerPoint's spell check feature. Your slides may contain different misspelled words, depending upon the accuracy of your typing.

1 Display Slide 3 and then type **Develop a Family Comunication Plan** in the title text placeholder. The word, Comunication, is intentionally misspelled; the red wavy line indicates the misspelling (Figure 2-12).

Figure 2-12

BTW
The Ribbon and Screen Resolution
PowerPoint may change how the groups and buttons within the groups appear on the ribbon, depending on the computer's screen resolution. Thus, your ribbon may look different from the ones in this book if you are using a screen resolution other than 1366 × 768.

To Save a Presentation

You have performed many tasks while creating this presentation and do not want to risk losing work completed thus far. Accordingly, you should save the presentation on your hard disk, SkyDrive, or a location that is most appropriate to your situation.

The following steps assume you already have created folders for storing your files, for example, a CIS 101 folder (for your class) that contains a PowerPoint folder (for your assignments). Thus, these steps save the presentation in the PowerPoint folder in the CIS 101 folder on your desired save location. For a detailed example of the procedure for saving a file in a folder or saving a file on SkyDrive, refer to the Office and Windows chapter at the beginning of this book.

① Tap or click the Save button on the Quick Access Toolbar, which depending on settings, will display either the Save As gallery in the Backstage view or the Save As dialog box.

② To save on a hard disk or other storage media on your computer, proceed to Step 2a. To save on SkyDrive, proceed to Step 2b.

②a If your screen opens the Backstage view and you want to save on storage media on your computer, tap or click Computer in the left pane, if necessary, to display options in the right pane related to saving on your computer. If your screen already displays the Save As dialog box, proceed to Step 3.

②b If your screen opens the Backstage view and you want to save on SkyDrive, tap or click SkyDrive in the left pane to display SkyDrive saving options or a Sign In button. If your screen displays a Sign In button, tap or click it and then sign in to SkyDrive.

③ Tap or click the Browse button in the right pane to display the Save As dialog box associated with the selected save location (i.e., Computer or SkyDrive).

④ Type **Emergency Plan** in the File name box to change the file name. Do not press the ENTER key after typing the file name because you do not want to close the dialog box at this time.

⑤ Navigate to the desired save location (in this case, the PowerPoint folder in the CIS 101 folder [or your class folder] on your computer or SkyDrive).

⑥ Tap or click the Save button (Save As dialog box) to save the presentation in the selected folder on the selected save location with the entered file name.

Inserting and Formatting Pictures in a Presentation

BTW
Organizing Files and Folders
You should organize and store files in folders so that you easily can find the files later. For example, if you are taking an introductory computer class called CIS 101, a good practice would be to save all PowerPoint files in a PowerPoint folder in a CIS 101 folder. For a discussion of folders and detailed examples of creating folders, refer to the Office and Windows chapter at the beginning of this book.

With the text entered in three of the four slides, the next step is to insert pictures into Slides 1 and 2 and then format the pictures. These graphical images draw the viewers' eyes to the slides and help them retain the information presented.

In the following pages, you will perform these tasks:

1. Insert the illustration into Slide 1.
2. Resize the illustration.
3. Change the Slide 2 photo.
4. Change the photo's brightness and contrast.
5. Change the photo's style and effect.
6. Add and modify the photo's border.

To Insert a Picture into a Slide without a Content Placeholder

1 DOWNLOAD & SELECT SLIDES | 2 INSERT & FORMAT PICTURES | 3 INSERT & FORMAT SHAPES
4 INSERT & FORMAT WORDART | 5 FORMAT SLIDE BACKGROUNDS | 6 REVIEW & REVISE SLIDES

In Chapter 1, you inserted photos and an illustration into slides without a content placeholder. *Why? Some slide layouts do not have a content placeholder, so you must insert and move the pictures to appropriate locations on the slide.* The illustration for Slide 1 is available on the Data Files for Students. Visit www.cengage.com/ ct/studentdownload for detailed instructions or contact your instructor for information about accessing the required files. The instructions in this chapter show the required files in the PowerPoint Chapter 2 folder in the CIS 101 folder on your computer. The following steps insert an illustration into the title slide.

- Display Slide 1 and then tap or click INSERT on the ribbon to display the INSERT tab.
- Tap or click the Pictures button (INSERT tab | Images group) to display the Insert Picture dialog box.

2

- If Computer is not displayed in the navigation pane, press and drag or drag the navigation pane scroll bar (Insert Picture dialog box) until Computer appears.
- Tap or click Computer in the navigation pane to display a list of available storage locations in the Insert Picture dialog box. If necessary, scroll through the dialog box until your class folder appears in the list.
- Double-tap or double-click your folder in the list of available storage locations to display a list of files and folders. Double-tap or double-click the Data Files for Students folder, double-tap or double-click the PowerPoint folder, and then double-tap or double-click the Chapter 02 folder to display a list of files in that folder.

- Slide or scroll down and then tap or click Fire Truck to select the file name (Figure 2–13).

Q&A What if the picture is not in the folder?
Use the same process, but select the location containing the Chapter 2 data file pictures or search for the picture on Office.com.

Why do I see thumbnails of the pictures along with the file names in my folder?
Your view is different from the view shown in Figure 2–13.

Figure 2–13

3

- Tap or click the Insert button (Insert Picture dialog box) to insert the illustration into Slide 1.
- Drag the upper-right sizing handle diagonally toward the upper-right corner of the slide until the crosshair is positioned approximately as shown in Figure 2–14.

Figure 2–14

4

- Release to resize the illustration.

- Drag the illustration downward until the horizontal Smart Guide is displayed under the title text placeholder and the vertical Smart Guide is displayed near the right side of the slide, as shown in Figure 2–15, and then release.

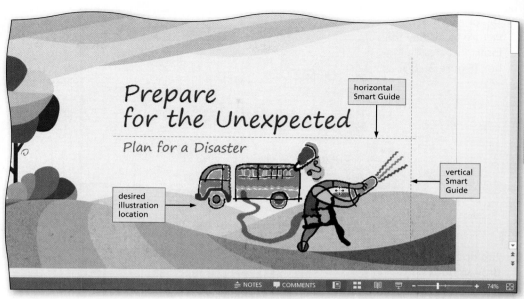

Figure 2–15

To Change a Picture

1 DOWNLOAD & SELECT SLIDES | 2 INSERT & FORMAT PICTURES | 3 INSERT & FORMAT SHAPES
4 INSERT & FORMAT WORDART | 5 FORMAT SLIDE BACKGROUNDS | 6 REVIEW & REVISE SLIDES

Why? *The downloaded theme included the photo of three children on Slide 2. You need to change the photo to reflect the emergency kit concept presented on this slide.* The next task in the presentation is to change the default picture on Slide 2 with one of the emergency pictures on the Data Files for Students. The following steps change the Slide 2 photo to the Emergency Kit photo, which, in this example, is located in the PowerPoint Chapter 02 folder that contains the saved presentation.

1

- Display Slide 2 and then press and hold or right-click the picture to display the shortcut menu (Figure 2–16).

Q&A Why are the Style and Crop buttons displayed above the shortcut menu on my screen?
These two buttons display either above or below the shortcut menu depending upon where you press and hold or right-click on the screen.

Figure 2–16

2

● Tap or click Change Picture to display the Insert Pictures dialog box (Figure 2–17).

Figure 2–17

3

● Tap or click the Browse button in the From a file area to display the Insert Pictures dialog box.

● If necessary, navigate to the PowerPoint Chapter 02 folder, slide or scroll down, and then click First Aid Kit to select the file name (Figure 2–18).

Figure 2–18

4

● Tap or click the Insert button (Insert Picture dialog box) to insert the photo into the Slide 2 picture placeholder (Figure 2–19).

Figure 2–19

Other Ways

1. Tap or click Change Picture button (PICTURE TOOLS FORMAT tab | Adjust group)

To Correct a Picture

1 DOWNLOAD & SELECT SLIDES | 2 INSERT & FORMAT PICTURES | 3 INSERT & FORMAT SHAPES
4 INSERT & FORMAT WORDART | 5 FORMAT SLIDE BACKGROUNDS | 6 REVIEW & REVISE SLIDES

A photo's color intensity can be modified by changing the brightness and contrast. **Brightness** determines the overall lightness or darkness of the entire image, whereas **contrast** is the difference between the darkest and lightest areas of the image. The brightness and contrast are changed in predefined percentage increments. The following step increases the brightness and decreases the contrast. *Why?* *Altering the photo's brightness will coordinate with the vibrant colors in the slide design while decreasing the contrast will soften the image. It is important for the audience to recognize the first aid kit but not focus on each individual supply in the kit.*

- With the First Aid Kit photo on Slide 2 still selected, tap or click FORMAT on the ribbon to display the PICTURE TOOLS FORMAT tab.

- Tap or click the Corrections button (PICTURE TOOLS FORMAT tab | Adjust group) to display the Corrections gallery.

- If you are using a mouse, point to Brightness: +20% Contrast: −40% (the fourth picture in the first Brightness/Contrast row) to display a live preview of these corrections on the picture (Figure 2–20).

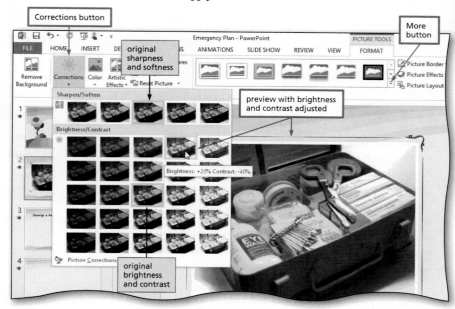

Figure 2–20

Q&A Can I use live preview on a touch screen?
Live preview is not available on a touch screen.

Why is a pink border surrounding the pictures in the center of the Sharpen/Soften and Brightness/Contrast areas of the gallery?
The image on Slide 2 currently has normal sharpness, brightness, and contrast (0%), which is represented by these center images in the gallery.

Experiment

- If you are using a mouse, point to various pictures in the Brightness and Contrast area and watch the brightness and contrast change on the picture in Slide 2.

- Tap or click Brightness: +20% Contrast: −40% to apply this correction to the First Aid Kit photo.

Q&A How can I remove all effects from the picture?
Tap or click the Reset Picture button (PICTURE TOOLS FORMAT tab | Adjust group).

Other Ways

1. Tap or click Picture Corrections Options (Corrections gallery), move Brightness or Contrast sliders or enter number in box next to slider (Format Picture task pane)

To Apply a Picture Style

1 DOWNLOAD & SELECT SLIDES | 2 INSERT & FORMAT PICTURES | 3 INSERT & FORMAT SHAPES
4 INSERT & FORMAT WORDART | 5 FORMAT SLIDE BACKGROUNDS | 6 REVIEW & REVISE SLIDES

A **style** is a named group of formatting characteristics. The picture on Slide 2 emphasizes the concept of assembling a supply kit, and you can increase its visual appeal by applying a style. *Why?* *PowerPoint provides more than 25 picture styles that enable you easily to change a picture's look to a more visually appealing style, including a variety of shapes, angles, borders, and reflections.* You want to use a style that applies a shadow to the First Aid Kit photo. The following steps apply a picture style to the Slide 2 photo.

- With the Slide 2 picture selected, if necessary tap or click the PICTURE TOOLS FORMAT tab and then tap or click the More button in the Picture Styles gallery (PICTURE TOOLS FORMAT tab | Picture Styles group) (shown in Figure 2–20) to expand the gallery.

- If you are using a mouse, point to Center Shadow Rectangle in the Picture Styles gallery (the sixth style in the second row) to display a live preview of that style applied to the picture in the document (Figure 2–21).

Figure 2–21

- If you are using a mouse, point to various picture styles in the Picture Styles gallery and watch the style of the picture change in the document window.

- Tap or click Center Shadow Rectangle in the Picture Styles gallery to apply the style to the selected picture (Figure 2–22).

BTW
Touch Screen Differences
The Office and Windows interfaces may vary if you are using a touch screen. For this reason, you might notice that the function or appearance of your touch screen differs slightly from this chapter's presentation.

Figure 2–22

To Add a Picture Border

1 DOWNLOAD & SELECT SLIDES | 2 INSERT & FORMAT PICTURES | 3 INSERT & FORMAT SHAPES
4 INSERT & FORMAT WORDART | 5 FORMAT SLIDE BACKGROUNDS | 6 REVIEW & REVISE SLIDES

The next step is to add a border to the Slide 2 picture. *Why? Some picture styles do not have a border; others, such as the Center Shadow Rectangle style you applied to this picture, do have this edging. This border is small, and you want a larger edge around the photo to draw attention to the graphic.* The following steps add a border to the First Aid Kit picture.

1

- With the Slide 2 picture still selected, tap or click the Picture Border arrow (PICTURE TOOLS FORMAT tab | Picture Styles group) to display the Picture Border gallery.

Q&A What if the PICTURE TOOLS FORMAT tab no longer is displayed on my ribbon?
Tap or click the picture to display the PICTURE TOOLS FORMAT tab.

2

- Point to Weight on the Picture Border gallery to display the Weight gallery (Figure 2–23).

3

- If you are using a mouse, point to 3 pt to display a live preview of this line weight on the picture.

Figure 2–23

Q&A Can I make the line width more than 6 pt?
Yes. Tap or click More Lines, tap or click Solid line in the LINE section of the Format Picture task pane, and then increase the amount in the Width box.

Experiment

- If you are using a mouse, point to various line weights in the Weight gallery and watch the line thickness change.

- Tap or click 3 pt to add this line weight to the picture.

To Change a Picture Border Color

1 DOWNLOAD & SELECT SLIDES | 2 INSERT & FORMAT PICTURES | 3 INSERT & FORMAT SHAPES
4 INSERT & FORMAT WORDART | 5 FORMAT SLIDE BACKGROUNDS | 6 REVIEW & REVISE SLIDES

The default color for the border you added to the Slide 2 picture is brown, but you will change the border color to light blue. *Why? The light blue color coordinates with other elements on the slide, especially the blue sky.* The following steps change the Slide 2 picture border color.

1

- With the Slide 2 photo still selected, tap or click the Picture Border arrow (PICTURE TOOLS FORMAT tab | Picture Styles group) to display the Picture Border gallery.

2

- If you are using a mouse, point to Light Blue, Background 2 (the third color in the first row) in the Picture Border gallery to display a live preview of that border color on the picture (Figure 2–24).

Figure 2–24

Experiment

- If you are using a mouse, point to various colors in the Picture Border gallery and watch the border on the picture change in the slide.

3

- Tap or click Light Blue, Background 2 in the Picture Border gallery to change the picture border color.

To Apply Picture Effects

Why? The picture effect allows you to further customize a picture. PowerPoint provides a variety of picture effects, including shadows, reflections, glow, soft edges, bevel, and 3-D rotation. The difference between the effects and the styles is that each effect has several options, providing you with more control over the exact look of the image.

In this presentation, the photo on Slide 2 has a blue glow effect and a bevel applied to its edges. The following steps apply picture effects to the selected picture.

1

- With the Slide 2 picture selected, tap or click the Picture Effects button (PICTURE TOOLS FORMAT tab | Picture Styles group) to display the Picture Effects menu.

Q&A What if the PICTURE TOOLS FORMAT tab no longer is displayed on my ribbon?
Tap or double-click the picture to display the PICTURE TOOLS FORMAT tab.

- Point to Glow on the Picture Effects menu to display the Glow gallery.

Figure 2–25

- If you are using a mouse, point to Light Blue, 18 pt glow, Accent color 2 in the Glow Variations area (the second glow in the last row) to display a live preview of the selected glow effect applied to the picture in the document window (Figure 2–25).

Experiment

- If you are using a mouse, point to various glow effects in the Glow gallery and watch the picture change in the document window.

2

- Tap or click Light Blue, 18 pt glow, Accent color 2 in the Glow gallery to apply the selected picture effect.

3

- Tap or click the Picture Effects button (PICTURE TOOLS FORMAT tab | Picture Styles group) to display the Picture Effects menu again.

- Point to Bevel on the Picture Effects menu to display the Bevel gallery.

- If you are using a mouse, point to Relaxed Inset (the second bevel in the first row) to display a live preview of the selected bevel effect applied to the Slide 2 picture (Figure 2–26).

 Experiment

- If you are using a mouse, point to various bevel effects in the Bevel gallery and watch the picture change in the slide.

Figure 2–26

4

- Tap or click Relaxed Inset in the Bevel gallery to apply the selected picture effect.

Other Ways

1. Press and hold or right-click picture, click Format Picture on shortcut menu, select desired options (Format Picture task pane), tap or click Close button

2. Tap or click Format Shape task pane launcher (PICTURE TOOLS FORMAT tab | Picture Styles group), select desired options (Format Picture task pane), tap or click Close button

Break Point: If you wish to take a break, this is a good place to do so. Be sure to save the Emergency Plan file again and then you can exit PowerPoint. To resume at a later time, run PowerPoint, open the file called Emergency Plan, and continue following the steps from this location forward.

Inserting and Formatting a Shape

One method of getting the audience's attention and reinforcing the major concepts being presented is to have graphical elements on the title slide. PowerPoint provides a wide variety of predefined shapes that can add visual interest to a slide. Shape elements include lines, basic geometrical shapes, arrows, equation shapes, flowchart symbols, stars, banners, and callouts. After adding a shape to a slide, you can change its default characteristics by adding text, bullets, numbers, and styles. You also can combine multiple shapes to create a more complex graphic.

Slide 3 in this presentation is enhanced in a variety of ways. First, a scroll and a plus shape are inserted on Slide 4. Then, a rectangle is added and copied, and text is added to each rectangle and then formatted.

To Add a Shape

Many of the shapes included in the Shapes gallery can direct the viewer to important aspects of the presentation. The following steps add a scroll shape to Slide 3. *Why? A scroll shape helps emphasize the presentation's theme of drafting and finalizing a plan for dealing with emergencies in the household.*

1
- Display Slide 3 and then display the HOME tab (Figure 2–27).

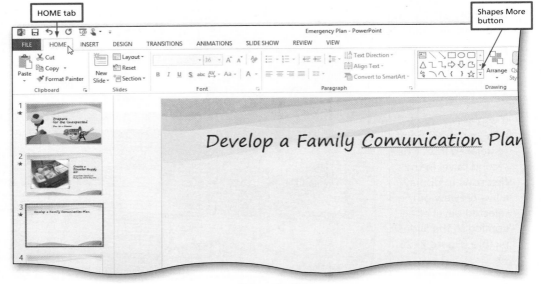

Figure 2–27

2
- Tap or click the Shapes More button (HOME tab | Drawing group) shown in Figure 2–27 to display the Shapes gallery (Figure 2–28).

Q&A | I do not see a Shapes More button and the three rows of the shapes shown in Figure 2–28. Instead, I have a Shapes button. Why?
Monitor dimensions and resolution affect how buttons display on the ribbon. Tap or click the Shapes button to display the entire Shapes gallery.

Figure 2–28

- Tap or click the Vertical Scroll shape in the Stars and Banners area of the Shapes gallery.

Q&A Why did my pointer change shape?

The pointer changed to a plus shape to indicate the Vertical Scroll shape has been added to the Clipboard.

- Position the pointer (a crosshair) below the word, Develop, as shown in Figure 2–29.

- Tap or click Slide 3 to insert the Vertical Scroll shape.

Figure 2–29

Other Ways

1. Tap or click Shapes button (INSERT tab | Illustrations group)

To Resize a Shape

1 DOWNLOAD & SELECT SLIDES | 2 INSERT & FORMAT PICTURES | 3 INSERT & FORMAT SHAPES
4 INSERT & FORMAT WORDART | 5 FORMAT SLIDE BACKGROUNDS | 6 REVIEW & REVISE SLIDES

The next step is to resize the Vertical Scroll shape. **Why?** *The shape should be enlarged so that it fills the middle area of the left side of the slide.* The following steps resize the selected Vertical Scroll shape.

- Press and hold down the SHIFT key and then drag the lower-right corner sizing handle until the Vertical Scroll shape is resized approximately as shown in Figure 2–30.

Q&A Why did I need to press the SHIFT key while enlarging the shape?

Holding down the SHIFT key while dragging keeps the proportions of the original shape.

What if my shape is not selected?

To select a shape, click it.

If I am using a touch screen, how can I maintain the shape's original proportion?

If you drag one of the corner sizing handles, the object should stay in proportion.

Figure 2–30

2

- Release to resize the shape.

- Drag the scroll shape until the vertical Smart Guide is displayed along the left side of the slide, as shown in Figure 2–31, and then release.

Q&A

What if I want to move the shape to a precise location on the slide? With the shape selected, press the ARROW keys or the CTRL+ARROW keys to move the shape to the desired location.

Figure 2–31

Other Ways

1. Enter shape height and width in Height and Width boxes (DRAWING TOOLS FORMAT tab | Size group)

2. Tap or click Size and Position task pane launcher (DRAWING TOOLS FORMAT tab | Size group), tap or click Size tab, enter desired height and width values in boxes, tap or click Close button

---

To Add Other Shapes

1 DOWNLOAD & SELECT SLIDES | 2 INSERT & FORMAT PICTURES | **3 INSERT & FORMAT SHAPES**
4 INSERT & FORMAT WORDART | 5 FORMAT SLIDE BACKGROUNDS | 6 REVIEW & REVISE SLIDES

Circles, squares, arrows, stars, and equation shapes are among the items included in the Shapes gallery. These shapes can be combined to show relationships among the elements, and they can help illustrate the basic concepts presented in your slide show. The following steps add the Plus and Rectangle shapes to Slide 3.

1

- Tap or click the Shapes More button (HOME tab | Drawing group) to display the Shapes gallery (Figure 2–32).

Figure 2–32

- Tap or click the Plus shape in the Equation Shapes area of the Shapes gallery.

- Position the pointer in the center of Slide 3 and then tap or click to insert the Plus shape.

- Press and hold down the SHIFT key and then drag a corner sizing handle until the Plus shape is the size shown in Figure 2–33.

Q&A If I am using a touch screen, how can I maintain the Plus shape's original proportion?
The object should stay in proportion when you drag one of the corner sizing handles.

Figure 2–33

- Drag the Plus shape until the horizontal Smart Guide is displayed in the middle of the two shapes and the vertical Smart Guide is displayed between the two shapes, as shown in Figure 2–33, and then release.

- Display the Shapes gallery and then tap or click the Rectangle shape in the Rectangles area of the gallery.

- Position the pointer toward the upper-right side of the Plus shape and then tap or click to insert the Rectangle shape.

- Resize the Rectangle shape so that it is the size shown in Figure 2–34.

- Drag the Rectangle shape until the horizontal Smart Guide is displayed below the title text and the vertical Smart Guide is displayed between the Plus and the Rectangle shapes, as shown in Figure 2–34, and then release.

Figure 2–34

To Apply a Shape Style

1 DOWNLOAD & SELECT SLIDES | 2 INSERT & FORMAT PICTURES | 3 INSERT & FORMAT SHAPES
4 INSERT & FORMAT WORDART | 5 FORMAT SLIDE BACKGROUNDS | 6 REVIEW & REVISE SLIDES

Formatting text in a shape follows the same techniques as formatting text in a placeholder. You can change font, font color and size, and alignment. You later will add contact information to the scroll, but now you want to apply a shape style to the scroll. *Why? The style will give depth to the object so that it appears three-dimensional.* The Quick Styles gallery has a variety of styles that change depending upon the theme applied to the presentation. The following steps apply a style to the Vertical Scroll shape.

- Tap or click the Vertical Scroll shape to select it and then tap or click the Quick Styles button (HOME tab | Drawing group) (Figure 2–35).

Figure 2–35

- If you are using a mouse, point to Subtle Effect – Lavender, Accent 6 in the Quick Styles gallery (the last shape in the fourth row) to display a live preview of that style applied to the Vertical Scroll shape in the slide (Figure 2–36).

  Experiment

- If you are using a mouse, point to various styles in the Quick Styles gallery and watch the style of the shape change.

Figure 2–36

- Tap or click Subtle Effect – Lavender, Accent 6 in the Quick Styles gallery to apply the selected style to the Vertical Scroll shape.

Other Ways

1. Tap or click Shape Styles More button (DRAWING TOOLS FORMAT tab | Shape Styles group), select style

2. Press and hold or right-click shape, tap or click Format Shape on shortcut menu, select desired style (Format Shape task pane), tap or click Close button

To Apply Another Style

You later will add meeting place information to the rectangle, but now you want to format this shape. *Why? The formatting will add interest. In addition, the Plus shape helps join the scroll and the rectangle, both of which will contain components of the family communication plan. You can apply a coordinating shape style to the Plus sign.* The following steps apply styles to the Rectangle and Plus shapes.

1 Tap or click the Rectangle shape on Slide 3 to select it.

2 Tap or click the Quick Styles button (HOME tab | Drawing group) to display the Quick Styles gallery and then apply the Subtle Effect – Lavender, Accent 6 style to the Rectangle shape.

3 Tap or click the Plus shape on Slide 3 to select it and then tap or click the Quick Styles button.

4 Tap or click Colored Outline – Lavender, Accent 6 (the last style in the first row) to apply that style to the Plus shape (Figure 2–37).

Figure 2–37

To Add Text to a Shape

1 DOWNLOAD & SELECT SLIDES | 2 INSERT & FORMAT PICTURES | 3 INSERT & FORMAT SHAPES
4 INSERT & FORMAT WORDART | 5 FORMAT SLIDE BACKGROUNDS | 6 REVIEW & REVISE SLIDES

The scroll and rectangle shapes on Slide 3 help call attention to the key aspects of your presentation. *Why? Your goal is to urge families to develop a communication plan by gathering contact information and determining meeting locations.* The next step is to add this information to Slide 3. The following steps add text to the two shapes.

- Tap or click the Vertical Scroll shape to select it and then type `Contact names & phone numbers` in the shape.

- Tap or click the Rectangle shape to select it and then type `Meeting place near house` in the shape (Figure 2–38).

Figure 2–38

To Change the Font

The default theme font is Segoe Print. To draw more attention to text in the shapes and to help differentiate these slide elements from the title text, you want to change the font to Courier New. *Why? This font resembles the letters that typewriters produced.* To change the font, you must select the letters you want to format. In Chapter 1, you selected a paragraph and then formatted the characters, and you follow the same procedure to change the font. The following steps change the text font in the shape.

- Be certain the Rectangle shape is selected. If you are using a touch screen, tap to position the insertion point in the text to select and then drag the selection handles as necessary until all the characters are selected and the mini toolbar is displayed; if you are using a mouse, triple-click the text to select all the characters and display the mini toolbar (Figure 2–39).

Figure 2–39

2

● Tap or click the Font arrow to display the Font gallery (Figure 2–40).

Q&A Will the fonts in my Font gallery be the same as those shown in Figure 2–40?
Your list of available fonts may differ, depending on what fonts you have installed and the type of printer you are using.

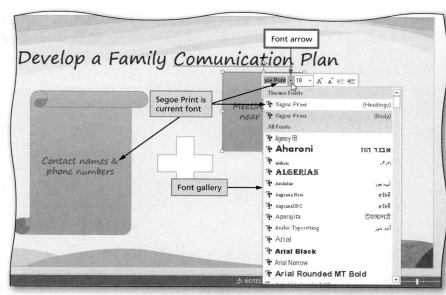

Figure 2–40

3

● If you are using a mouse, drag or scroll through the Font gallery and then point to Courier New (or a similar font) to display a live preview of the title text in the Courier New font (Figure 2–41).

 Experiment

● If you are using a mouse, point to various fonts in the Font gallery and watch the subtitle text font change in the slide.

● Tap or click Courier New (or a similar font) to change the font of the selected text to Courier New.

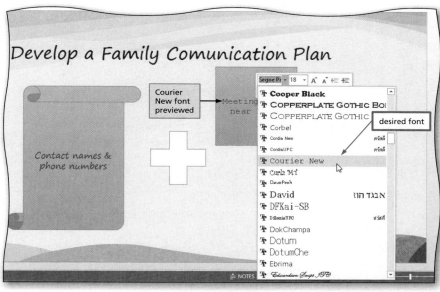

Figure 2–41

Other Ways

1. Tap or click Font arrow (HOME tab | Font group), tap or click desired font in Font gallery

2. Press and hold or right-click selected text, click Font on shortcut menu (Font dialog box), tap or click Font tab, select desired font in Font list, tap or click OK button

3. Tap or click Font dialog box launcher (HOME tab | Font group), tap or click Font tab (Font dialog box), select desired font in Font list, tap or click OK button

4. Press CTRL+SHIFT+F, click Font tab (Font dialog box), select desired font in the Font list, tap or click OK button

To Format the Text

To increase readability, you can format the Rectangle shape text by increasing the font size, bolding the characters, and changing the font color to black. The following steps format the Rectangle shape text.

① With the Rectangle shape text selected, tap or click the Increase Font Size button (HOME tab | Font group) three times to increase the font size to 28 pt.

② Tap or click the Bold button (HOME tab | Font group) to bold the text.

③ Tap or click the Font Color arrow and change the color to Black (the fourth color in the first row) (Figure 2–42).

Q&A Could I also add a shadow behind the text to add depth and help the letters display prominently?

Yes. Select the text and then tap or click the Text Shadow button (HOME tab | Font group).

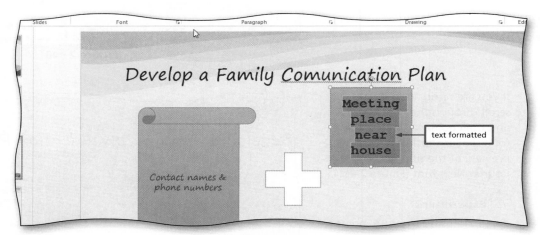

Figure 2–42

Other Ways

1. Select text, tap 'Show Context Menu' button on mini toolbar or right-click selected text, tap or click desired text format button on mini toolbar

BTW

Shadowing Text
Adding a shadow to text adds depth and helps the letters display prominently by adding a shadow behind them. To add a shadow, select the text and then tap or click the Text Shadow button (HOME tab | Font group).

Format Painter

To save time and avoid formatting errors, you can use the Format Painter to apply custom formatting to other places in your presentation quickly and easily. You can use this feature in three ways:

• To copy only character attributes, such as font and font effects, select text that has these qualities.

• To copy both character attributes and paragraph attributes, such as alignment and indentation, select the entire paragraph.

• To apply the same formatting to multiple words, phrases, or paragraphs, double-tap or double-click the Format Painter button and then select each item you want to format. You then can press the ESC key or click the Format Painter button to turn off this feature.

To Format Text Using the Format Painter

Why? To save time and duplicated effort, you quickly can use the Format Painter to copy formatting attributes from the Rectangle shape text and apply them to Vertical Scroll text. The following steps use the Format Painter to copy formatting features.

- With the Rectangle shape text still selected, double-tap or double-click the Format Painter button (HOME tab | Clipboard group).
- Move the pointer off the ribbon (Figure 2–43).

Q&A Why did my pointer change shape?
The pointer changed shape by adding a paintbrush to indicate that the Format Painter function is active.

Figure 2–43

- Tap and drag the selection handles as necessary or triple-click the Vertical Scroll text to apply the format to all characters (Figure 2–44).
- Tap the Format Painter button or press the ESC key to turn off the Format Painter feature.

Figure 2–44

Other Ways

1. Select text, tap or click Format Painter button on mini toolbar

To Copy and Paste a Shape

When developing a communication plan, family members need to determine two meeting places: one near the house and a second outside the neighborhood. You already have created the shape stating the first meeting location. You now need to create a second shape with the instruction to decide where to meet away from the house. The following steps copy the Rectangle shape and then move the copy. *Why? You could repeat all the steps you performed to create the first rectangle, but it is much more efficient to duplicate the shape and then edit the text.*

- Select the Rectangle shape and then tap or click the Copy button (HOME tab | Clipboard group) (Figure 2–45).

Figure 2–45

2

- Tap or click the Paste button (HOME tab | Clipboard group) to insert a duplicate Rectangle shape on Slide 3.

- Drag the Rectangle shape below the first Rectangle shape (Figure 2–46).

Figure 2–46

3

- In the second Rectangle shape, select the text, near house, and then type **away from vicinity** as the replacement text (Figure 2–47).

Figure 2–47

Other Ways

1. Press and hold or right-click selected shape, tap or click Copy on shortcut menu, press and hold or right-click, tap or click Paste on shortcut menu

2. Select shape, press CTRL+C, press CTRL+V

Break Point: If you wish to take a break, this is a good place to do so. Be sure to save the Emergency Plan file again and then you can exit PowerPoint. To resume at a later time, run PowerPoint, open the file called Emergency Plan, and continue following the steps from this location forward.

Inserting and Formatting WordArt

One method of adding appealing visual elements to a presentation is by using **WordArt** styles. This feature is found in other Microsoft Office applications, including Word and Excel. This gallery of decorative effects allows you to type new text or convert existing text to WordArt. You then can add elements such as fills, outlines, and effects.

WordArt **fill** in the interior of a letter can consist of a solid color, texture, picture, or gradient. The WordArt **outline** is the exterior border surrounding each letter or symbol. PowerPoint allows you to change the outline color, weight, and style. You also can add an **effect**, which helps add emphasis or depth to the characters. Some effects are shadows, reflections, glows, bevels, and 3-D rotations.

BTW

Undo Text Formatting Changes
To remove a formatting change you have made to text, such as an underline or bolding, select the text and then tap or click the button that originally applied the format. For example, to undo bolding, select the text and then click the Bold button. If you apply a format and then immediately decide to remove this effect, click the Undo button on the Quick Access Toolbar.

To Insert WordArt

1 DOWNLOAD & SELECT SLIDES | 2 INSERT & FORMAT PICTURES | 3 INSERT & FORMAT SHAPES
4 INSERT & FORMAT WORDART | 5 FORMAT SLIDE BACKGROUNDS | 6 REVIEW & REVISE SLIDES

Having a communication plan is of utmost importance to prepare for the unexpected. You want to emphasize this concept, and the last slide in the presentation is an excellent location to urge your audience to take action. ***Why?*** *Audience members remember the first and last things they see and hear.* You quickly can add a visual element to the slide by selecting a WordArt style from the WordArt Styles gallery and then applying it to some text. The following steps insert WordArt.

- Display Slide 4 and then display the INSERT tab.

- Tap or click the WordArt button (INSERT tab | Text group) to display the WordArt gallery (Figure 2–48).

Figure 2–48

- Tap or click Fill – Brown, Text 1, Outline – Background 1, Hard Shadow – Background 1 (the first style in the third row) to insert the WordArt object (Figure 2–49).

Figure 2–49

3

- Type **Be Prepared** in the object as the WordArt text (Figure 2–50).

Q&A Why did the DRAWING TOOLS FORMAT tab appear automatically in the ribbon?
It appears when you select text to which you could add a WordArt style or other effect.

Figure 2–50

To Change the WordArt Shape

1 DOWNLOAD & SELECT SLIDES | 2 INSERT & FORMAT PICTURES | 3 INSERT & FORMAT SHAPES

4 INSERT & FORMAT WORDART | **5 FORMAT SLIDE BACKGROUNDS** | 6 REVIEW & REVISE SLIDES

Why? *The WordArt text is useful to emphasize the need to prepare for emergencies. You further can emphasize this text by changing its shape.* PowerPoint provides a variety of graphical shapes that add interest to WordArt text. The following steps change the WordArt shape to Inflate Bottom.

1

- With the WordArt object still selected, click the Text Effects button (DRAWING TOOLS FORMAT tab | WordArt Styles group) to display the Text Effects menu (Figure 2–51).

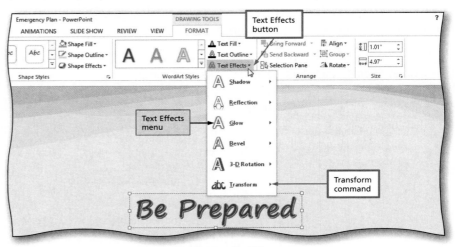

Figure 2–51

2

- Point to Transform in the Text Effects menu to display the WordArt Transform gallery (Figure 2–52).

Figure 2–52

3

- If you are using a mouse, point to the Inflate Bottom shape in the Warp area (the third shape in the last row) to display a live preview of that text effect applied to the WordArt object (Figure 2–53).

 Experiment

- If you are using a mouse, point to various effects in the Transform gallery and watch the format of the text and borders change.

Q&A How can I see the preview of a Transform effect if the gallery is overlaying the WordArt letters?
Move the WordArt box to the left or right side of the slide and then repeat Steps 1 and 2.

Figure 2–53

4

- Tap or click the Inflate Bottom shape to apply this text effect to the WordArt object.

Q&A Can I change the shape I applied to the WordArt?
Yes. Position the insertion point in the box and then repeat Steps 1 and 2.

5

- Drag the upper-left sizing handle diagonally toward the upper-left corner of the slide until the crosshair is positioned approximately as shown in Figure 2–54.

Figure 2–54

6

- Release to resize the WordArt object.

- Drag the WordArt object toward the center of the slide until it is positioned approximately as shown in Figure 2–55.

Figure 2–55

To Apply a WordArt Text Fill

Various texture fills are available to give your WordArt characters a unique look. The 24 pictures in the Texture gallery give the appearance of a physical object, such as water drops, sand, tissue paper, and a paper bag. The following steps add the Purple Mesh texture as a fill for the WordArt characters. *Why? Purple coordinates well with the shapes on Slide 3 and is similar to the color in the Slide1 flower and firefighter's hose.*

1

• With the WordArt object selected, click the Text Fill arrow (DRAWING TOOLS FORMAT tab | WordArt Styles group) to display the Text Fill gallery.

• Point to Texture in the Text Fill gallery to display the Texture gallery.

2

• If you are using a mouse, point to the Purple mesh texture (the third texture in the fifth row) to display a live preview of that texture applied to the WordArt object (Figure 2–56).

🔍 **Experiment**

• If you are using a mouse, point to various styles in the Texture gallery and watch the fill change.

3

• Tap or click the Purple mesh texture to apply this texture as the fill for the WordArt object.

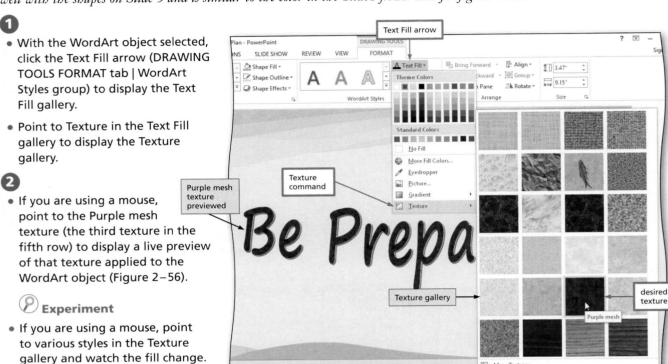

Figure 2–56

Q&A Can I apply this texture simultaneously to text that appears in more than one place on my slide?

Yes. If you are not using a touch screen, you can select one area of text, press and then hold the CTRL key while you select the other text, and then apply the texture.

To Change the Weight of the WordArt Outline

The letters in the WordArt style applied have an outline around the edges. You can increase the width of the lines. *Why? The thicker line will emphasize this characteristic and add another visual element.* As with fonts, lines also are measured in point size, and PowerPoint gives you the option to change the line **weight**, or thickness, starting with ¼ point (pt) and increasing in one-fourth-point increments. Other outline options include modifying the color and the line style, such as changing to dots or dashes or a combination of dots and dashes. The following steps change the WordArt outline weight to 3 pt.

1

- With the WordArt object still selected, click the Text Outline arrow (DRAWING TOOLS FORMAT tab | WordArt Styles group) to display the Text Outline gallery.

- Point to Weight in the gallery to display the Weight list.

- If you are using a mouse, point to 3 pt to display a live preview of this line weight on the WordArt text outline (Figure 2–57).

Q&A Can I make the line width more than 6 pt?
Yes. Tap or click More Lines and increase the amount in the Width box.

Experiment

- If you are using a mouse, point to various line weights in the Weight list and watch the line thickness change.

Figure 2–57

2

- Tap or click 3 pt to apply this line weight to the WordArt text outline.

Q&A Must my text have an outline?
No. To delete the outline, click No Outline in the Text Outline gallery.

To Change the Color of the WordArt Outline

1 DOWNLOAD & SELECT SLIDES | 2 INSERT & FORMAT PICTURES | 3 INSERT & FORMAT SHAPES
4 INSERT & FORMAT WORDART | **5 FORMAT SLIDE BACKGROUNDS** | 6 REVIEW & REVISE SLIDES

Why? *The WordArt outline color and the slide background color are similar, so you can add contrast by changing one of these slide elements.* The following steps change the WordArt outline color.

1

- With the WordArt object still selected, display the Text Outline gallery.

- If you are using a mouse, point to Red (the second color in the Standard Colors row) to display a live preview of this outline color.

Experiment

- If you are using a mouse, point to various colors in the gallery and watch the outline colors change.

2

- Tap or click Red to apply this color to the WordArt outline.

- Tap or click outside of the WordArt box to deselect this slide element (Figure 2–58).

Figure 2–58

Formatting Slide Backgrounds

A slide's background is an integral part of a presentation because it can generate audience interest. Every slide can have the same background, or different backgrounds can be used in a presentation. This background is considered fill, which is the content that makes up the interior of a shape, line, or character. Four fills are available: solid, gradient, picture or texture, and pattern. **Solid fill** is one color used throughout the entire slide. **Gradient fill** is one color shade gradually progressing to another shade of the same color or one color progressing to another color. **Picture** or **texture fill** uses a specific file or an image that simulates a material, such as cork, granite, marble, or canvas. **Pattern fill** adds designs, such as dots or diamonds, that repeat in rows across the slide.

Once you add a fill, you can adjust its appearance. For example, you can adjust its **transparency**, which allows you to see through the background, so that any text on the slide is visible. You also can select a color that is part of the theme or a custom color. You can use **offsets**, another background feature, to move the background away from the slide borders in varying distances by percentage. **Tiling options** repeat the background image many times vertically and horizontally on the slide; the smaller the tiling percentage, the greater the number of times the image is repeated.

To Insert a Picture to Create a Background

1 DOWNLOAD & SELECT SLIDES | 2 INSERT & FORMAT PICTURES | 3 INSERT & FORMAT SHAPES
4 INSERT & FORMAT WORDART | 5 FORMAT SLIDE BACKGROUNDS | 6 REVIEW & REVISE SLIDES

Why? *For variety and interest, you want to use an illustration as the Slide 4 background.* This picture is stored on the Data Files for Students. PowerPoint will stretch the height and width of this picture to fill the slide area. The following steps insert the picture, Emergency Collage, on Slide 4 only.

• With Slide 4 displaying, display the DESIGN tab and then click the Format Background button (DESIGN tab | Customize group).

• With the FILL section displaying (Format Background task pane) and 'Picture or texture fill' selected, tap or click the File button to display the Insert Picture dialog box (Figure 2–59).

• If necessary, navigate to the PowerPoint Chapter 02 folder or the location where your Data Files for Students folder is located.

Figure 2–59

2

- If necessary, slide or scroll down and then click Emergency Collage to select the file name (Figure 2–60).

Figure 2–60

3

- Tap or click the Insert button (Insert Picture dialog box) to insert the Emergency Collage illustration as the Slide 4 background (Figure 2–61).

◄ **Q&A** What if I do not want to use this picture?

Tap or click the Undo button on the Quick Access Toolbar or tap or click the Reset Background button at the bottom of the Format Background task pane.

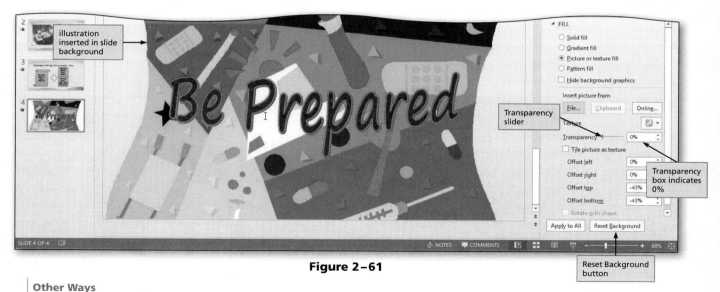

Figure 2–61

Other Ways

1. Tap or click Format Background on shortcut menu, click Picture or Texture Fill, Insert from File (Format Background pane)

To Format the Background Picture Fill Transparency

1 DOWNLOAD & SELECT SLIDES | 2 INSERT & FORMAT PICTURES | 3 INSERT & FORMAT SHAPES
4 INSERT & FORMAT WORDART | 5 FORMAT SLIDE BACKGROUNDS | 6 REVIEW & REVISE SLIDES

The Emergency Collage illustration on Slide 4 has vibrant colors and conflicts with the WordArt. One method of reducing this richness is to change the transparency. The **Transparency slider** indicates the amount of opaqueness. The default setting is 0, which is fully opaque. The opposite extreme is 100%, which is fully transparent. To change the transparency, you can move the Transparency slider or enter a number in the box next to the slider. The following step adjusts the transparency of the background picture to 60%.

1

• Tap or click the Transparency slider and drag it to the right until 60% is displayed in the Transparency box (Figure 2–62).

Q&A Can I move the slider in small increments so that I can get a precise percentage easily?
Yes. Tap or click the up or down arrows in the Transparency box to move the slider in one-percent increments.

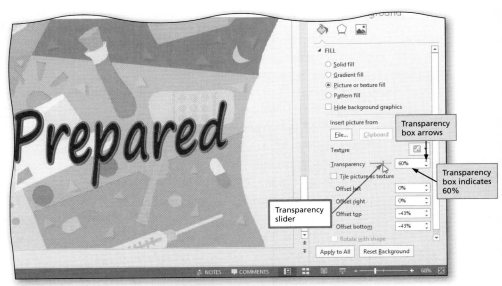

Figure 2–62

To Insert a Texture Fill

You used a texture fill to add interest to the WordArt characters. These same fills are available to add as a slide background. You also can use your own texture pictures for custom backgrounds. The following steps insert the Bouquet fill on Slide 3 in the presentation.

1

• Display Slide 3 and, if necessary, tap or click the Format Background button (DESIGN tab | Customize group) to display the Format Background task pane.

• Tap or click the Texture button to display the Texture gallery (Figure 2–63).

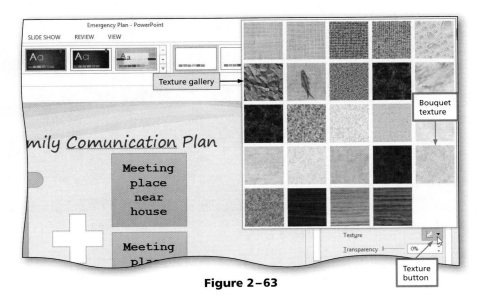

Figure 2–63

2

• Tap or click the Bouquet texture (the last texture in the fourth row) to insert this texture fill as the background on Slide 3 (Figure 2–64).

Q&A Is a live preview available to see the various textures on this slide?
No. Live preview is not an option with the background textures and fills.

Could I insert this background on all four slides simultaneously?
Yes. You would click the 'Apply to All' button to insert the Bouquet background on all slides.

Figure 2–64

To Format the Background Texture Fill Transparency

1 DOWNLOAD & SELECT SLIDES | 2 INSERT & FORMAT PICTURES | 3 INSERT & FORMAT SHAPES
4 INSERT & FORMAT WORDART | 5 FORMAT SLIDE BACKGROUNDS | 6 REVIEW & REVISE SLIDES

The Bouquet texture on Slide 3 may detract from the three shapes because it does not offer sufficient contrast with the symbols and text. You can adjust the transparency of a slide texture in the same manner that you change a picture transparency. The following step adjusts the texture transparency to 35%.

1

• Click the Transparency slider and drag it to the right until 35% is displayed in the Transparency box (Figure 2–65).

Figure 2–65

To Insert a Gradient Fill

1 DOWNLOAD & SELECT SLIDES | 2 INSERT & FORMAT PICTURES | 3 INSERT & FORMAT SHAPES
4 INSERT & FORMAT WORDART | 5 FORMAT SLIDE BACKGROUNDS | 6 REVIEW & REVISE SLIDES

Although you selected Bouquet texture fill on Slide 3 and changed the transparency, you decide that another type of background may be more suitable for your presentation. *Why? The Bouquet texture is very colorful and may detract from the messages presented in the symbols.* For each theme, PowerPoint provides 30 preset **gradient fills** with five designs for each of the six major theme colors. Each fill has one dark color shade that gradually lightens to either another shade of the same color or another color. The following steps replace the texture fill on Slide 3 to a preset gradient fill.

1

- Tap or click Gradient fill in the Format Background pane and then click the Preset gradients button to display the Preset gradients gallery (Figure 2–66).

Q&A Are the backgrounds displayed in a specific order?
Yes. The first row has light colors at the top of the background; the middle rows have darker fills at the bottom; the bottom row has overall dark fills on all edges.

Is a live preview available to see the various gradients on this slide?
No. Live preview is not an option with the background textures and fills.

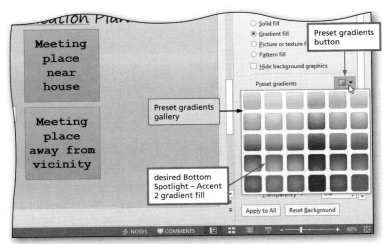

Figure 2–66

2

- Tap or click Bottom Spotlight – Accent 2 (the second fill in the fourth row) to apply that style to Slide 3 (Figure 2–67).

Q&A If I decide later that this background gradient does not fit the theme of my presentation, can I apply a different background?
Yes. You can repeat these steps at any time while creating your presentation.

What if I want to apply this background gradient to all slides in the presentation?
Tap or click the desired style or click the 'Apply to All' button at the bottom of the pane.

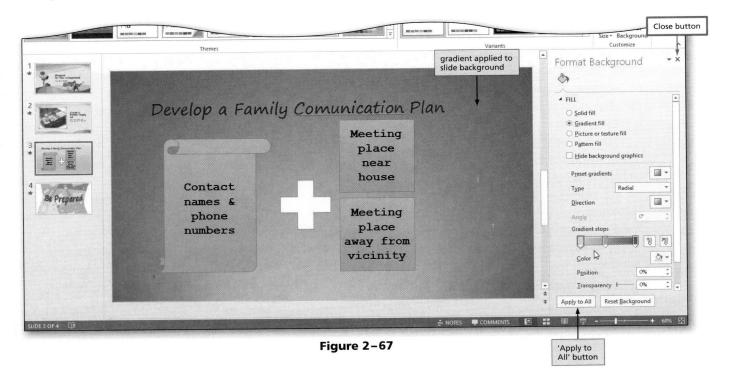

Figure 2–67

3

- Tap or click the Close button (Format Background pane) to close the pane and return to Slide 3.

Other Ways

1. Tap or click DESIGN tab on ribbon, tap or click Format Background button (Customize group), select desired options (Format Background pane)
2. Press and hold or right-click background, click Format Background on shortcut menu, select desired options (Format Background pane)

Reviewing and Revising Individual Slides

The text, pictures, and shapes for all slides in the Emergency Plan presentation have been entered. Once you complete a slide show, you might decide to change elements. PowerPoint provides several tools to assist you with making changes. They include finding and replacing text, inserting a synonym, and checking spelling. The following pages discuss these tools.

Replace Dialog Box

At times, you might want to change all occurrences of a word or phrase to another word or phrase. For example, an instructor may have one slide show to accompany a lecture for several introductory classes, and he wants to update slides with the particular class name and section that appear on several slides. He manually could change the characters, but PowerPoint includes an efficient method of replacing one word with another. The Find and Replace feature automatically locates specific text and then replaces it with desired text.

In some cases, you may want to replace only certain occurrences of a word or phrase, not all of them. To instruct PowerPoint to confirm each change, click the Find Next button in the Replace dialog box instead of the Replace All button. When PowerPoint locates an occurrence of the text, it pauses and waits for you to click either the Replace button or the Find Next button. Clicking the Replace button changes the text; clicking the Find Next button instructs PowerPoint to disregard that particular instance and look for the next occurrence of the Find what text.

To Find and Replace Text

1 DOWNLOAD & SELECT SLIDES | 2 INSERT & FORMAT PICTURES | 3 INSERT & FORMAT SHAPES
4 INSERT & FORMAT WORDART | 5 FORMAT SLIDE BACKGROUNDS | 6 REVIEW & REVISE SLIDES

While reviewing your slides, you realize that the word, Emergency, would be a better choice than the word, Disaster. To change these words throughout a presentation, you could view each slide, look for the word, Disaster, delete the word, and then type the replacement word, Emergency. A more efficient and effective method of performing this action is to use PowerPoint's Find and Replace feature, which automatically locates each occurrence of a word or phrase and then replaces it with specified text. The word, Disaster, displays twice in the presentation. The following steps use Find and Replace to replace all occurrences of the words, a Disaster, with the words, an Emergency.

- Display the HOME tab and then tap or click the Replace button (HOME tab | Editing group) to display the Replace dialog box.

- Type **a Disaster** in the Find what box (Replace dialog box).

- Tap or click the Replace with box and then type **an Emergency** in the box (Figure 2–68).

Figure 2–68

2

- Tap or click the Replace All button (Replace dialog box) to instruct PowerPoint to replace all occurrences of the Find what words, a Disaster, with the Replace with words, an Emergency (Figure 2–69).

Q&A If I accidentally replaced the wrong text, can I undo this replacement?
Yes. Tap or click the Undo button on the Quick Access Toolbar to undo all replacements. If you had tapped or clicked the Replace button instead of the Replace All button, PowerPoint would undo only the most recent replacement.

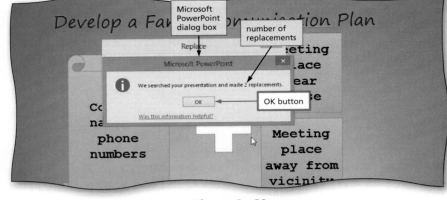

Figure 2–69

3

- Tap or click the OK button (Microsoft PowerPoint dialog box).

- Tap or click the Close btton (Replace dialog box).

BTW
Finding and Replacing Text
When finding and replacing text, you do not need to display the slide that contains the word for which you are searching. You can perform this action when any slide is displayed. To see the results of the search and replace action, however, you need to display the slide where the change occurred.

Other Ways

1. Press CTRL+H

1 DOWNLOAD & SELECT SLIDES | 2 INSERT & FORMAT PICTURES | 3 INSERT & FORMAT SHAPES
4 INSERT & FORMAT WORDART | 5 FORMAT SLIDE BACKGROUNDS | 6 REVIEW & REVISE SLIDES

To Find and Insert a Synonym

When reviewing your slide show, you may decide that a particular word does not express the exact usage you intended or that you used the same word on multiple slides. In these cases, you could find a **synonym**, or word similar in meaning, to replace the inappropriate or duplicate word. PowerPoint provides a **thesaurus**, which is a list of synonyms and antonyms, to help you find a replacement word.

In this project, you want to find a synonym to replace the words, stay alive, on Slide 2. The following steps locate an appropriate synonym and replace the word.

1

- Display Slide 2 and then select the words, stay alive.

- If you are using a mouse, right-click to display a shortcut menu related to the words you right-clicked. Then, point to Synonyms on the shortcut menu to display a list of synonyms for these words (Figure 2–70).

Q&A If I want to locate a synonym for only one word, do I need to select it?
No. You simply need to place the insertion point in the word and then press and hold or right-click to display the shortcut menu.

- If you are using a touch screen, tap the Thesaurus button (REVIEW

Figure 2–70

tab | Proofing group) to display the Thesaurus task pane for the selected words. Then, in the task pane, tap the arrow next to the word survive if necessary to display a shortcut menu.

- Tap Insert or click the synonym you want (survive) on the Synonyms submenu to replace the words, stay alive, in the presentation with the word, survive (Figure 2–71).

Q&A What if a suitable word does not display in the Synonyms submenu?

You can display the Thesaurus task pane by tapping or clicking Thesaurus on the Synonyms submenu. A complete thesaurus with synonyms displays in the task pane along with an antonym, which is a word with an opposite meaning.

Figure 2–71

Other Ways

1. Tap or click Thesaurus (REVIEW tab | Proofing group) 2. Press SHIFT+F7

To Add Notes

1 DOWNLOAD & SELECT SLIDES | 2 INSERT & FORMAT PICTURES | 3 INSERT & FORMAT SHAPES
4 INSERT & FORMAT WORDART | 5 FORMAT SLIDE BACKGROUNDS | 6 REVIEW & REVISE SLIDES

As you create slides, you may find material you want to state verbally and do not want to include on the slide. You can type and format notes in the **Notes pane** as you work in Normal view and then print this information as **notes pages**. The Notes pane is hidden until you tap or click the Notes button on the status bar to open the pane. If you want to close the Notes pane, tap or click the Notes button again. After adding comments, you can print a set of speaker notes. These notes will print below a small image of the slide. Charts, tables, and pictures added to the Notes pane also print on these pages. The following steps add text to the Notes pane on Slides 2, 3, and 4.

Note: In the following step, the word, whistle, has been misspelled intentionally as wistle to illustrate the use of PowerPoint's spell check feature. Your slides may contain different misspelled words, depending upon the accuracy of your typing.

- Display Slide 2 and then if necessary tap or click the Notes button on the status bar to display the Notes pane.

Q&A Why might I need to tap or click the Notes pane?

By default, the Notes pane is closed when you begin a new presentation. Once you display the Notes pane for any slide, the Notes pane will remain open unless you tap or click the Notes button to close it.

- Tap or click the Notes pane and then type **The kit should include a flashlight, wistle, water, radio, batteries, three-day supply of food, three gallons of water for each family member, change of clothing, tools, and first aid kit.** (Figure 2–72).

Q&A What if I cannot see all the lines I typed?

You can drag the splitter bar up to enlarge the Notes pane. Clicking the Notes pane scroll arrows or swiping up or down on the Notes pane allows you to view the entire text.

Figure 2–72

2

- Display Slide 3, tap or click the Notes pane, and then type `One meeting place should be near the home, and the second should be outside the neighborhood. One out-of-state relative should be included in the contacts list.` (Figure 2–73).

Figure 2–73

3

- Display Slide 4 and then type `The Federal Emergency Management Agency (FEMA) has additional information about helping people prepare for emergency situations. Visit www.ready.gov.` in the Notes pane (Figure 2–74).

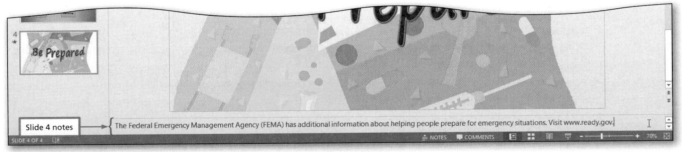

Figure 2–74

BTW
Formatting Notes Pane Text
You can format text in the Notes pane in the same manner you format text on a slide. For example, you can bold key words or change the font size and color to add emphasis.

BTW
Detecting Spelling Errors
The x in the Spell Check icon indicates PowerPoint detected a possible spelling error. A check mark in the icon indicates the entered text contains no spelling errors.

Checking Spelling

After you create a presentation, you should check it visually for spelling errors and style consistency. In addition, you use PowerPoint's Spelling tool to identify possible misspellings on the slides and in the notes. Do not rely on the spelling checker to catch all your mistakes. Although PowerPoint's spelling checker is a valuable tool, it is not infallible. You should proofread your presentation carefully by pointing to each word and saying it aloud as you point to it. Be mindful of commonly misused words such as its and it's, through and though, and to and too.

PowerPoint checks the entire presentation for spelling mistakes using a standard dictionary contained in the Microsoft Office group. This dictionary is shared with the other Microsoft Office applications such as Word and Excel. A custom dictionary is available if you want to add special words such as proper names, cities, and acronyms. When checking a presentation for spelling errors, PowerPoint opens the standard dictionary and the custom dictionary file, if one exists. When a word appears in the Spelling pane, you can perform one of several actions, as described in Table 2–1.

The standard dictionary contains commonly used English words. It does not, however, contain many proper names, abbreviations, technical terms, poetic contractions, or antiquated terms. PowerPoint treats words not found in the dictionaries as misspellings.

Table 2–1 Spelling Pane Buttons and Actions

Button Name/Action	When to Use	Action
Ignore	Word is spelled correctly but not found in dictionaries	PowerPoint continues checking rest of the presentation but will flag that word again if it appears later in document.
Ignore All	Word is spelled correctly but not found in dictionaries	PowerPoint ignores all occurrences of the word and continues checking rest of presentation.
Add	Add word to custom dictionary	PowerPoint opens custom dictionary, adds word, and continues checking rest of presentation.
Change	Word is misspelled	Click proper spelling of the word in Suggestions list. PowerPoint corrects word, continues checking rest of presentation, but will flag that word again if it appears later in document.
Change All	Word is misspelled	Click proper spelling of word in Suggestions list. PowerPoint changes all occurrences of misspelled word and continues checking rest of presentation.
Listen to the pronunciation	To hear the pronunciation of a word	Tap or click the audio speaker icon next to the properly spelled word near the bottom of the Spelling pane.
View synonyms	See some synonyms for the correctly spelled word	View the bullet list of synonyms below the correctly spelled word near the bottom of the Spelling pane.
Close	Stop spelling checker	PowerPoint closes spelling checker and returns to PowerPoint window.

© 2014 Cengage Learning

To Check Spelling

1 DOWNLOAD & SELECT SLIDES | 2 INSERT & FORMAT PICTURES | 3 INSERT & FORMAT SHAPES
4 INSERT & FORMAT WORDART | 5 FORMAT SLIDE BACKGROUNDS | 6 REVIEW & REVISE SLIDES

The following steps check the spelling on all slides in the Emergency Plan presentation.

1

- Tap or click REVIEW on the Ribbon to display the REVIEW tab.

- Tap or click the Spelling button (REVIEW Tab | Proofing group) to start the spelling checker and display the Spelling pane (Figure 2–75).

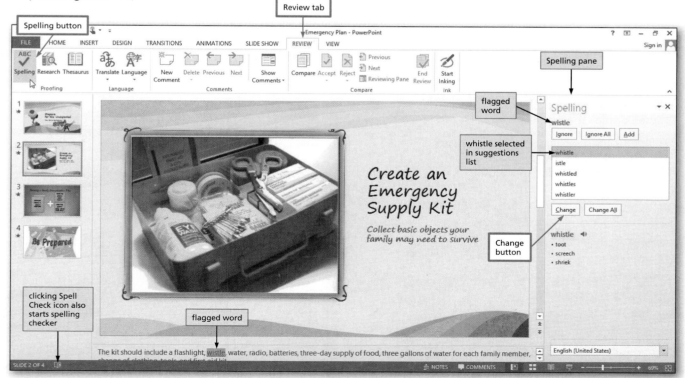

Figure 2–75

2

- With the word, wistle, selected in the list, tap or click the Change button (Spelling pane) to replace the misspelled flagged word, wistle, with the selected correctly spelled word, whistle, and then continue the spelling check (Figure 2–76).

Q&A Could I have tapped or clicked the Change All button instead of the Change button?

Yes. When you tap or click the Change All button, you change the current and future occurrences of the misspelled word. The misspelled word, wistle, appears only once in the presentation, so tapping or clicking the Change or the Change All button in this instance produces identical results.

Occasionally a correctly spelled word is flagged as a possible misspelled word. Why?

Your custom dictionary does not contain the word, so it is seen as spelled incorrectly. You can add this word to a custom dictionary to prevent the spelling checker from flagging it as a mistake.

Figure 2–76

3

- Replace the misspelled word, Comunication, with the word, Communication.

- Continue checking all flagged words in the presentation. When the Microsoft PowerPoint dialog box appears, tap or click the OK button (Microsoft PowerPoint dialog box) to close the spelling checker and return to the slide where a possible misspelled word appeared.

Other Ways

1. Tap or click Spell Check icon on status bar	2. Press and hold or right-click flagged word, tap or click correct word	3. Press F7

To Insert a Slide Number

1 DOWNLOAD & SELECT SLIDES | 2 INSERT & FORMAT PICTURES | 3 INSERT & FORMAT SHAPES
4 INSERT & FORMAT WORDART | 5 FORMAT SLIDE BACKGROUNDS | **6 REVIEW & REVISE SLIDES**

PowerPoint can insert the slide number on your slides automatically to indicate where the slide is positioned within the presentation. The number location on the slide is determined by the presentation theme. You have the option to not display this slide number on the title slide. The following steps insert the slide number on all slides except the title slide.

1

- If necessary, display Slide 3 and then display the INSERT tab.

- Tap or click the Slide Number button (INSERT tab | Text group) to display the Header and Footer dialog box (Figure 2–77).

Q&A Why might I need to tap or click the Thumbnail pane?

If the final flagged word had been located in the Notes pane during the spell check, the insertion point would have been in the Notes pane. The page number, consequently, would have been inserted in the Notes pane instead of on the slide.

Figure 2–77

2

- Tap or click the Slide number check box (Header and Footer dialog box) to place a check mark in it.

- Tap or click the 'Don't show on title slide' check box (Header and Footer dialog box) to place a check mark in it (Figure 2–78).

Q&A Where does the slide number display on the slide?

Each theme determines where the slide number is displayed in the footer. In this theme, the slide number location is the left side of the footer, as indicated by the black box at the bottom of the Preview area.

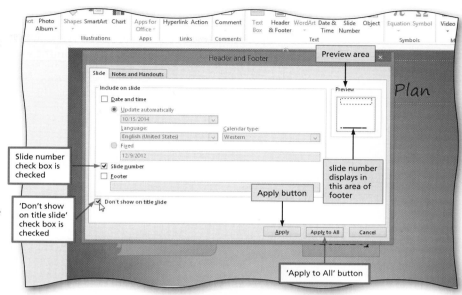

Figure 2–78

3

- Tap or click the Apply to All button (Header and Footer dialog box) to close the dialog box and insert the slide number on all slides except Slide 1 (Figure 2–79).

Q&A How does tapping or clicking the Apply to All button differ from tapping or clicking the Apply button?

The Apply button inserts the slide number only on the currently displayed slide whereas the Apply to All button inserts the slide number on every slide.

Figure 2–79

Other Ways

1. Tap or click Header & Footer button (INSERT tab | Text group), tap or click Slide Number box (Header and Footer dialog box), tap or click 'Slide number' and 'Don't show on title slide' boxes, tap or click Apply to All button

To Add a Transition between Slides

A final enhancement you will make in this presentation is to apply the Fracture transition in the Exciting category to all slides and increase the transition duration. The following steps apply this transition to the presentation.

1 Tap or click TRANSITIONS on the ribbon. Tap or click the More button (TRANSITIONS tab | Transition to This Slide group) to expand the Transitions gallery.

2 Tap or click the Fracture transition in the Exciting category to apply this transition.

3 Tap or click the Duration up arrow in the Timing group four times to change the transition speed from 02.00 to 03.00.

BTW

Certification
The Microsoft Office Specialist (MOS) program provides an opportunity for you to obtain a valuable industry credential — proof that you have the PowerPoint 2013 skills required by employers. For more information, visit the Certification resource on the Student Companion Site located on www.cengagebrain. com. For detailed instructions about accessing available resources, visit www.cengage.com/ct/ studentdownload or see the inside back cover of this book.

4 Tap or click the Preview Transitions button (TRANSITIONS tab | Preview area) to view the new transition time.

5 Tap or click the Apply To All button (TRANSITIONS tab | Timing group) to apply this transition and speed to all four slides in the presentation (Figure 2–80).

Q&A Can I apply a particular transition or duration to one slide and then change the transition or timing for a different slide in the presentation?

Yes. Select a slide and then select a transition and duration. Do not tap or click the Apply To All button. Repeat this process to apply the transition and duration to individual slides.

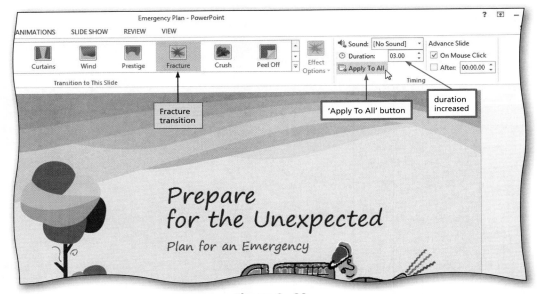

Figure 2–80

CONSIDER THIS

How can I use handouts to organize my speech?

As you develop a lengthy presentation with many visuals, handouts may help you organize your material. Print handouts with the maximum number of slides per page. Use scissors to cut each thumbnail and then place these miniature slide images adjacent to each other on a flat surface. Any type on the thumbnails will be too small to read, so the images will need to work with only the support of the verbal message you provide. You can rearrange these thumbnails as you organize your speech. When you return to your computer, you can rearrange the slides on your screen to match the order of your thumbnail printouts. Begin speaking the actual words you want to incorporate in the body of the talk. This process of glancing at the thumbnails and hearing yourself say the key ideas of the speech is one of the best methods of organizing and preparing for the actual presentation. Ultimately, when you deliver your speech in front of an audience, the images on the slides or on your note cards should be sufficient to remind you of the accompanying verbal message.

To Print Speaker Notes

Comments added to slides in the Notes pane give the speaker information that supplements the text on the slide. They will print with a small image of the slide at the top and the comments below the slide. The following steps print the speaker notes.

- Display Slide 1, tap or click FILE on the ribbon to open the Backstage view, and then tap or click the Print tab in the Backstage view to display Slide 1 in the Print gallery.

- Tap or click 'Full Page Slides' in the Settings area to display the Print gallery (Figure 2–81).

Q&A Why does the preview of my slide appear in color?
Your printer determines how the preview appears. If your printer is not capable of printing color images, the preview will not appear in color.

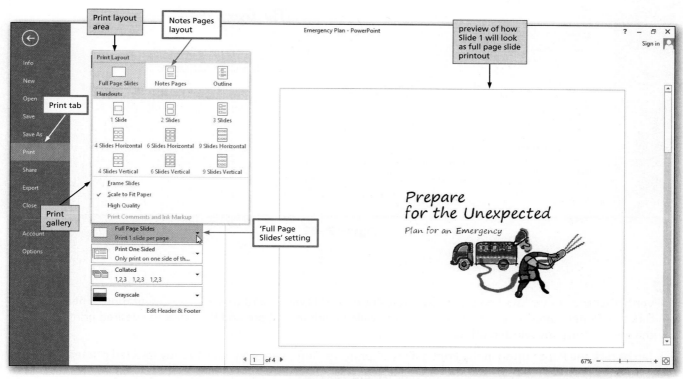

Figure 2–81

2

● Tap or click Notes Pages in the Print Layout area to select this option and then tap or click the Next Page button three times to display a preview of Slide 4 (Figure 2–82).

Q&A Can I preview Slides 1, 2, or 3 now?
Yes. Click the Previous Page button to preview the other slides.

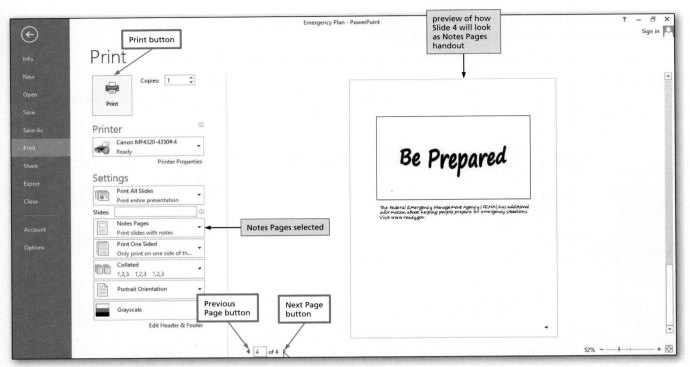

Figure 2–82

3

● Verify that the printer listed on the Printer Status button will print a hard copy of the presentation. If necessary, click the Printer Status button to display a list of available printer options and then click the desired printer to change the currently selected printer.

● Tap or click the Print button in the Print gallery to print the notes pages on the currently selected printer.

● When the printer stops, retrieve the hard copy (Figure 2–83).

Q&A Why does the background display on my printout but not in the figure?
Graphics are displayed depending upon the settings in the Print gallery. For example, the background will print if Color is specified whereas it will not with a Grayscale or Pure Black and White setting.

BTW
Printing Document Properties
To print document properties, tap or click FILE on the ribbon to open the Backstage view, tap or click the Print tab in the Backstage view to display the Print gallery, tap or click the first button in the Settings area to display a list of options specifying what you can print, tap or click Document Info in the list to specify you want to print the document properties instead of the actual document, and then tap or click the Print button in the Print gallery to print the document properties on the currently selected printer.

(a) Slide 1 – Speaker Notes

(b) Slide 2 – Speaker Notes

Figure 2–83 (Continued)

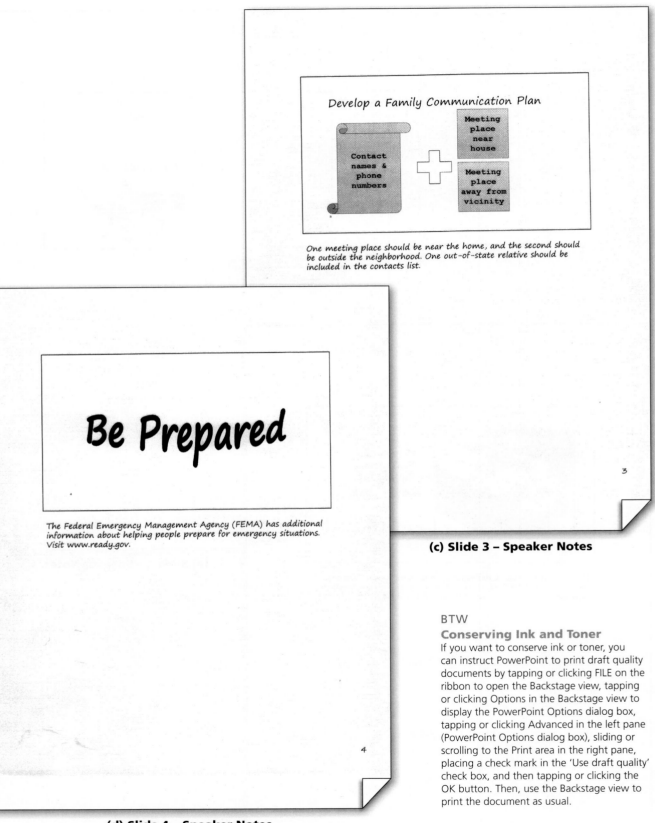

(c) Slide 3 – Speaker Notes

(d) Slide 4 – Speaker Notes

Figure 2–83 (Handouts printed using a black-and-white printer) (Continued)

BTW

Conserving Ink and Toner
If you want to conserve ink or toner, you can instruct PowerPoint to print draft quality documents by tapping or clicking FILE on the ribbon to open the Backstage view, tapping or clicking Options in the Backstage view to display the PowerPoint Options dialog box, tapping or clicking Advanced in the left pane (PowerPoint Options dialog box), sliding or scrolling to the Print area in the right pane, placing a check mark in the 'Use draft quality' check box, and then tapping or clicking the OK button. Then, use the Backstage view to print the document as usual.

Other Ways

1. Press CTRL+P, press ENTER

To Save the Presentation, Sign Out of a Microsoft Account, and Exit PowerPoint

You have made several changes to the presentation since you last saved it. Thus, you should save it again. The following steps save the presentation, sign out of your Microsoft account, and exit PowerPoint.

1 Tap or click the Save button on the Quick Access Toolbar.

2 If you wish to sign out of your Microsoft account, open the Backstage view, tap or click the Account tab to display the Account gallery, and then tap or click the Sign out link, which displays the Remove Account dialog box. If a Can't remove Windows accounts dialog box appears instead of the Remove Account dialog box, click the OK button and skip the remaining steps.

3 Tap or click the Yes button (Remove Account dialog box) to sign out of your Microsoft account on this computer.

4 Tap or click the Back button in the upper-left corner of the Backstage view to return to the presentation.

5a If you have one PowerPoint presentation open, tap or click the Close button on the right side of the title bar to close the open document and exit PowerPoint.

5b If you have multiple PowerPoint presentations open, press and hold or right-click the PowerPoint app button on the taskbar and then tap or click 'Close all windows' on the shortcut menu, or press ALT+F4 to close all open presentations and exit PowerPoint.

BTW
Quick Reference
For a table that lists how to complete the tasks covered in this book using touch gestures, the mouse, ribbon, shortcut menu, and keyboard, see the Quick Reference Summary at the back of this book, or visit the Quick Reference resource on the Student Companion Site located on www.cengagebrain.com. For detailed instructions about accessing available resources, visit www.cengage.com/ct/studentdownload or see the inside back cover of this book.

Chapter Summary

In this chapter you have learned how to insert and format pictures, add and format shapes, insert and format WordArt, add slide backgrounds, find and replace text, check spelling, add notes, and print speaker notes. The items listed below include all the new PowerPoint skills you have learned in this chapter, with the tasks grouped by activity.

Download and Modify Themes
Search for and Download an Online Theme (PPT 77)
Delete a Slide (PPT 79)

Format Fonts
Change the Font (PPT 98)
Format Text Using the Format Painter (PPT 101)

Format Slide Backgrounds
Insert a Picture to Create a Background (PPT 108)
Format the Background Picture Fill Transparency (PPT 109)
Insert a Texture Fill (PPT 110)
Format the Background Texture Fill Transparency (PPT 111)
Insert a Gradient Fill (PPT 111)

Insert and Format Pictures
Insert a Picture into a Slide without a Content Placeholder (PPT 83)
Change a Picture (PPT 85)
Correct a Picture (PPT 87)
Apply a Picture Style (PPT 87)
Add a Picture Border (PPT 88)
Change a Picture Border Color (PPT 89)
Apply Picture Effects (PPT 90)

Insert and Format Shapes
Add a Shape (PPT 92)
Resize a Shape (PPT 93)
Add Other Shapes (PPT 94)
Apply a Shape Style (PPT 95)
Add Text to a Shape (PPT 97)
Copy and Paste a Shape (PPT 101)

Insert and Format WordArt
    Insert WordArt (PPT 103)
    Change the WordArt Shape (PPT 104)
    Apply a WordArt Text Fill (PPT 106)
    Change the Weight of the WordArt Outline
        (PPT 106)
    Change the Color of the WordArt Outline
        (PPT 107)

Review and Enhance Slides and Printouts
    Find and Replace Text (PPT 113)
    Find and Insert a Synonym (PPT 114)
    Add Notes (PPT 115)
    Check Spelling (PPT 117)
    Insert a Slide Number (PPT 118)
    Print Speaker Notes (PPT 121)

CONSIDER THIS

What decisions will you need to make when creating your next presentation?
Use these guidelines as you complete the assignments in this chapter and create your own slide show decks outside of this class.

1. Determine if an online theme can help you design and develop the presentation efficiently and effectively.

2. Identify personal pictures that would create interest and promote the message being presented.

3. Consider modifying pictures.

    a) Add corrections.

    b) Add styles.

    c) Add effects.

    d) Add and format borders.

4. Locate shapes that supplement the verbal and written message.

    a) Size and position them aesthetically on slides.

    b) Add styles.

5. Develop WordArt that emphasizes major presentation messages.

    a) Modify the shape.

    b) Change the weight and color to coordinate with slide elements.

6. Format individual slide backgrounds.

    a) Add and modify fills.

    b) Insert a picture.

7. Change fonts to emphasize particular slide components.

8. Search for synonyms that help express your thoughts.

9. Create speaker notes.

10. Check spelling.

Apply Your Knowledge

Reinforce the skills and apply the concepts you learned in this chapter.

Changing the Background and Adding Photos and WordArt

Note: To complete this assignment, you will be required to use the Data Files for Students. Visit www.cengage.com/ct/studentdownload for detailed instructions or contact your instructor for information about accessing the required files.

Instructions: Run PowerPoint. Open the presentation, Apply 2-1 Bicycle, from the Data Files for Students.

The five slides in the presentation discuss bicycle safety. The document you open is an unformatted presentation. You are to add photos, apply picture styles, add WordArt, change slide layouts, apply a transition, and use the Format Painter so the slides look like Figures 2–84a through 2–84e on pages PPT 127 through 130.

Perform the following tasks:

1. On the title slide, use your name in place of Student Name and bold and italicize your name.

2. If requested by your instructor, change your first name to your mother's first name on the title slide.

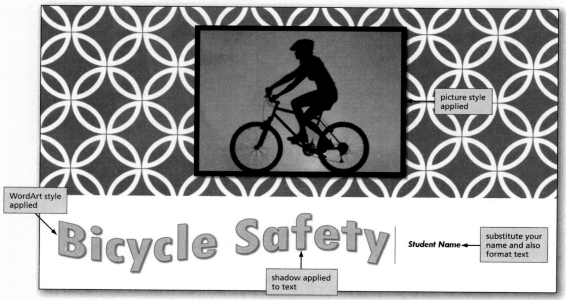

(a) Slide 1

Figure 2–84 (Continued)

Continued >

Apply Your Knowledge *continued*

(b) Slide 2

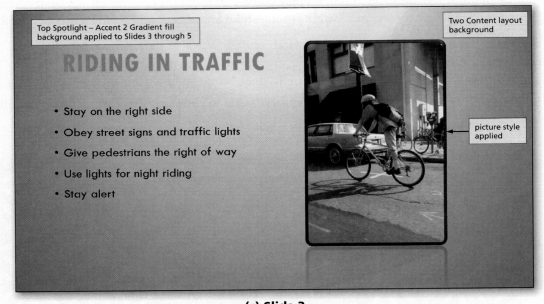

(c) Slide 3

Figure 2–84

3. Increase the title text font size to 60 point. Apply the WordArt style, Fill – Blue, Accent 2, Outline – Accent 2 (the third style in the first row). Apply the Transform text effect, Wave 2 (the second effect in the fifth Warp area row) to this text. Also add a shadow to this text.

4. Apply the Moderate Frame, Black picture style (the fifth style in the second row) to the photo on Slide 1, as shown in Figure 2–84a on the previous page.

5. On Slide 2, change the layout to Title and Content. Increase the title text font to 54 point, change the font color to Green (the sixth color in the Standard Colors row), and then bold this text. Increase the bulleted list font to 24 point, as shown in Figure 2–84b.

6. Create a background on Slide 2 by inserting the photo called Cyclist, which is available on the Data Files for Students.

7. On Slide 2, type **The average cost for a routine bike inspection is $20.** in the Notes pane.

8. On Slides 3 through 5, change the layout to Two Content. Insert the photos, as shown in Figures 2–84c through 2–84e on the next page. The photos to be inserted are called Bicycle2, Bicycle3, and Bicycle4 and are available on the Data Files for Students. Also, change the background to Top Spotlight – Accent 2 gradient fill (the second gradient in the second row) in the Preset gradients gallery on Slides 3 through 5.

9. On Slide 3, adjust the size of the photo and apply the Reflected Bevel, Black picture style (the fourth style in the fourth row) and change the photo brightness to +20% (the fourth picture in the third row in the Brightness and Contrast area).

10. On Slide 3, type **Laws for bicycles on the road vary in every state and country.** in the Notes pane.

11. On Slide 4, adjust the size of the photo, apply the Metal Oval picture style (the seventh style in the fourth row), and then change the photo border to Black, Text 1 (the second color in the first Theme Colors row), as shown in Figure 2–84d.

12. Use the thesaurus to change the word, suitable, to appropriate.

13. Type **Hydration is critical. Make sure your bike is equipped with a bottle holder.** in the Notes pane.

14. On Slide 5, adjust the size of the photo and apply the Bevel Perspective picture style (the first style in the fourth row) to the photo, as shown in Figure 2–84e on the next page.

15. Use the Format Painter to format the title text and the bulleted lists on Slides 3 through 5 with the same features as the title text and bulleted list on Slide 2.

16. Apply the Wind transition in the Exciting category to all slides. Change the duration to 2.50 seconds.

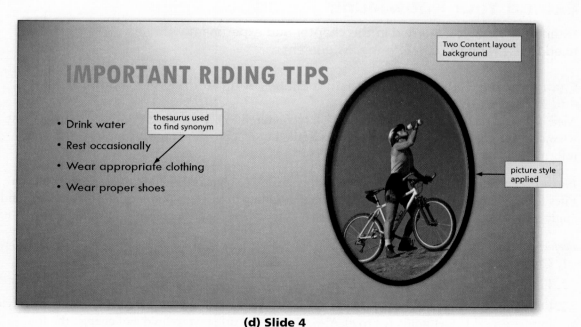

(d) Slide 4

Figure 2–84 (Continued)

Continued >

Apply Your Knowledge *continued*

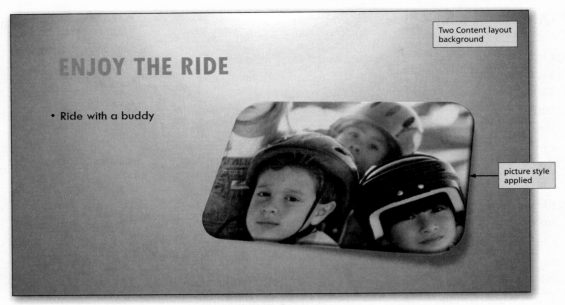

(e) Slide 5
Figure 2–84 (Continued)

17. Save the presentation using the file name, Apply 2-1 Bicycle Safety.

18. Submit the revised document in the format specified by your instructor.

19. ✳ In Step 4 you applied the Moderate Frame, Black picture style. How did this style improve the slide?

Extend Your Knowledge

Extend the skills you learned in this chapter and experiment with new skills. You may need to use Help to complete the assignment.

Changing Slide Backgrounds, Inserting Shapes and WordArt, and Finding and Replacing Text

Note: To complete this assignment, you will be required to use the Data Files for Students. Visit www.cengage.com/ct/studentdownload for detailed instructions or contact your instructor for information about accessing the required files.

Instructions: Run PowerPoint. Open the presentation, Extend 2-1 Field Archery, from the Data Files for Students. You will create backgrounds including inserting a photo to create a background, apply a WordArt Style and Effect, and add shapes to create the presentation shown in Figure 2–85.

Perform the following tasks:
1. Change the theme to Wisp and choose the second variant.

2. Find and replace the words, Bow and Arrow, with the word, Archery, on all slides.

3. On Slides 2 through 4, change the background style to Top Spotlight – Accent 5 (the fifth style in the second Preset gradients row). Also, change the title text to bold and change the font color to Orange, Accent 1 (the fifth color in the first Theme Colors row) on Slides 2 through 4.

4. On the title slide (Figure 2–85a), create a background by inserting the photo called Bow and Arrow, which is available on the Data Files for Students. Change the transparency to 50%.

5. Apply the WordArt style, Fill - Orange, Accent 1, Shadow (the second style in the first row), to the title text, center the text, and increase the font size to 72 point. Apply the WordArt Transform text effect, Arch Up (the first effect in the first Follow Path row), and then bold this text. Also, move the title text above the archer in the photo on the title slide.

6. If requested by your instructor, add your current or previous pet's name as the Slide 1 subtitle text.

7. On Slides 2 through 4, increase the font size of the first-level bulleted text to 22 point and the second-level bulleted text to 20 point.

8. On Slide 2, enlarge the illustration to the size shown in Figure 2–85b on the next page, apply the Reflected Bevel, Black picture style (the fourth style in the fourth row), and then move it to the location shown in the figure.

9. On Slide 3, apply the Soft Edge Oval picture style (the sixth style in the third row) to the photo and move the photo to the upper-right area of the slide. Also, apply the Orange, 18 pt glow, Accent color 1 glow variation (the first variation in the fourth Glow Variations row) to this photo, as shown in Figure 2–85c on the next page.

10. On Slide 4, select the Oval shape and while holding down the Shift key, draw a circle 6" × 6", as shown in Figure 2–85d on page PPT 133. Fill this shape with Black, Text 1, Lighter 15% and then change the shape outline to No Outline. Then copy and paste this shape two times. Change the shape size of the first pasted circle to 4" × 4". Hint: Use the Size and Position group on the PICTURE TOOLS FORMAT tab to enter the exact measurement of the shape. Change the Shape Fill to White and then center this shape over the original black circle using the Smart Guides. Select the second pasted circle and change the shape size to 2" × 2", the Shape Fill to Black, Text 1, Lighter 15% and then center this shape over the white circle shape using the Smart Guides.

photo inserted as background and transparency changed

bold and shadow the WordArt text and move up to new location

color variant changed

Wisp document theme

(a) Slide 1

Figure 2–85 (Continued)

Continued >

Extend Your Knowledge *continued*

(b) Slide 2

(c) Slide 3
Figure 2–85

11. Insert an arrow on Slide 4 by using the Right Arrow shape under Block Arrows. Size the arrow to 1.5" × 6" and then copy and paste this arrow shape two times. Copy and paste the three paragraphs from the bulleted list into the three arrow shapes. Select the text on one of these shapes, change the font size to 28 point, change the font color to black, center the text, and

(d) Slide 4
Figure 2–85 (Continued)

then bold the text. Use the Format Painter to format the text in the two arrows with the same features as the first arrow. Move the arrows so that each one points to the correct ring, as shown in Figure 2–85d. Delete the bulleted text in the text placeholder.

12. Apply an appropriate transition to all slides.

13. Save the presentation using the file name, Extend 2-1 Field Archery Scoring.

14. Submit the revised document in the format specified by your instructor.

15. ✸ In this assignment, you changed the transparency of the inserted background photo on the title slide to 50%. How did this transparency change enhance your title slide?

Analyze, Correct, Improve

Analyze a presentation, correct all errors, and improve it.

***

Correcting Formatting, Adding Slide Numbers, and Correcting Spelling
Note: To complete this assignment, you will be required to use the Data Files for Students. Visit www.cengage.com/ct/studentdownload for detailed instructions or contact your instructor for information about accessing the required files.

Instructions: Run PowerPoint. Open the presentation, Analyze 2-1 Avoid the Flu, from the Data Files for Students. This presentation contains four slides and explains why doctors recommend you should get an annual flu shot. Figure 2–86 on the next page shows the uncorrected title slide. Modify the slides by making the indicated corrections and improvements.

1. Correct

   a. Change the variant to blue (the second variant in the gallery).

   b. Decrease the font size of the Slide 1 title text and change the font color. Also, capitalize the letter F in the word, flu.

   c. Use your name in place of Student Name on Slide 1.

Continued >

Analyze, Correct, Improve *continued*

d. If requested by your instructor, change your first name on Slide 1 to your mother's first name.

e. On Slides 2 through 4, adjust the photo sizes and move them so they do not overlap text and are the appropriate dimensions for the slide content.

f. On all slides, adjust font sizes and font color so they are the appropriate size and enhance the presentation.

g. Correct the spelling errors on all slides.

2. Improve

a. Increase the size of the medical symbol on the title slide and move the symbol to the right side of the slide.

b. On Slides 2 through 4, change the color of the title text and bold all the titles.

c. Change the photo border colors on all slides to make them more visually attractive.

d. Add the slide number to all slides except the title slide.

e. Apply the same transition and duration to all slides.

f. Save the presentation using the file name, Analyze 2-1 – Get Your Flu Shot.

g. Submit the revised document in the format specified by your instructor.

3. ✳ Which errors existed in the starting file? How did changing the variant color help? When you adjusted the photo sizes, how did you determine their final sizes?

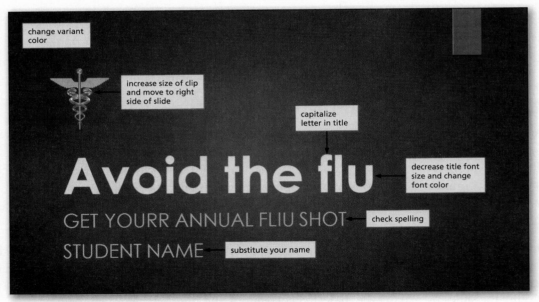

Slide 1

Figure 2–86

In the Labs

Design and/or create a presentation using the guidelines, concepts, and skills presented in this chapter. Labs 1 and 2, which increase in difficulty, require you to create solutions based on what you learned in the chapter; Lab 3 requires you to create a solution, which uses cloud and web technologies, by learning and investigating on your own from general guidance.

Lab 1: Creating a Presentation Inserting Photos, Applying Picture Styles, and Inserting Shapes

Problem: Your creative cooking class has volunteered to manage a bake sale to raise funds for victims of a tornado in a neighboring town. To encourage more students to participate in the bake sale, you decide to put together a presentation that would run in the cafeteria. You want to show your audience how easy it is to make an apple pie. Create the slides shown in Figure 2–87.

Instructions: Perform the following tasks:

1. Create a new presentation using the Retrospect theme. Do not change the brown variant.

2. On Slide 1, create a background by inserting the photo called Apple Pie from the Data Files for Students, as shown in Figure 2–87a. Change the transparency to 53%.

3. Type **Homemade Apple Pie** as the Slide 1 title text. Press the ENTER key after the word, Homemade, so the text is on two lines, and then center the text. Apply the WordArt style Fill – Orange, Accent 2, Outline – Accent 2 (the third style in the first row). Change the text fill to Dark Red (the first color in the Standard Colors row), and then change the text outline color to Green (the sixth color in the Standard Colors row) and the text outline weight to 3 pt. Also, apply the Transform text Effect, Chevron Up (the first effect in the second Warp row), to this text. Position this WordArt, as shown in Figure 2–87a. Type **BAKE SALE – SATURDAY JANUARY 20** in the subtitle placeholder. Change the font to MV Boli, increase the font size to 30 point, bold this text, and then center the text, as shown in the figure.

4. Create Slides 2 through 4 with the Two Content layout, Slide 5 with the Content with Caption layout, and Slide 6 with the Picture with Caption layout.

(a) Slide 1

Figure 2–87 (Continued)

Continued >

In the Labs *continued*

5. Type the title and content and insert all photos on Slides 2 through 5, as shown in Figures 2–87b through 2–87e. The photos to be inserted are called Apples, Ingredients, Cooks, and Apple Pie Slice, and are available on the Data Files for Students. Size the photos and then use the Smart Guides to position these images. You may want to zoom the slides to help you align these graphic elements.

6. On Slide 2, increase the title text size to 54 point, change the font color to Dark Red, and then bold this text. Use the Format Painter to apply these formatting changes to the title text on Slides 3 and 4. On Slide 2, change the list font size to 24 point. Apply the Bevel Perspective picture style (the first style in the fourth row) to the photo, change the border color to Light Green (the fifth color in the Standard Colors row), and then change the border weight to 6 pt, as shown in Figure 2–87b.

(b) Slide 2

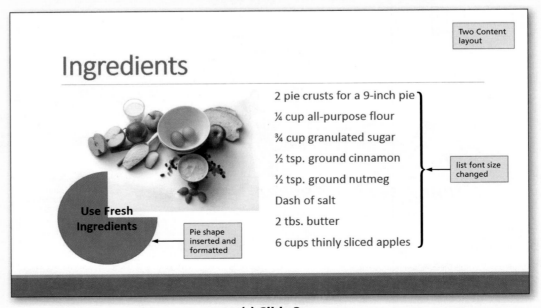

(c) Slide 3

Figure 2–87

7. On Slide 3, change the list font size to 24 point. Insert the Pie shape located in the Basic Shapes area to the lower-left corner of the slide. Apply the Colored Fill – Brown, Accent 4 (the eighth color in the first row) to the shape. Size the shape as shown in the figure. Type the text, **Use Fresh Ingredients** in the shape. Bold this text, and change the font size to 24 point, as shown in Figure 2–87c.

8. On Slide 4, change the list font size to 20 point. Apply the Snip Diagonal Corner, White picture style (the first style in the third row) to the photo, change the border color to Dark Red (the first color in the Standard Colors row), and then apply the Reflection picture effect, Tight Reflection, touching (the first effect in the first Reflection Variations row). Copy the pie shape from Slide 3 and paste it in the bottom center of the slide. Type the text, **Bake 40 to 50 Minutes,** as shown in Figure 2–87d.

(d) Slide 4

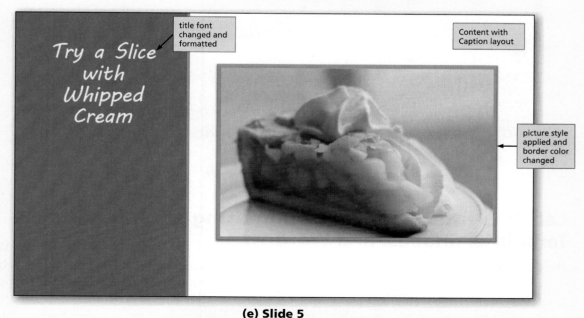

(e) Slide 5

Figure 2–87 (Continued)

Continued >

In the Labs *continued*

9. On Slide 5, change the title text font to MV Boli, change the font size to 40 point, and then center this text. Apply the Simple Frame, White picture style (the first style in the first row) to the slice of pie photo and then change the border color to Orange, Accent 1 (the fifth color in the Theme Colors row), as shown in Figure 2–87e on the previous page.

10. On Slide 6, change the caption title font to MV Boli, change the font size to 32 point, and then bold this text. Select the photo, click the Change Picture button (PICTURE TOOLS FORMAT tab | Adjust group), and then insert the Bake Sale illustration from the Data Files for Students, as shown in Figure 2–87f.

11. If requested by your instructor, type the name of the city or county in which you were born into the subtitle text placeholder on Slide 6.

12. Apply the Peel Off transition in the Exciting category to all slides. Change the duration to 2.5 seconds.

13. Check the spelling and correct any errors. Save the presentation using the file name, Lab 2-1 Homemade Apple Pie.

14. Submit the document in the format specified by your instructor.

15. ✸ What is the significance of changing the transparency of the photo on the title slide? Why did you put a red border on the photo on Slide 4? Explain why you did not follow the 7 × 7 rule on Slides 3 and 4.

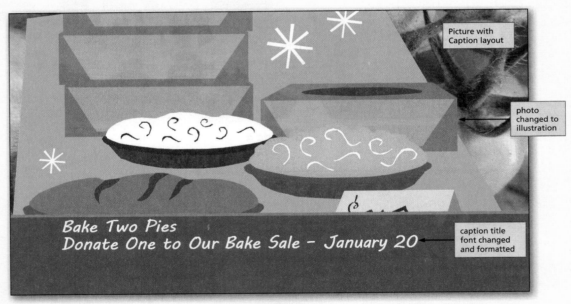

(f) Slide 6
Figure 2–87 (Continued)

Lab 2: Creating a Presentation Using an Online Theme Template, Shapes, and WordArt

Problem: Your local Chamber of Commerce is presenting a seminar to local business owners about ways to expand their business. Because you are majoring in business, your teacher thought that attending this meeting would be a good experience for you. He asked the Chamber of Commerce president if you could submit some ideas for the seminar. You decide to put together the presentation shown in Figure 2–88.

Instructions: Perform the following tasks:

1. Create a new presentation using the Business project plan presentation (widescreen) in the Business category under Suggested searches.

2. Delete Slides 7 through 14.

3. Apply the Two Content layout to Slide 2, the Alternate Content with Caption layout to Slide 3, the Content with Caption layout to Slide 4, the Title only layout to Slide 5, and the Section Header layout to Slide 6. Delete all titles and text content from Slides 2 through 6. Type the new title and text content for Slides 2, 3, and 4, as shown in Figures 2–88b through 2–88d on the next page.

4. Insert the photos and illustration shown in Figures 2–88b through 2–88e from the Data Files for Students. The photos and illustration are called Advertising, Delivery, Customer, and Call Center. Apply the Canvas texture fill (the second texture in the first row) to Slides 2 through 5 and change the transparency to 35%.

5. On the title slide, type the new title and subtitle content, increase the font size of the subtitle text to 28 point, and then change the font color to Orange (the third color in the Standard Colors row), as shown in Figure 2–88a.

6. If requested by your instructor, add the name of your hometown after the word, Business, in the subtitle placeholder. Type the word **in** before the name of your hometown.

7. On Slide 2, increase the font size of the title to 40 point, change the font color to Indigo, Text 2, Darker 25% (the fourth color in the fifth Theme Colors row), and then bold this text. Increase the font size of the bulleted list to 24 point. Apply the Perspective Shadow, White picture style (the fourth style in the third row) and resize the photo, as shown in Figure 2–88b.

8. On Slide 3, increase the font size of the title to 40 point and then bold this text. Increase the font size of the text to 24 point. Apply the Simple Frame picture style (the first style in the first row) to the photo, as shown in Figure 2–88c.

9. On Slide 4, increase the font size of the title text to 40 point, change the font color to Indigo, Text 2, Darker 25% (the fourth color in the fifth Theme Colors row), and then bold this text. Increase the font size of the bulleted list text to 24 point. Apply the Metal Frame picture style (the third style in the first row) to the photo, as shown in Figure 2–88d.

10. On Slide 5, increase the font size of the title to 40 point, change the font color to Indigo, Text 2, Darker 25% (the fourth color in the fifth Theme Colors row), and then bold this text. Move

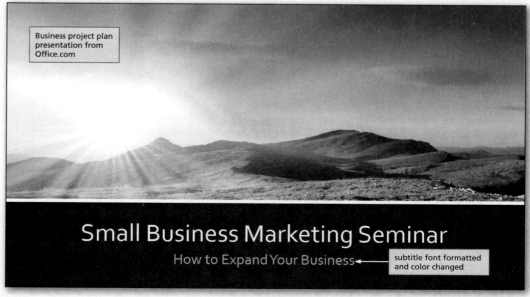

(a) Slide 1

Figure 2–88 (Continued)

Continued >

In the Labs *continued*

(b) Slide 2

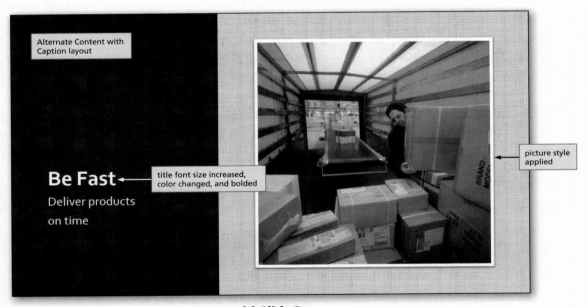

(c) Slide 3

Figure 2–88

the photo to the right side of the slide and then apply the Soft Edge Oval picture style (the sixth style in the third row) to the photo, as shown in Figure 2–88e.

11. Insert the Diamond shape located in the Basic Shapes area, resize the shape so that it is approximately 3.42" × 3.93", and then right-click the shape, click Style, and apply the Subtle Effect – Red, Accent 6 Shape Quick Style (the seventh style in the fourth row). Copy and paste the shape two times and move the shapes, as shown in Figure 2–88e. Type the text into the shape and then increase the text size to 24 point.

12. On Slide 6, type the new title and subtitle content, and create a background by inserting the Ladder photo from the Data Files for Students. Change the transparency to 40%. Decrease the title font size to 44 point, change the font color to Indigo, Text 2, Darker 25% (the fourth color in the fifth Theme Colors row), right-align the text, and then bold this text. Increase the font size of the subtitle text to 28 point, change the font color to Indigo, Text 2 (the fourth color in the first Theme

(d) Slide 4

(e) Slide 5

Figure 2–88 (Continued)

Colors row), and then right-align this text, as shown in Figure 2–88f. Insert the Pentagon shape located in the Block Arrows area and then apply the Subtle Effect - Lime, Accent 1 Quick Style (the second style in the fourth row) to the shape. Type **Success** in the shape, change the font to Forte, change the font size to 60 point, and then change the font color to Gray – 80%, Text 1.

13. Change the transition to Doors in the Exciting category to all slides. Change the duration to 2.75 seconds.

14. Check spelling and correct all errors. Save the presentation using the file name, Lab 2-2 Small Business Seminar.

15. Submit the revised document in the format specified by your instructor.

16. ✳ You searched for an online theme under Business. Why? Do you think any of the other themes would have worked well for your presentation? How does changing the slide layouts help your presentation?

Continued >

In the Labs *continued*

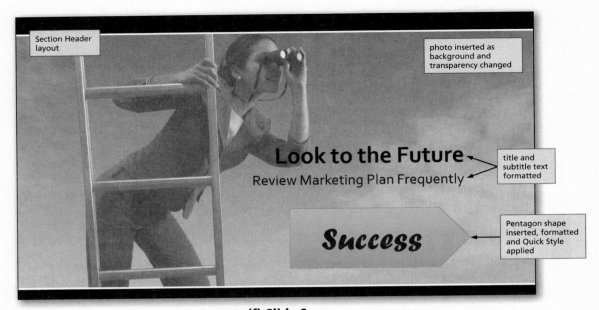

(f) Slide 6
Figure 2–88 (Continued)

Lab 3: Expand Your World: Cloud and Web Technologies
Modifying a Presentation Using the PowerPoint Web App

Problem: The fire chief in your community is planning a family security and safety workshop at your local hardware store. He has asked you to help him publicize the event, and he wants to focus on urging families to prepare for unexpected situations. You inform him that you have created an Emergency Plan presentation for your computer class, and he would like you to customize the content of these slides slightly to promote the workshop.

Instructions:

1. Sign in to your Microsoft account and run the PowerPoint web app.

2. Create a presentation with content similar to what you used for the Emergency Plan presentation.

3. On the title slide, add the name and address of the nearest hardware store. In addition, add the date that is exactly one month from today and a starting time of noon. Add the name of one of your elementary school teachers as the fire chief's name on this slide.

4. Save the presentation using the file name, Lab 2-3 Local Safety Workshop.

5. Submit the assignment in the format specified by your instructor.

6. ✺ Other than the content the chief asked you to include on the title slide, how does the presentation you created using the PowerPoint web app differ from the presentation you created in the Chapter 2 project? Which formatting features are not available in the web app? Do you think using the web app has sufficient functions to develop effective presentations? Why or why not?

✳ Consider This: Your Turn

Apply your creative thinking and problem-solving skills to design and implement a solution.

1. Design and Create a Presentation about Skydiving from New Heights

Personal

Part 1: Members of your skydiving club are discussing free-falling records of new heights reached by skydivers over the past years. They've been following the news reports about the man from Austria, 43-year-old Felix Baumgartner, who broke a record by completing the highest skydive and traveling faster than the speed of sound without being in an aircraft. At a recent meeting with your fellow sky-divers, many questions arose as to how this man was able to accomplish this, what risks were involved, and how long he trained for this venture. You researched facts about this record-breaking skydive and learned that the height he dove from (128,100 feet above Earth) was more than three times the cruising altitude of a passenger jet (hitting Mach 1.24 or 833.9 mph). It was the height at which wa-ter boils. If his pressurized spacesuit had malfunctioned, it would have been disastrous: a leak in his spacesuit would have caused his blood to boil instantly. Half of his nine-minute descent was a free fall of 119,846 feet. He trained for seven years. Use the concepts and techniques presented in this chapter to prepare a presentation with a minimum of four slides that explores this subject. Select a suitable theme, and include a title slide, bulleted lists, shapes, and WordArt. The presentation should contain photos and illustrations appropriately resized. Eight photos and illustrations are available on the Data Files for Students: Skydiving1, Skydiving2, Skydiving3, Skydiving4, Skydiving5, Skydiving6, Skydiv-ing7, and Skydiving8. You can add your own digital photos or photos from Office.com if they are ap-propriate for this topic. Apply picture styles and effects. Add a title slide and closing slide to complete your presentation. Format the title slide with a shape. Format the background with at least one photo and apply a background texture to at least one slide. Review and revise your presentation as needed. Submit your assignment in the format specified by your instructor.

Part 2: ✳ You made several decisions while creating the presentation in this assignment: where to place text, how to format the text (such as font, font size, and where to use WordArt), which graphi-cal image(s) to use, what styles and effects to apply, where to position the graphical image, how to format the graphical images, and which shapes to use to add interest to the presentation. What was the rationale behind each of these decisions? When you reviewed the document, what further revi-sions did you make and why? Where would you recommend showing this slide show?

2. Design and Create a Presentation about Teaching Geometry to Elementary Students

Professional

Part 1: You work part time for a tutoring agency. Because you are majoring in math, your boss asked if you would put together a teaching aid for teaching geometry to the elementary students. You decide to create a presentation with some basic shapes: squares, circles, and triangles. To make the slides appeal to your young students, you decide to use shapes and add photos and illustra-tions. Geometry for elementary students also can cover parallel lines, intersecting lines, and how intersecting lines form angles. You can show them shapes such as pentagons, heptagons, and octa-gons. They can look for shapes in their environment and draw them. You can teach them that even though a shape is turned upside down or rotated, it is still the same shape even if it looks different. Use the concepts and techniques presented in this chapter to create a presentation with at least four slides. Select a suitable theme, include a title slide, and add WordArt. Review and revise your pre-sentation as needed. Submit your assignment in the format specified by your instructor.

Part 2: ✳ You made several decisions while creating the presentation in this assignment: where to place text, how to format the text (such as font, font size, and where to use WordArt), which graphical image(s) to use, what styles and effects to apply, where to position the graphical images,

Continued >

Consider This: Your Turn *continued*

and which shapes to use to add interest to the presentation. What was the rationale behind each of these decisions? When you reviewed the document, what further revisions did you make and why? Where would you recommend showing this slide show?

3. Design and Create a Presentation about Coyotes Roaming in Your Neighborhood
Research and Collaboration

Part 1: Many of your neighbors are concerned about the coyotes that have been spotted in your neighborhood. With the help of a friend who works part time at a local wildlife refuge, you suggest that each of you do some research about coyotes and discuss your findings and put together a presentation to share at the next town hall meeting. Your main concern is that the coyotes are finding outdoor food sources such as pet food, uncovered garbage cans, and areas near homes where rodents may be nesting. You want to make suggestions to your neighbors about how to deter the coyotes from staying in your neighborhood. You ask your friend who works at the wildlife refuge to research the habits of coyotes. You will gather information from the local newspaper where there have been articles written about the coyotes and your other neighbor will talk to other people in the neighbor about sightings of coyotes and possible photographs. After coordinating all the facts about the coyotes, use the concepts and techniques presented in this chapter to prepare a presentation with a minimum of four slides that explores the subject of coyotes. Summarize your research findings and type this information in the Notes pane of each slide. Select a suitable theme, include a title slide, bulleted lists, shapes, and WordArt. Seven photos and illustrations are available on the Data Files for Students: Coyote1, Coyote2, Coyote3, Coyote4, Coyote5, Coyote6, and Coyote7. Change the brightness and contrast for at least one photo. Insert shapes and WordArt to enhance your presentation. Apply a transition in the Subtle area to all slides and increase the duration. Review and revise your presentation as needed. Submit your assignment in the format specified by your instructor.

Part 2: ☀ You made several decisions while creating the presentation in this assignment: where to place text, how to format the text (such as font, font size, and where to use WordArt), which graphical image(s) to use, what styles and effects to apply, where to position the graphical image, what shapes to use to add interest to the presentation. What was the rationale behind each of these decisions? When you reviewed the document, what further revisions did you make and why? Where would you recommend showing this slide show?

Learn Online
Reinforce what you learned in this chapter with games, exercises, training, and many other online activities and resources.

Student Companion Site Reinforcement activities and resources are available at no additional cost on www.cengagebrain.com. Visit www.cengage.com/ct/studentdownload for detailed instructions about accessing the resources available at the Student Companion Site.

SAM Put your skills into practice with SAM! If you have a SAM account, go to www.cengage.com/sam2013 to access SAM assignments for this chapter.

3 Reusing a Presentation and Adding Media and Animation

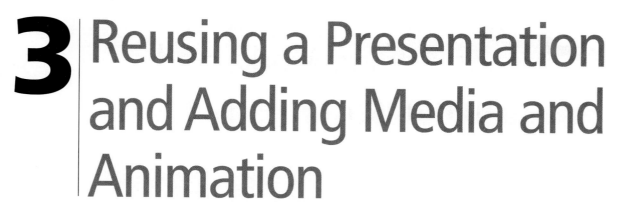

Microsoft product screenshots used with permission from Microsoft Corporation.

Objectives

You will have mastered the material in this chapter when you can:

- Color a photo

- Add an artistic effect to a photo

- Align paragraph text

- Change views

- Ungroup, change the color of, and regroup an illustration

- Copy a slide element from one slide to another

- Insert and edit a video clip

- Insert audio

- Control audio and video clips

- Insert entrance, emphasis, and exit effects

- Control animation timing

- Change theme colors

- Change a theme and variant on one slide

- Print handouts

3 | Reusing a Presentation and Adding Media and Animation

Introduction

At times, you will need to revise a PowerPoint presentation. Changes may include inserting and adding effects to photos, altering the colors of photos and illustrations, and updating visual elements displayed on a slide. Applying a different theme, changing fonts, and substituting graphical elements can give a slide show an entirely new look. Adding media, including sounds, video, and music, can enhance a presentation and help audience members retain the information being presented. Adding animation can reinforce important points and enliven a presentation.

Project — Presentation with Video, Audio, Animation, and Photos with Effects

The project in this chapter follows graphical guidelines and uses PowerPoint to create the presentation shown in Figure 3–1. The slides in this revised presentation, which discusses Watch for Motorcycles, have a variety of audio and visual elements. For example, the photos have artistic effects applied that soften the photos and help the audience focus on other elements on the slides. The car clip has colors that blend well with the background. The bullet list is animated with entrance, emphasis, and exit effects. The video has been edited to play only the portion with Watch for Motorcycles and has effects to add audience interest. Motorcycle sounds integrate with the visual elements. Overall, the slides have myriad media elements and effects that are exciting for your audience to watch and hear.

BTW

Using Media in Presentations

PowerPoint makes it easy to insert media into a presentation. Well-produced video clips add value when they help explain a procedure or show movement that cannot be captured in a photo or illustration. A sound can emphasize an action. Before you insert these files on a slide, however, consider whether they really add any value to your overall slide show. If you are inserting them just because you can, you might want to reconsider your decision. Audiences quickly tire of extraneous movement and sounds on slides, and they will find these media clips annoying. Keep in mind that the audience's attention should focus primarily on the presenter; extraneous or inappropriate media files may divert their attention and, in turn, decrease the quality of the presentation.

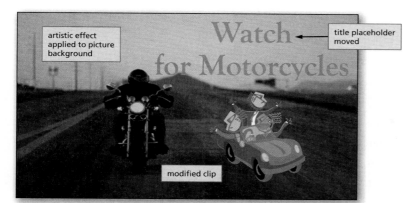

(a) Slide 1 (Title Slide with Picture Background, Modified Clip, and Animated Clip)

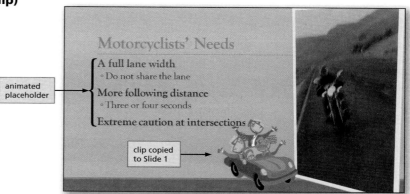

(b) Slide 2 (Bulleted List)

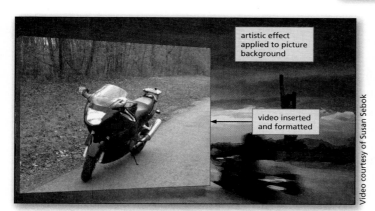

(c) Slide 3 (Picture Background and Video Clip)

(d) Slide 4 (Video Playing Full Screen)

Figure 3–1

For an introduction to Windows and instruction about how to perform basic Windows tasks, read the Office and Windows chapter at the beginning of this book, where you can learn how to resize windows, change screen resolution, create folders, move and rename files, use Windows Help, and much more.

One of the few differences between Windows 7 and Windows 8 occurs in the steps to run PowerPoint. If you are using Windows 7, click the Start button, type **PowerPoint** in the 'Search programs and files' box, click PowerPoint 2013, and then, if necessary, maximize the PowerPoint window. For detailed steps to run PowerPoint in Windows 7, refer to the Office and Windows chapter at the beginning of this book. For a summary of the steps, refer to the Quick Reference located at the back of this book.

Roadmap

In this chapter, you will learn how to create the slides shown in Figure 3–1 on the previous page. The following roadmap identifies general activities you will perform as you progress through this chapter:

1. INSERT and ADD EFFECTS to photos, including changing colors and styles.
2. MODIFY PLACEHOLDERS on the slides by moving and changing sizes.
3. MODIFY and COPY an ILLUSTRATION to customize its appearance.
4. ADD MEDIA files to slides.
5. ANIMATE SLIDE CONTENT with entrance, emphasis, and exit effects.
6. CUSTOMIZE SLIDE ELEMENTS by changing a theme and variant on one slide and changing the theme colors.

At the beginning of step instructions throughout the chapter, you will see an abbreviated form of this roadmap. The abbreviated roadmap uses colors to indicate chapter progress: gray means the chapter is beyond that activity; blue means the task being shown is covered in that activity, and black means that activity is yet to be covered. For example, the following abbreviated roadmap indicates the chapter would be showing a task in the 5 ANIMATE SLIDE CONTENT activity.

1 INSERT & ADD EFFECTS | 2 MODIFY PLACEHOLDERS | 3 MODIFY & COPY ILLUSTRATIONS
4 ADD MEDIA | 5 ANIMATE SLIDE CONTENT | 6 CUSTOMIZE SLIDE ELEMENTS

Use the abbreviated roadmap as a progress guide while you read or step through the instructions in this chapter.

To Run PowerPoint

If you are using a computer to step through the project in this chapter and you want your screens to match the figures in this book, you should change your screen's resolution to 1366 × 768. For information about how to change a computer's resolution, refer to the Office and Windows chapter at the beginning of this book.

The following steps, which assume Windows 8 is running, use the Start screen or the search box to run PowerPoint based on a typical installation. You may need to ask your instructor how to run PowerPoint on your computer. For a detailed example of the procedure summarized below, refer to the Office and Windows chapter.

1 Scroll the Start screen for a PowerPoint 2013 tile. If your Start screen contains a PowerPoint 2013 tile, tap or click it to run PowerPoint and then proceed to Step 5; if the Start screen does not contain the PowerPoint 2013 tile, proceed to the next step to search for the PowerPoint app.

2 Swipe in from the right edge of the screen or point to the upper-right corner of the screen to display the Charms bar and then tap or click the Search charm on the Charms bar to display the Search menu.

3 Type **PowerPoint** as the search text in the Search text box and watch the search results appear in the Apps list.

4 Tap or click PowerPoint 2013 in the search results to run PowerPoint.

5 If the PowerPoint window is not maximized, tap or click the Maximize button on its title bar to maximize the window.

6 If necessary, navigate to the PowerPoint files location (in this case, the PowerPoint folder in the CIS 101 folder [or your class folder]). Visit www.cengage.com/ct/ studentdownload for detailed instructions or contact your instructor for information about accessing the required files. Open the presentation, Motorcycle, from the Data Files for Students.

7 Save the presentation using the file name, Watch for Motorcycles.

Inserting Photos and Adding Effects

The Watch for Motorcycles presentation consists of three slides that have some text, a clip art image, a formatted background, and a transition applied to all slides. You will insert a photo into one slide and then modify it and another photo by adding artistic effects and recoloring. You also will copy the clip art from Slide 2 to Slide 1 and modify the objects in this clip. In Chapter 2, you inserted photos, made corrections, and added styles and effects; the new effects you apply in this chapter will add to your repertoire of photo enhancements that increase interest in your presentation.

In the following pages, you will perform these tasks:

1. Insert the first photo into Slide 1.
2. Recolor the Slide 1 photo.
3. Add an artistic effect to the Slide 3 photo.
4. Send the Slide 1 photo back behind all other slide objects.

> For an introduction to Office and instruction about how to perform basic tasks in Office apps, read the Office and Windows chapter at the beginning of this book, where you can learn how to run an application, use the ribbon, save a file, open a file, exit an application, use Help, and much more.

To Insert and Resize a Photo into a Slide without Content Placeholders

The first step is to insert a photo into Slide 1. This photo is available on the Data Files for Students. Visit www.cengage.com/ct/studentdownload for detailed instructions or contact your instructor for information about accessing the required file.

The following steps insert a photo into Slide 1.

1 With Slide 1 displaying, tap or click INSERT on the ribbon to display the INSERT tab and then tap or click the Pictures button (INSERT tab | Images group) to display the Insert Picture dialog box.

2 If necessary, navigate to the photo location (in this case, the PowerPoint folder in the CIS 101 folder [or your class folder]).

3 Tap or click Highway Motorcycle to select the file.

4 Tap or click the Insert button (Insert Picture dialog box) to insert the photo into Slide 1.

5 Drag the sizing handles to resize the photo so that it covers the entire slide. You can tap or click the Height and Width arrows (PICTURE TOOLS FORMAT tab | Size group) to adjust the picture size (Figure 3–2 on the next page).

> BTW
> **Organizing Files and Folders**
> You should organize and store files in folders so that you easily can find the files later. For example, if you are taking an introductory computer class called CIS 101, a good practice would be to save all PowerPoint files in a PowerPoint folder in a CIS 101 folder. For a discussion of folders and detailed examples of creating folders, refer to the Office and Windows chapter at the beginning of this book.

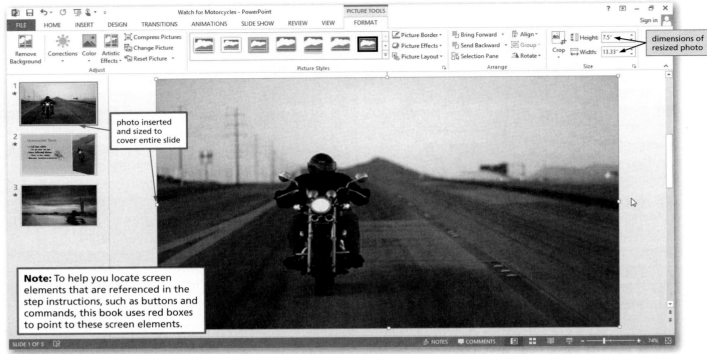

Figure 3–2

Adjusting Photo Colors

BTW
Touch Screen Differences
The Office and Windows interfaces may vary if you are using a touch screen. For this reason, you might notice that the function or appearance of your touch screen differs slightly from this chapter's presentation.

PowerPoint allows you to adjust colors to match or add contrast to slide elements by coloring photos. The Color gallery has a wide variety of preset formatting combinations. The thumbnails in the gallery display the more common color saturation, color tone, and recolor adjustments. **Color saturation** changes the intensity of colors. High saturation produces vivid colors; low saturation produces gray tones. **Color tone** affects the coolness, called blue, or the warmness, called orange, of photos. When a digital camera does not measure the tone correctly, a **color cast** occurs, and, as a result, one color dominates the photo. **Recolor** effects convert the photo into a wide variety of hues. The more common are **grayscale**, which changes the color photo into black, white, and shades of gray, and **sepia**, which changes the photo colors into brown, gold, and yellow, reminiscent of a faded photo. You also can fine-tune the color adjustments by tapping or clicking the Picture Color Options and More Variations commands in the Color gallery.

To Color a Photo

1 INSERT & ADD EFFECTS | 2 MODIFY PLACEHOLDERS | 3 MODIFY & COPY ILLUSTRATIONS
4 ADD MEDIA | 5 ANIMATE SLIDE CONTENT | 6 CUSTOMIZE SLIDE ELEMENTS

The Office theme and text on Slides 1 and 2 are simple and fulfill the need to communicate the presentation's safety message. The photos on Slides 1 and 3, in contrast, help set the tone of riding on an open road and enjoying the freedom that biking brings. You may want to add an effect to photos. *Why? An effect adds variety to the presentation and helps enhance ordinary photos.* The following steps recolor the Slide 1 photo to coordinate with the brown colors of a highway and barren desert landscape.

1

- With Slide 1 displaying and the Highway Motorcycle photo selected, tap or click the Color button (PICTURE TOOLS FORMAT tab | Adjust group) to display the Color gallery (Figure 3–3).

Q&A Why does the Adjust group look different on my screen?
Your monitor is set to a different resolution. See the Office and Windows chapter for an explanation of screen resolution and the appearance of the ribbon.

Why are pink borders surrounding the thumbnails in the Color Saturation, Color Tone, and Recolor areas in the gallery?
The image on Slide 1 currently has normal color saturation and a normal color tone.

Figure 3–3

2

- If you are using a mouse, point to Sepia (third photo in the first Recolor area row) to display a live preview of this adjustment on the photo.

 Experiment

- If you are using a mouse, point to various thumbnails in the Recolor area and watch the hues change on the photo in Slide 1.

- Tap or click Sepia to apply this recoloring to the Highway Motorcycle photo (Figure 3–4).

Q&A Could I have applied this recoloring to the photo if it had been a background instead of a file inserted into the slide?
No. Artistic effects and recoloring cannot be applied to backgrounds.

Figure 3–4

Other Ways

1. Tap or click Format Picture on shortcut menu, tap or click Picture icon, tap or click PICTURE COLOR, tap or click Recolor button (Format Picture pane)

To Add an Artistic Effect to a Photo

Artists use a variety of techniques to create effects in their paintings. They can vary the amount of paint on their brushstroke, use fine bristles to add details, mix colors to increase or decrease intensity, and smooth their paints together to blend the colors. You, likewise, can add similar effects to your photos using PowerPoint's built-in artistic effects. ***Why?*** *The completed Slide 3 will have both the photo and a video, so applying an artistic effect to the photo will provide a contrast between the two images.* The following steps add an artistic effect to the Slide 3 photo.

- Display Slide 3 and select the photo.

- Tap or click the Artistic Effects button (PICTURE TOOLS FORMAT tab | Adjust group) to display the Artistic Effects gallery (Figure 3–5).

Figure 3–5

- If you are using a mouse, point to Paint Brush (third photo in the second row) to display a live preview of this adjustment on the photo.

Experiment

- If you are using a mouse, point to various artistic effects and watch the hues change on the photo in Slide 3.

- Tap or click Paint Brush to apply this artistic effect to the photo (Figure 3–6).

Q&A Can I adjust a photo by recoloring and applying an artistic effect?
Yes. You can apply both a color and an effect. You may prefer at times to mix these adjustments to create a unique image.

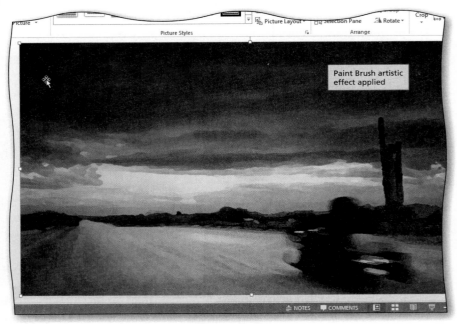

Figure 3–6

Other Ways

1. Tap or click Format Picture on shortcut menu, tap or click Effects icon, tap or click ARTISTIC EFFECTS

To Change the Stacking Order

The objects on a slide stack on top of each other, much like individual cards in a deck. To change the order of these objects, you use the Bring Forward and Send Backward commands. **Bring Forward** moves an object toward the top of the stack, and **Send Backward** moves an object underneath another object. When you tap or click the Bring Forward arrow, PowerPoint displays a menu with an additional command, **Bring to Front**, which moves a selected object to the top of the stack. Likewise, when you tap or click the Send Backward arrow, the **Send to Back** command moves the selected object underneath all objects on the slide. The following steps arrange the Slide 1 photo. *Why? On this slide, the photo is on top of the placeholders, so you no longer can see the text. If you send the photo to the bottom of the stack on the slide, the letters will become visible.*

- Display Slide 1 and then select the Highway Motorcycle photo.

- Tap or click the Send Backward arrow (PICTURE TOOLS FORMAT tab | Arrange group) to display the Send Backward menu (Figure 3–7).

Q&A How can I see objects that are not on the top of the stack?
Press TAB or SHIFT+TAB to display each slide object.

Figure 3–7

- Tap or click Send to Back to move the photo underneath all slide objects (Figure 3–8).

Figure 3–8

Other Ways

1. Tap or click Send Backward arrow (PICTURE TOOLS FORMAT tab | Arrange group), press K

2. Press and hold or right-click photo, tap or click Send to Back on shortcut menu

Modifying Placeholders

You have become familiar with inserting text and graphical content in the three types of placeholders: title, subtitle, and content. These placeholders can be moved, resized, and deleted to meet desired design requirements. In addition, placeholders can be added to a slide when needed. After you have modified the placeholder locations, you can view thumbnails of all your slides simultaneously by changing views.

In the following pages, you will perform these tasks:

1. Resize the Slide 1 title placeholder.
2. Align the Slide 1 title text.
3. Move the Slide 1 title placeholder.
4. Delete the Slide 1 subtitle placeholder.
5. Change views.

BTW

Q&As

For a complete list of the Q&As found in many of the step-by-step sequences in this book, visit the Q&A resource on the Student Companion Site located on www.cengagebrain.com. For detailed instructions about accessing available resources, visit www.cengage.com/ct/studentdownload or see the inside back cover of this book.

To Resize a Placeholder

The AutoFit button displays on the left side of the Slide 1 title placeholder because the two lines of text exceed the placeholder's borders. PowerPoint attempts to reduce the font size when the text does not fit, and you can tap or click this button to resize the existing text in the placeholder so the spillover text will fit within the borders. The following step increases the Slide 1 title placeholder size. **Why?** *The two lines of text exceed the placeholder's borders, so you can resize the placeholder and fit the letters within the rectangle.*

1

- With Slide 1 displaying, tap or click somewhere in the title text paragraph to position the insertion point in the paragraph. Tap or click the border of the title placeholder to select it. Point to the top-middle sizing handle.

- Drag the top title placeholder border upward to enlarge the placeholder (Figure 3–9).

Q&A
Can I drag other sizing handles to enlarge or shrink the placeholder?
Yes, you also can drag the left, right, top, and corner sizing handles to resize a placeholder. When you drag a corner sizing handle, the box keeps the same proportion and simply enlarges the overall shape.

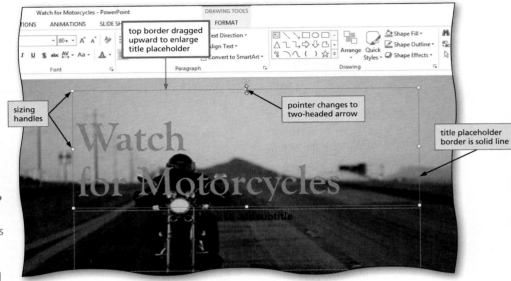

Figure 3–9

To Align Paragraph Text

The presentation theme determines the formatting characteristics of fonts and colors. It also establishes paragraph formatting, including the alignment of text. Some themes **center** the text paragraphs between the left and right placeholder borders, while others **left-align** the paragraph so that the first character of a text line is near the left border or **right-align** the paragraph so that the last character of a text line is near the right border. The paragraph also can be **justified** so that the text is aligned to both the left and right borders. When PowerPoint justifies text, it adds extras spaces between the words to fill the entire line.

The words, Watch for Motorcycles, are left-aligned in the Slide 1 title placeholder. Later, you will add an illustration below the words, for Motorcycles, so you desire to center the paragraph. **Why?** *Both the text and the picture will be centered, so the alignments complement each other.* The following steps change the alignment of the Slide 1 title placeholder.

1

- With the HOME tab displayed, tap or click somewhere in the title text paragraph of Slide 1 to position the insertion point in the paragraph to be formatted (Figure 3–10).

Figure 3–10

- Tap or click the Center button (HOME tab | Paragraph group) to center the paragraph (Figure 3–11).

Q&A What if I want to return the paragraph to left-alignment?
Tap or click the Align Left button (HOME tab | Paragraph group).

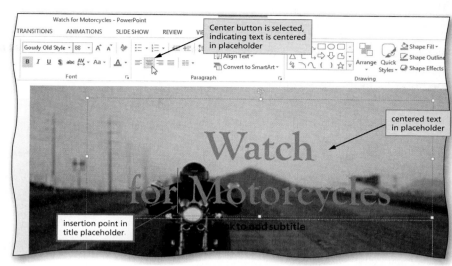

Figure 3–11

Other Ways

1. Press and hold or right-click paragraph, tap or click Center button on mini toolbar	2. Press and hold or right-click paragraph, tap or click Paragraph on shortcut menu, tap or click Indents and Spacing tab (Paragraph dialog box), tap or click Alignment arrow, tap or click Centered, tap or click OK button	3. Tap or click Paragraph dialog box launcher (HOME tab | Paragraph group), tap or click Indents and Spacing tab (Paragraph dialog box), tap or click Alignment arrow, tap or click Centered, tap or click OK button	4. Press CTRL+E

To Move a Placeholder

1 INSERT & ADD EFFECTS | 2 MODIFY PLACEHOLDERS | 3 MODIFY & COPY ILLUSTRATIONS
4 ADD MEDIA | 5 ANIMATE SLIDE CONTENT | 6 CUSTOMIZE SLIDE ELEMENTS

Why? *If you desire to have a placeholder appear in a different area of the slide, you can move it to a new location.* The theme layouts determine where the text and content placeholders display on the slide. The Slide 1 title placeholder currently displays in the upper third of the slide, but the text in this placeholder would be more aesthetically pleasing if it were moved to the upper-right corner of the slide. The following step moves the Slide 1 title placeholder.

- Tap or click the border of the Slide 1 title placeholder to select it.

- With the title placeholder border displaying as a solid line or fine dots, point to an area of the left border between the middle and lower sizing handles so that the pointer changes to a four-headed arrow.

Q&A Can I tap or click any part of the border to select it?
Yes. You can tap or click any of the four border lines.

How do I know if the placeholder is selected?
The selection handles are displayed.

- Drag the placeholder upward and to the right so that the text is centered between the motorcyclist's helmet and the right edge of the slide (Figure 3–12).

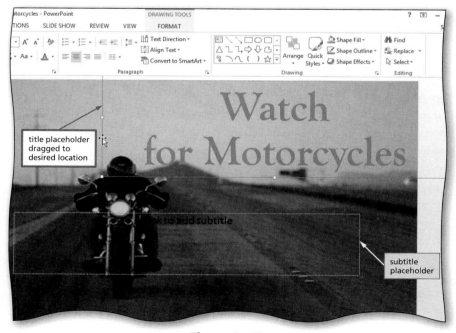

Figure 3–12

To Delete a Placeholder

When you run a slide show, empty placeholders do not display. You may desire to delete unused placeholders from a slide. *Why? So they are not a distraction when you are designing slide content.* The subtitle placeholder on Slide 1 is not required for this presentation, so you can remove it. The following steps remove the Slide 1 subtitle placeholder.

- Tap or click a border of the subtitle placeholder so that it displays as a solid line or fine dots (Figure 3–13).

Figure 3–13

- Tap or click the Cut button (HOME tab | Clipboard group) to remove the placeholder.

Other Ways
1. Select placeholder, press DELETE or BACKSPACE
2. Press and hold or right-click placeholder border, tap Cut on shortcut menu

TO ADD A TEXT BOX

You occasionally may need to insert a small amount of text in an area of a slide where no content placeholder is located. A text box allows you to emphasize or set off text that you consider important for your audience to read. To add a text box to a slide, you would perform the following steps.

1. Tap or click the Text Box button (INSERT tab | Text group), click or tap the slide, and then drag the object to the desired location on the slide.

2. Click inside the text box to add or paste text.

3. If necessary, change the look and style of the text box characters by using formatting features (HOME tab | Font group).

Changing Views

You have been using Normal view to create and edit your slides. Once you completed your slides, you reviewed the final products by displaying each slide in Slide Show view, which occupies the full computer screen. You were able to view how the transitions, graphics, and effects will display in an actual presentation before an audience.

PowerPoint has other views to help review a presentation for content, organization, and overall appearance. Slide Sorter view allows you to look at several slides at one time. Reading view is similar to Slide Show view because each slide displays individually, but the slides do not fill the entire screen. Using this view, you easily can progress through the slides forward or backward with simple controls at the bottom of the window. Switching between Slide Sorter view, Reading view, and Normal view helps you review your presentation, assess whether the slides have an attractive design and adequate content, and make sure they are organized for the most impact. After reviewing the slides, you can change the view to Normal so that you may continue working on the presentation.

To Change Views

1 INSERT & ADD EFFECTS | 2 MODIFY PLACEHOLDERS | 3 MODIFY & COPY ILLUSTRATIONS
4 ADD MEDIA | 5 ANIMATE SLIDE CONTENT | 6 CUSTOMIZE SLIDE ELEMENTS

Why? *You have made several modifications to the slides, so you should check for balance and consistency.* The following steps change the view from Normal view to Slide Sorter view, then Reading view, and back to Normal view.

- Tap or click the Slide Sorter view button in the lower right of the PowerPoint window to display the presentation in Slide Sorter view (Figure 3–14).

Q&A | Why is Slide 1 selected?
It is the current slide in the Thumbnails pane.

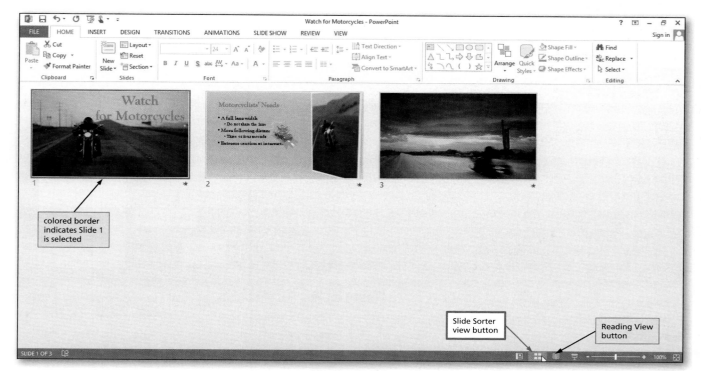

Figure 3–14

②

● Tap or click the Reading View button in the lower right of the PowerPoint window to display Slide 1 of the presentation in Reading view (Figure 3–15).

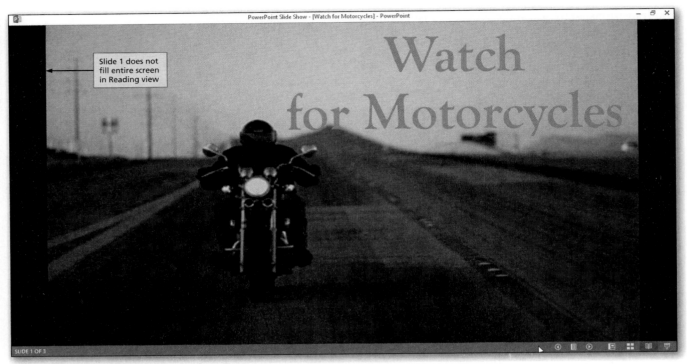

Figure 3–15

③

● Tap or click the Next button two times to advance through the presentation.

● Tap or click the Previous button two times to display Slide 2 and then Slide 1.

● Tap or click the Menu button to display commonly used commands (Figure 3–16).

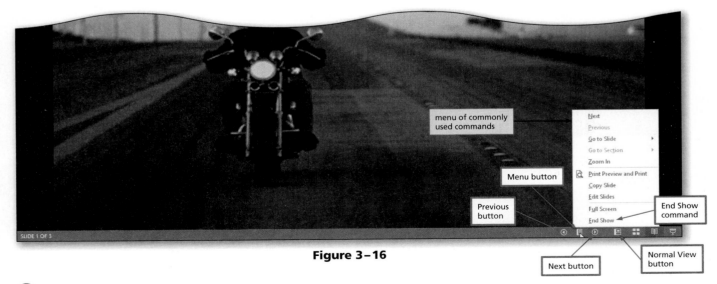

Figure 3–16

④

● Tap or click End Show to return to Slide Sorter view, which is the view you were using before Reading view.

● Tap or click the Normal view button to display the presentation in Normal view.

Modifying and Copying an Illustration

Slides 1 and 2 (shown in Figures 3–1a and 3–1b on PPT 147) contain an illustration of a car that was downloaded from Office.com and then modified. You may want to modify an illustration for various reasons. Many times, you cannot find an illustration that precisely represents your topic. For example, you want a picture of a person wearing a red sweater, but the only available picture has a person with a blue sweater.

Occasionally, you may want to remove or change a portion of an illustration or you might want to combine two or more illustrations. For example, you can use one illustration for the background and another photo as the foreground. Other times, you may want to combine an illustration with another type of object. In this presentation, the tires on the car are orange, and you want to change the color to black. In addition, the car illustration has a highway below the tires and a colorful background, which are not required to display on the slide, so you will ungroup the illustration, change the color of the tires, and remove the highway and the background.

Modifying the clip on Slide 2 and then copying it to Slide 1 requires several steps. In the following pages, you will perform these tasks:

1. Zoom Slide 2 to examine the illustration.
2. Ungroup the illustration.
3. Change a color.
4. Delete objects.
5. Regroup the illustration.
6. Copy the illustration from Slide 2 to Slide 1.

BTW

BTWs
For a complete list of the BTWs found in the margins of this book, visit the BTW resource on the Student Companion Site located on www.cengagebrain.com. For detailed instructions about accessing available resources, visit www.cengage.com/ct/studentdownload or see the inside back cover of this book.

To Zoom a Slide

You will be modifying small areas of the illustration, so it will help you select the relevant pieces if the graphic is enlarged. The following step changes the zoom to 200 percent.

1 Display Slide 2 and then drag the Zoom slider or tap or click the Zoom level button or the Zoom In button to change the zoom level to 200% (Figure 3–17).

Figure 3–17

To Ungroup an Illustration

The next step is to ungroup the car illustration, also called a clip, on Slide 2. When you **ungroup** an illustration, PowerPoint breaks it into its component objects. A clip may be composed of a few individual objects or several complex groups of objects. These groups can be ungrouped repeatedly until they decompose into individual objects. **Why?** *Because an illustration is a collection of complex groups of objects, you may need to ungroup a complex object into less complex objects before being able to modify a specific object.* When you ungroup a clip and tap or click the Yes button in the Microsoft PowerPoint dialog box, PowerPoint converts the clip to a PowerPoint object. The following steps ungroup an illustration.

- Tap or click the car clip to select it and then tap or click FORMAT on the ribbon to display the PICTURE TOOLS FORMAT tab.

- Tap or click the Group button (PICTURE TOOLS FORMAT tab | Arrange group) to display the Group menu (Figure 3–18).

Q&A

Why does the Group button look different on my screen?
Your monitor is set to a different resolution. See Chapter 1 for an explanation of screen resolution and the appearance of the ribbon.

Figure 3–18

- Tap or click Ungroup on the Group menu to display the Microsoft PowerPoint dialog box (Figure 3–19).

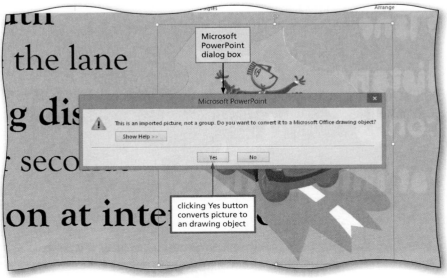

Figure 3–19

3

- Tap or click the Yes button (Microsoft PowerPoint dialog box) to convert the clip to a Microsoft Office drawing.

Q&A What happens if I tap or click the No button?
The clip will remain displayed on the slide as an illustration and will not ungroup.

- Tap or click FORMAT on the ribbon to display the DRAWING TOOLS FORMAT tab. Tap or click the Group button (DRAWING TOOLS FORMAT tab | Arrange group) and then tap or click Ungroup again to display the objects that constitute the car clip (Figure 3–20).

Q&A Why does the ribbon change from the PICTURE TOOLS DRAWING tab to the DRAWING TOOLS FORMAT tab and show different options this time?
The illustration has become a drawing object, so tools related to drawing now display.

Why do all those circles and squares display in the clip?
The circles and squares are sizing handles for each of the clip's objects, which resemble pieces of a jigsaw puzzle.

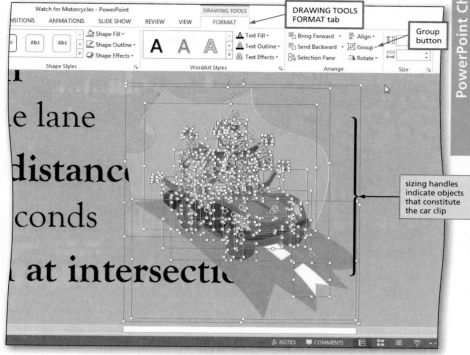

Figure 3–20

Other Ways

1. Press and hold or right-click clip, point to Group on shortcut menu, tap or click Ungroup
2. Press CTRL+SHIFT+G

To Change the Color of a Clip Object

1 INSERT & ADD EFFECTS | 2 MODIFY PLACEHOLDERS | 3 MODIFY & COPY ILLUSTRATIONS
4 ADD MEDIA | 5 ANIMATE SLIDE CONTENT | 6 CUSTOMIZE SLIDE ELEMENTS

Now that the car illustration is ungrouped, you can change the color of the objects. You must exercise care when selecting the correct object to modify. **Why?** *The clip is composed of hundreds of objects.* The following steps change the color of the car's tires from orange to black.

1

- Tap or click an area of the slide that is not part of the clip to deselect all the clip pieces.

- Tap or click the car's left front tire to display sizing handles around the orange colored area (Figure 3–21).

Q&A What if I selected a different area by mistake?
Tap or click outside the clip and retry.

Figure 3–21

- Tap or click the Shape Fill arrow (DRAWING TOOLS FORMAT tab | Shape Styles group) to display the Shape Fill gallery.

- If you are using a mouse, point to Black, Text 1 (second color in the first Theme Colors row) to display a live preview of the tire color (Figure 3–22).

 Experiment

- If you are using a mouse, point to various colors and watch the car's tire color change.

Figure 3–22

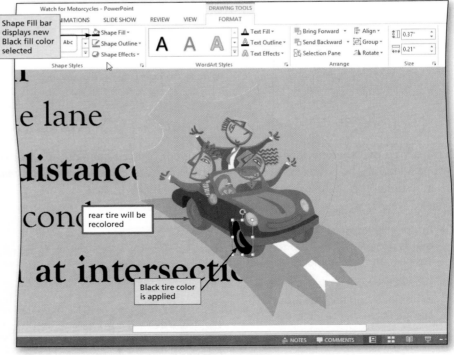

- Tap or click the color Black, Text 1 to change the car's tire color (Figure 3–23).

Q&A Why is the bar under the Shape Fill button now black?
The button displays the last fill color selected.

BTW

The Ribbon and Screen Resolution
PowerPoint may change how the groups and buttons within the groups appear on the ribbon, depending on the computer's screen resolution. Thus, your ribbon may look different from the ones in this book if you are using a screen resolution other than 1366 × 768.

Figure 3–23

- Tap or click the left rear tire to select it.

- Tap or click the Shape Fill button to change the tire color to Black, Text 1 (Figure 3–24).

Q&A Why did I not need to tap or click the Shape Fill arrow to select this color?
PowerPoint uses the last fill color selected. This color displays in the bar under the bucket icon on the button.

Figure 3–24

- Change the right front tire color to black (Figure 3–25).

Figure 3–25

Other Ways

1. Press and hold or right-click object, tap or click Fill button below shortcut menu

2. Press and hold or right-click object, tap or click Format Shape on shortcut menu, tap or click Fill & Line icon

To Delete a Clip Object

1 INSERT & ADD EFFECTS | 2 MODIFY PLACEHOLDERS | 3 MODIFY & COPY ILLUSTRATIONS
4 ADD MEDIA | 5 ANIMATE SLIDE CONTENT | 6 CUSTOMIZE SLIDE ELEMENTS

With the car tires' color changed, you want to delete the pink and purple background objects and the highway objects. *Why? These objects clutter the slide and are not necessary elements of the clip.* The following steps delete these objects.

- Tap or click the background in any area where the pink color displays to select this object (Figure 3–26).

Q&A Can I select multiple objects so I can delete them simultaneously?
Yes. While pressing the SHIFT key, tap or click the unwanted elements to select them.

Figure 3–26

2

- Display the HOME tab and then tap or click the Cut button (HOME tab | Clipboard group) to delete this object (Figure 3–27).

Q&A Should the purple background object display on the slide?
Yes. It is part of the car clip. You will remove it in the next step.

Figure 3–27

3

- Tap or click the purple background to select this object.
- Tap or click the Cut button to delete this object.

4

- Tap or click the mauve highway to select this object (Figure 3–28).
- Tap or click the Cut button to delete this object.

Q&A Should the white highway stripes display on the slide?
Yes. They are part of the car clip. You will remove them in the next step.

Figure 3–28

5

- If using a mouse, click one white highway stripe, press the SHIFT key, and then click the second white highway stripe to select both objects (Figure 3–29).
- If using a touch screen, select one stripe, tap the Cut button to delete this object, and then select the other stripe and tap the Cut button again.
- If using a mouse, click the Cut button to delete these objects.

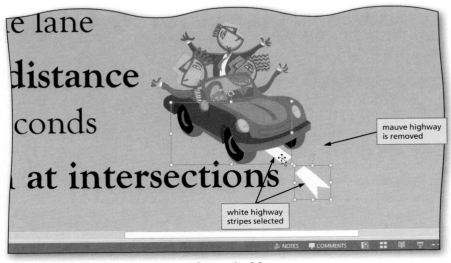

Figure 3–29

To Regroup Objects

When you ungrouped the car clip, you eliminated the embedding data or linking information that tied all the individual pieces together. If you attempt to move or size this clip now, you might encounter difficulties because it consists of hundreds of objects and is no longer one unified piece. Dragging or sizing affects only a selected object, not the entire collection of objects, so you must use caution when objects are not completely regrouped. All of the ungrouped objects in the car clip must be regrouped. *Why? So they are not accidentally moved or manipulated.* The following steps regroup these objects into one object.

- If necessary, select the clip, tap or click the DRAWING TOOLS FORMAT tab and then tap or click the Group button (DRAWING TOOLS FORMAT tab | Arrange group) to display the Group menu (Figure 3–30).

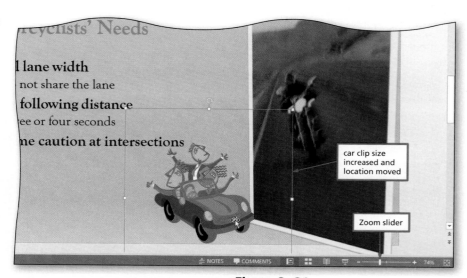

- Tap or click Regroup to recombine all the clip objects.

Figure 3–30

- Use the Zoom slider to change the zoom level to 74%.

- Increase the car's size by dragging one of the corner sizing handles outward until the illustration is the size shown in Figure 3–31 and then move the illustration to the location shown in the figure (Figure 3–31).

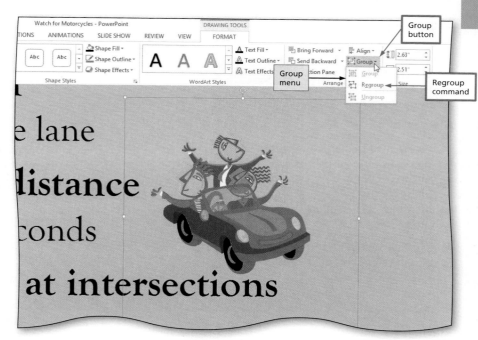

Figure 3–31

Other Ways

1. Press and hold or right-click clip, point to Group on shortcut menu, tap or click Regroup

To Copy a Clip from One Slide to Another

The car clip on Slide 2 also can display in its modified form on the title slide. You first must copy it using the Office Clipboard and then paste it in the desired location. *Why? The **Office Clipboard** is a temporary storage location that can hold a maximum of 24 text or graphics items copied from any Office program.* The same procedure of copying and pasting objects works for copying and pasting text from one placeholder to another. The following steps copy this slide element from Slide 2 to Slide 1.

1

- With the car illustration selected, display the HOME tab and then tap or click the Copy button (HOME tab | Clipboard group) (Figure 3–32).

2

- Display Slide 1 and then tap or click the Paste button (HOME tab | Clipboard group) to insert the car illustration into the title slide.

Q&A Is the clip deleted from the Office Clipboard when I paste it into the slide?
No.

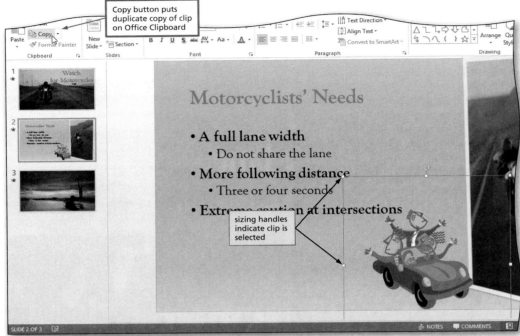

Figure 3–32

3

- Increase the car size by dragging one of the corner sizing handles outward until the car is the size shown in Figure 3–33. Drag the car to the location shown in this figure.

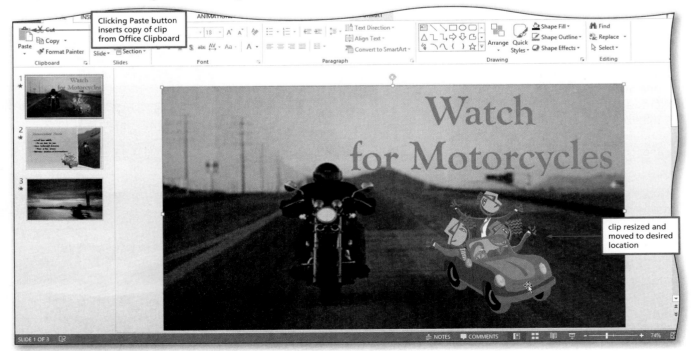

Figure 3–33

Break Point: If you wish to take a break, this is a good place to do so. Be sure to save the Watch for Motorcycles file again and then you can quit PowerPoint. To resume at a later time, start PowerPoint, open the file called Watch for Motorcycles, and continue following the steps from this location forward.

Adding Media to Slides

Media files can enrich a presentation if they are used correctly. Movie files can be produced with a camera and editing software, and sound files can come from the Office.com Clip Art collection, files stored on your computer, or an audio track on a CD. To hear the sounds, you need a sound card and speakers or headphones on your system.

Once an audio or video clip is inserted into a slide, you can specify options that affect how the file is displayed and played. For example, you can have the video play automatically when the slide is displayed, or you can tap or click the video frame when you are ready to start the playback. You also can have the video fill the entire slide, which is referred to as **full screen**. If you decide to play the slide show automatically and have it display full screen, you can drag the video frame to the gray area off the slide so that it does not display briefly before going to full screen. You can select the Loop until Stopped option to have the video repeat until you tap or click the next slide, or you can choose to not have the video frame display on the slide until you tap or click the slide.

If your video clip has recorded sounds, the volume controls give you the option to set how loudly this audio will play. They also allow you to mute the sound so that your audience will hear no background noise or music.

In the following pages, you will perform these tasks:

1. Insert a video file into Slide 3.
2. Trim the video file to shorten the play time.
3. Add video options that determine the clip's appearance and playback.
4. Insert an audio file into Slide 1.
5. Add audio options that determine the clip's appearance and playback.
6. Add a video style to the Slide 3 clip.
7. Resize the video.

> **BTW**
> **Using Codecs**
> Video and audio content developers use a codec (**co**mpressor/**dec**ompressor) to reduce the file size of digital media. The reduced file size helps transfer files across the Internet quickly and smoothly and helps save space on storage media. Your computer can play any compressed file if the specific codec used to compress the file is available on your computer. If the codec is not installed or is not recognized, your computer attempts to download this file from the Internet. Many codex files are available to download from the Internet at no cost.

To Insert a Video File

1 INSERT & ADD EFFECTS | 2 MODIFY PLACEHOLDERS | 3 MODIFY & COPY ILLUSTRATIONS
4 ADD MEDIA | 5 ANIMATE SLIDE CONTENT | 6 CUSTOMIZE SLIDE ELEMENTS

Slide 3 has another photo of a motorcyclist, and you have a video clip of a person mounting a motorcycle, putting the bike into gear, and riding out of the scene. You want to use a majority of the clip and eliminate a few seconds from the end. PowerPoint allows you to insert this clip into your slide and then trim the file. *Why?* *Just a portion will play when you preview the clip or run the slide show.* This clip is available on the Data Files for Students. See the inside back cover of this book for instructions on downloading the Data Files for Students, or contact your instructor for more information about accessing the required file. The following steps insert this video clip into Slide 3.

- Display Slide 3 and then display the INSERT tab. Tap or click the Video button (INSERT tab | Media group) to display the Video menu (Figure 3–34).

Figure 3–34

2

- Tap or click 'Video on My PC' on the Video menu to display the Insert Video dialog box.

- If the list of files and folders for Chapter 3 is not displayed in the Insert Video dialog box, navigate to the location where the files are located.

- Tap or click Motorcycle Rider to select the file (Figure 3–35).

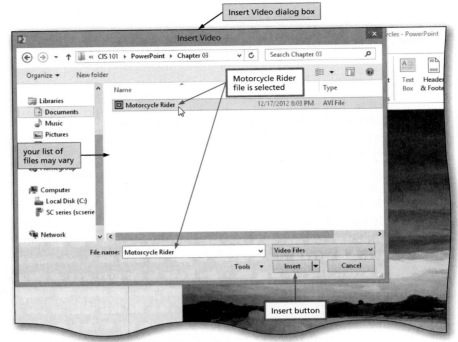

Figure 3–35

3

- Tap or click the Insert button (Insert Video dialog box) to insert the video clip into Slide 3 (Figure 3–36).

Q&A Can I adjust the color of a video clip?
Yes. You can correct the brightness and contrast, and you also can recolor a video clip using the same methods you learned in this chapter to color a photo.

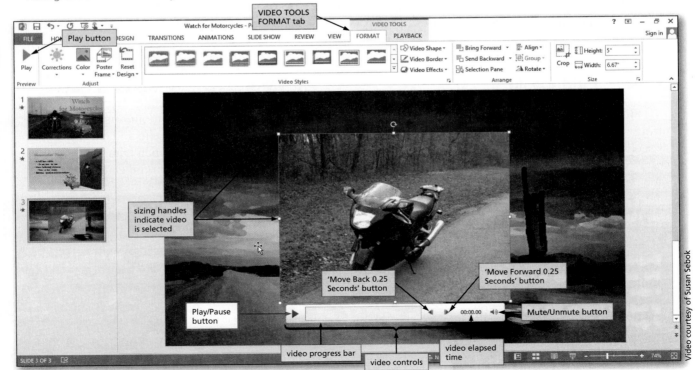

Figure 3–36

To Trim a Video File

Why? The Motorcycle Rider video has a running time of slightly more than 14 seconds. Near the end of the clip, the motorcyclist rides out of the frame, so you delete a few seconds from that portion of the file. PowerPoint's **Trim Video** feature allows you to trim the beginning and end of your clip by designating your desired Start Time and End Time. These precise time measurements are accurate to one-thousandth of a second. The start point is indicated by a green marker, and the end point is indicated by a red marker. The following steps trim the Motorcycle Rider video clip.

● With the video clip selected on Slide 3, tap or click the Play/Pause button to play the entire video.

Q&A Can I play the video by tapping or clicking the Play button in the Preview group?
Yes. This Play button plays the entire clip. You may prefer to tap or click the Play/Pause button displayed in the video controls to stop the video and examine one of the frames.

● Tap or click PLAYBACK on the ribbon to display the VIDEO TOOLS PLAYBACK tab. Tap or click the Trim Video button (VIDEO TOOLS PLAYBACK tab | Editing group) to display the Trim Video dialog box (Figure 3–37).

Figure 3–37

② Point to the end point, which is indicated by the red marker on the right side, so that the pointer changes to a two-headed arrow.

● Slide or drag the red marker to the left until the End Time is 00:13:365 (Figure 3–38).

Q&A Can I specify the start or end times without dragging the markers?
Yes. You can enter the time in the Start Time or End Time boxes, or you can tap or click the Start Time or End Time box arrows. You also can tap or click the Next Frame and Previous Frame buttons (Trim Video dialog box).

How would I indicate a start point if I want the clip to start at a time other than at the beginning of the clip?
You would drag the green marker to the right until the desired time displays in the Start Time box.

Figure 3–38

③

● Tap or click the Play/Pause button (Trim Video dialog box) to review the shortened video clip.

● Tap or click the OK button to set the Start Time and End Time and to close the Trim Video dialog box.

Other Ways

1. Press and hold or right-click clip, tap or click Trim on shortcut menu

To Add Video Options

Once the video clip is inserted into Slide 3, you can specify that the video plays automatically when the slide is displayed. *Why? When you are giving your presentation, you do not want to click the mouse or tap the screen to start the video.* You also can adjust the volume of the sound recorded on the file. The following steps add the option of playing the video full screen automatically and also decrease the volume of the motorcycle engine.

- If necessary, tap or click PLAYBACK on the ribbon to display the VIDEO TOOLS PLAYBACK tab. Tap or click the Start arrow (VIDEO TOOLS PLAYBACK tab | Video Options group) to display the Start menu (Figure 3–39).

Q&A What does the On Click option do?
The video clip would begin playing when a presenter taps or clicks the frame during the slide show.

Figure 3–39

- Tap or click Automatically in the Start menu to run the video clip automatically when the slide is displayed.

- Tap or click the 'Play Full Screen' check box (VIDEO TOOLS PLAYBACK tab | Video Options group) to place a check mark in it.

- Tap or click the Volume button (VIDEO TOOLS PLAYBACK tab | Video Options group) to display the Volume menu (Figure 3–40).

Figure 3–40

- Tap or click Medium on the Volume menu to set the audio volume.

Q&A Will the Mute option silence the video's background sounds?
Yes. Tap or click Mute if you do not want your audience to hear any recorded sounds.

To Insert an Audio File

If you have an active Internet connection, you can search Office.com to locate several motorcycle sounds in audio files that you can download and insert into your presentation. The following steps insert an audio clip into Slide 1. *Why? Avid motorcyclists enjoy hearing the sounds of their engines and often can identify a bike by the engine sounds it makes. A clip of a motorcycle engine adds interest to the start of your presentation when Slide 1 is displayed.*

- Display Slide 1 and then tap or click INSERT on the ribbon to display the INSERT tab.

- Tap or click the Audio button (INSERT tab | Media group) to display the Audio menu (Figure 3–41).

Figure 3–41

- Tap or click Online Audio on the Insert Audio menu to open the Insert Audio dialog box.

- With the insertion point in the Office.com Clip Art area, type **motorcycle** in the search text box (Figure 3–42).

- Tap or click the Search button (the magnifying glass) or press the ENTER key so that Office.com will search for and display all audio clips having the keyword, motorcycle.

Figure 3–42

- If you are using a mouse, point to the 1200cc Passby clip to display the total time of the clip and to hear a preview of this file (Figure 3–43).

Q&A What if the 1200cc Passby audio clip is not shown in my Office.com Clip Art dialog box?
Select a similar clip. Your clips may be different depending on the clips included in the Office.com Clip Art collection.

🔍 Experiment

- If you are using a mouse, point to other audio clips to hear the sounds and to view the clips' length.

- Tap or click the 1200cc Passby clip to select the clip (Figure 3–44).

Figure 3–43

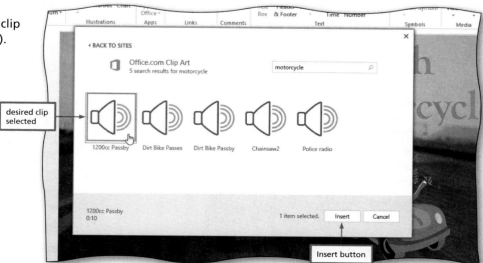

Figure 3–44

5

- Tap or click the Insert button in the dialog box to insert that file into Slide 1 (Figure 3–45).

Q&A | Why does a sound icon display on the slide?
The icon indicates an audio file is inserted.

Do the audio control buttons have the same functions as the video control buttons that displayed when I inserted the Motorcycle Rider clip?
Yes. The controls include playing and pausing the sound, moving back or forward 0.25 seconds, audio progress, elapsed time, and muting or unmuting the sound.

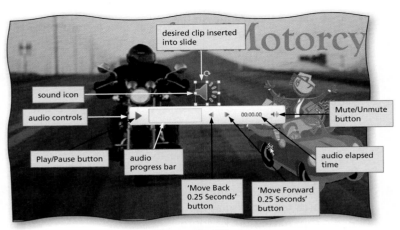

Figure 3–45

6

- Drag the sound icon to the lower-left corner of the slide (Figure 3–46).

Q&A | Must I move the icon on the slide?
No. Although your audience will not see the icon when you run the slide show, it is easier for you to see the audio controls in the dark area of this slide.

Figure 3–46

To Add Audio Options

1 INSERT & ADD EFFECTS | 2 MODIFY PLACEHOLDERS | 3 MODIFY & COPY ILLUSTRATIONS
4 ADD MEDIA | 5 ANIMATE SLIDE CONTENT | 6 CUSTOMIZE SLIDE ELEMENTS

Once an audio clip is inserted into a slide, you can specify options that control playback and appearance. As with the video options you applied to the Motorcycle Rider clip, the audio clip can play either automatically or when tapped or clicked, it can repeat the clip while a particular slide is displayed, and you can drag the sound icon off the slide and set the volume. The following steps add the options of starting automatically, playing until the slide no longer is displayed, and hiding the sound icon on the slide. *Why? You do not want to tap or click the screen to start the sound, so you do not need to see the icon. In addition, you want the engine sound to repeat while the slide is displayed to coordinate with the motorcycle picture prominently shown and to keep the audience's attention focused on the topic of listening for motorcycles while operating a vehicle.*

1

- If necessary, tap or click PLAYBACK on the ribbon to display the AUDIO TOOLS PLAYBACK tab. Tap or click the Start arrow (AUDIO TOOLS PLAYBACK tab | Audio Options group) to display the Start menu (Figure 3–47).

2

- Tap or click Automatically in the Start menu.

Figure 3–47

Q&A | Does the On Click option function the same way for an audio clip as On Click does for a video clip?
Yes. If you were to select On Click, the sound would begin playing only after the presenter taps or clicks Slide 1 during a presentation.

- Tap or click the 'Loop until Stopped' check box (AUDIO TOOLS PLAYBACK tab | Audio Options group) to place a check mark in it.

Q&A | What is the difference between the 'Loop until Stopped' option and the 'Play Across Slides' option?

The audio clip in the 'Loop until Stopped' option repeats for as long as one slide is displayed. In contrast, the 'Play Across Slides' option would play the clip only once, but it would continue to play while other slides in the presentation are displayed. Once the end of the clip is reached, the sound would end and not repeat.

- Tap or click the 'Hide During Show' check box (AUDIO TOOLS PLAYBACK tab | Audio Options group) to place a check mark in it (Figure 3–48).

Q&A | Why would I want the icon to display during the show?

If you had selected the On Click option, you would need to find this icon on the slide and tap or click it to start playing the clip.

Can I adjust the sound's volume?

Yes. You can adjust the volume or mute the sound by clicking the Volume button (AUDIO TOOLS PLAYBACK tab | Audio Options group) or by clicking the Mute/Unmute button on the Media Controls bar and using the volume slider.

Figure 3–48

To Add a Video Style

1 INSERT & ADD EFFECTS | 2 MODIFY PLACEHOLDERS | 3 MODIFY & COPY ILLUSTRATIONS
4 ADD MEDIA | 5 ANIMATE SLIDE CONTENT | 6 CUSTOMIZE SLIDE ELEMENTS

The video styles are similar to the photo styles you applied in Chapter 2 and include various shapes, angles, borders, and reflections. The following steps apply a video style to the Motorcycle Rider clip on Slide 3. *Why? The Motorcycle Rider video clip on Slide 3 displays full screen when it is playing, but you decide to increase the visual appeal of the clip when it is not playing by applying a video style.*

- Display Slide 3 and select the video frame. Tap or click FORMAT on the ribbon to display the VIDEO TOOLS FORMAT tab (Figure 3–49).

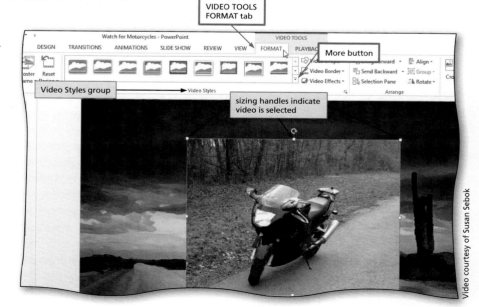

Video courtesy of Susan Sebok

Figure 3–49

- With the video frame selected, tap or click the More button in the Video Styles gallery (VIDEO TOOLS FORMAT tab | Video Styles group) (shown in Figure 3–49) to expand the gallery.

- If you are using a mouse, point to Canvas, Gray in the Intense area of the Video Styles gallery (third style in the second row) to display a live preview of that style applied to the video frame on the slide (Figure 3–50).

Experiment

- If you are using a mouse, point to various photo styles in the Video Styles gallery and watch the style of the video frame change in the document window.

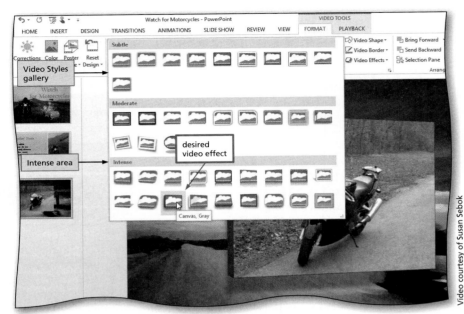

Figure 3–50

- Tap or click Canvas, Gray in the Video Styles gallery to apply the style to the selected video (Figure 3–51).

Q&A Can I preview the movie clip?
Yes. Point to the clip and then tap or click the Play button on the ribbon (Preview group) or the Play/Pause button on the video controls below the video.

Can I add a border to a video style? Yes. You add a border using the same method you learned in Chapter 2 to add a border to a photo. Tap or click the Video Border button (VIDEO TOOLS FORMAT tab | Video Styles group) and then select a border line weight and color.

Figure 3–51

Other Ways

1. Tap or click Format Video on shortcut menu, tap or click Video icon, tap or click VIDEO, tap or click Presets button

BTW

PowerPoint Help
At any time while using PowerPoint, you can find answers to questions and display information about various topics through PowerPoint Help. Used properly, this form of assistance can increase your productivity and reduce your frustrations by minimizing the time you spend learning how to use PowerPoint. For instruction about PowerPoint Help and exercises that will help you gain confidence in using it, read the Office and Windows chapter at the beginning of this book.

To Resize a Video

The default Motorcycle Rider frame size can be changed. You resize a video clip in the same manner that you resize photos and illustrations. The following steps will increase the Motorcycle Rider video using a sizing handle. *Why? You want to fill some space on the left side of the slide.*

- With the video selected, drag the lower-left corner sizing handle diagonally outward until the frame is resized to approximately 5.89" × 7.86".

- Drag the clip to the location shown in Figure 3–52.

Video courtesy of Susan Sebok

Figure 3–52

Break Point: If you wish to take a break, this is a good place to do so. Be sure to save the Watch for Motorcycles file again and then you can quit PowerPoint. To resume at a later time, start PowerPoint, open the file called Watch for Motorcycles, and continue following the steps from this location forward.

Animating Slide Content

Animation includes special visual and sound effects applied to text or other content. You already are familiar with one form of animation: transitions between slides. To add visual interest and clarity to a presentation, you can animate various parts of an individual slide, including pictures, shapes, text, and other slide elements. For example, each paragraph on the slide can spin as it is displayed. Individual letters and shapes also can spin or move in various motions. PowerPoint has a variety of built-in animations that will fade, wipe, or fly-in text and graphics.

Custom Animations

You can create your own **custom animations** to meet your unique needs. Custom animation effects are grouped in categories: entrance, exit, emphasis, and motion paths. **Entrance** effects, as the name implies, determine how slide elements first appear on a slide. **Exit** animations work in the opposite manner as entrance effects: They determine how slide elements disappear. **Emphasis** effects modify text and objects

BTW
Certification
The Microsoft Office Specialist (MOS) program provides an opportunity for you to obtain a valuable industry credential — proof that you have the PowerPoint 2013 skills required by employers. For more information, visit the Certification resource on the Student Companion Site located on www.cengagebrain.com. For detailed instructions about accessing available resources, visit www.cengage.com/ct/studentdownload or see the inside back cover of this book.

displayed on the screen. For example, letters may darken or increase in font size. The entrance, exit, and emphasis animations are grouped into categories: Basic, Subtle, Moderate, and Exciting. You can set the animation speed to Very Fast, Fast, Medium, Slow, or Very Slow.

The Slide 2 illustration shows three people in a car. When the slide is displayed, the audience will see this car enter from the upper-left corner, move diagonally across the slide and stop below the bulleted list, rock slightly, and then continue down the slide toward the lower-right corner.

In the following pages, you will perform these tasks:

1. Apply an entrance effect to the car illustration and then change the direction.
2. Apply emphasis and exit effects.
3. Change the exit effect direction.
4. Preview the animation sequence.
5. Modify the entrance, emphasis, and exit effects' timing.
6. Animate text paragraphs.

To Animate an Illustration Using an Entrance Effect

1 INSERT & ADD EFFECTS | 2 MODIFY PLACEHOLDERS | 3 MODIFY & COPY ILLUSTRATIONS
4 ADD MEDIA | 5 ANIMATE SLIDE CONTENT | 6 CUSTOMIZE SLIDE ELEMENTS

The car you modified will not appear on Slide 1 when you display the slide. Instead, it will enter the slide from the upper-left corner. *Why? To give the appearance it is driving toward the motorcycle photo.* It will then continue downward until it reaches the lower-left side of the photo. Entrance effects are colored green in the Animation gallery. The following step applies an entrance effect to the car illustration.

- Display Slide 2, select the car clip, and then tap or click ANIMATIONS on the ribbon to display the ANIMATIONS tab.

- If you are using a mouse, click the Fly In animation in the Animation gallery (ANIMATIONS tab | Animation group) to display a live preview of this animation and to apply this entrance animation to the car illustration; if you are using a touch screen, tap Fly In animation to apply this entrance animation to the car illustration (Figure 3–53).

Q&A Are more entrance animations available?
Yes. Tap or click the More button in the Animation gallery to see additional animations. You can select one of the 13 entrance animations that are displayed, or you can tap or click the More Entrance Effects command to expand the selection. You can tap or click any animation to see a preview of the effect.

Why does the number 1 appear in a box on the left side of the clip?
The 1 is a sequence number and indicates Fly In is the first animation that will appear on the slide when you tap or click the slide.

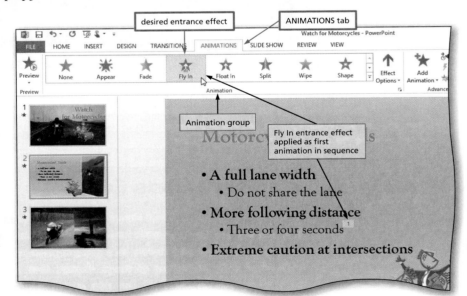

Figure 3–53

To Change Animation Direction

Why? *By default, the illustration appears on the slide by entering from the bottom edge, and you want it to enter from the top left.* You can modify this direction and specify that it enters from another side or from a corner. The following steps change the car entrance animation direction to the upper-left corner.

1

- Tap or click the Effect Options button (ANIMATIONS tab | Animation group) to display the Direction gallery (Figure 3–54).

Q&A Why does a pink box appear around the From Bottom arrow? From Bottom is the default entrance direction applied to the animation.

2

- Tap or click the From Top-Left arrow to apply this direction to the entrance animation.

Q&A Can I change this entrance effect? Yes. Repeat Step 1 to select another direction.

Figure 3–54

To Animate an Illustration Using an Emphasis Effect

Why? *The car will enter the slide from the upper-left corner and stop beside the motorcycle photo. You then want it to rock slightly.* PowerPoint provides several effects that you can apply to a picture once it appears on a slide. These movements are categorized as emphasis effects, and they are colored yellow in the Animation gallery. You already have applied an entrance effect to the car, so you want to add another animation to this illustration. The following steps apply an emphasis effect to the car after the entrance effect.

1

- Select the car illustration and then tap or click the Add Animation button (ANIMATIONS tab | Advanced Animation group) to display the Animation gallery (Figure 3–55).

Q&A Are more emphasis effects available in addition to those shown in the Animation gallery? Yes. To see additional emphasis effects, tap or click 'More Emphasis Effects' in the lower portion of the Animation gallery. The effects are arranged in the Basic, Subtle, Moderate, and Exciting categories.

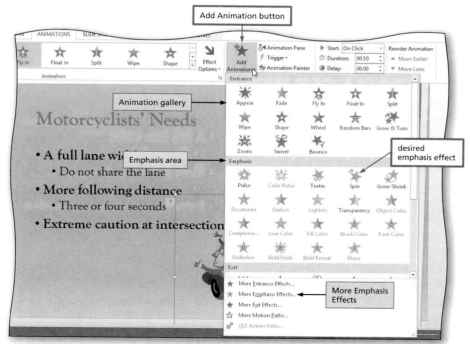

Figure 3–55

2

- Tap or click Teeter (third effect in the first Emphasis row) to see a preview of this animation and to apply this emphasis effect to the car illustration (Figure 3–56).

Q&A Do I need to use both an entrance and an emphasis effect, or can I use only an emphasis effect?
You can use one or the other effect, or both effects.

Why does the number 2 appear in a box below the number 1 on the left side of the illustration?
The 2 in the numbered tag indicates a second animation is applied in the animation sequence.

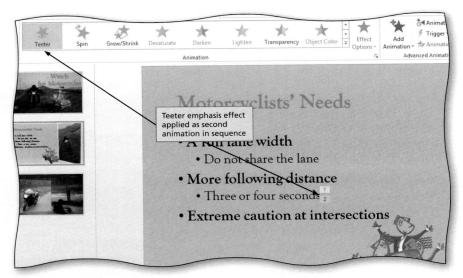

Figure 3–56

To Animate an Illustration Using an Exit Effect

1 INSERT & ADD EFFECTS | 2 MODIFY PLACEHOLDERS | 3 MODIFY & COPY ILLUSTRATIONS
4 ADD MEDIA | 5 ANIMATE SLIDE CONTENT | 6 CUSTOMIZE SLIDE ELEMENTS

The animated car will enter the slide from the upper-left corner, stop beside the motorcycle photo, and then teeter. It then will continue across the slide and exit in the lower-right corner. To continue this animation sequence, you first need to apply an exit effect. As with the entrance and emphasis effects, PowerPoint provides a wide variety of effects that you can apply to remove an illustration from a slide. These exit effects are colored red in the Animation gallery. You already have applied the Fly In entrance effect, so you will apply the Fly Out exit effect. *Why? It would give continuity to the animation sequence.* The following steps add this exit effect to the car illustration after the emphasis effect.

1

- Select the car illustration and then tap or click the Add Animation button (ANIMATIONS tab | Advanced Animation group) again to display the Animation gallery.

- Scroll down to display all the exit effects in the gallery (Figure 3–57).

Q&A Are more exit effects available in addition to those shown in the Animation gallery?
Yes. To see additional exit effects, tap or click 'More Exit Effects' in the lower portion of the Animation gallery. The effects are arranged in the Basic, Subtle, Moderate, and Exciting categories.

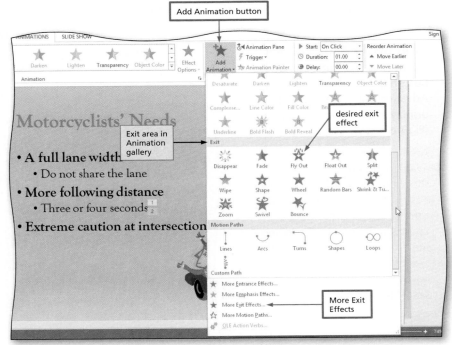

Figure 3–57

2

- Tap or click Fly Out to see a preview of this animation and to add this exit effect to the sequence of car illustration animations (Figure 3–58).

Q&A

How can I tell that this exit effect has been applied?

The Fly Out effect is displayed in the Animation gallery (ANIMATIONS tab | Animation group), and the number 3 is displayed to the left of the car illustration.

How can I delete an animation effect?

Tap or click the number associated with the animation you wish to delete and then press the DELETE key.

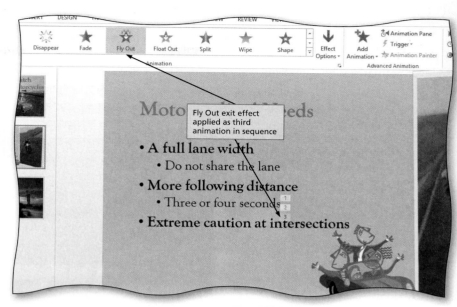

Figure 3–58

To Change Exit Animation Direction

The default direction for a picture to exit a slide is To Bottom. In this presentation, you want the car to exit in the lower-right corner. ***Why?*** *To give the impression it is continuing down an invisible highway.* The following steps change the exit animation direction from To Bottom to To Bottom-Right.

1 Tap or click the Effect Options button (ANIMATIONS tab | Animation group) to display the Direction gallery (Figure 3–59).

2 Tap or click the To Bottom-Right arrow to apply this direction to the exit animation effect.

Figure 3–59

To Preview an Animation Sequence

Why? *Although you have not completed developing the presentation, you should view the animation you have added to check for continuity and verify that the animation is displaying as you expected.* By default, the entrance, emphasis, and exit animations will be displayed when you run the presentation and tap or click the slide. The following step runs the presentation and displays the three animations.

- Tap or click the Preview button (ANIMATIONS tab | Preview group) to view all the Slide 1 animations (Figure 3–60).

Q&A Why does a red square appear in the middle of the circle on the Preview button when I tap or click that button? The red square indicates the animation sequence is in progress. Ordinarily, a green arrow is displayed in the circle.

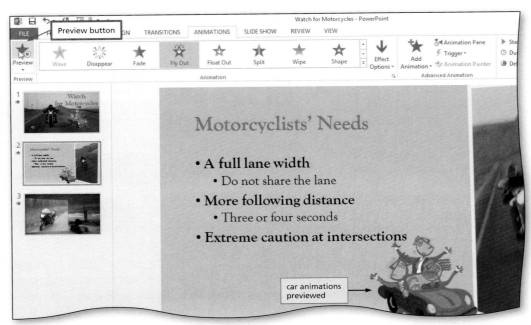

Figure 3–60

To Modify Entrance Animation Timing

The three animation effects are displayed quickly. To create a dramatic effect, you can change the timing. The default setting is to start each animation with a tap or click, but you can change this setting so that the entrance effect is delayed until a specified number of seconds has passed. The following steps modify the start, delay, and duration settings for the entrance animation. *Why?* *You want the slide title text to display and then, a few seconds later, the car to start to drive down the slide slowly.*

- Tap or click the tag numbered 1 on the left side of the car illustration and then tap or click the Start arrow (ANIMATIONS tab | Timing group) to display the Start menu (Figure 3–61).

Figure 3–61

- Tap or click After Previous to change the start option.

Q&A Why did the numbered tags change from 1, 2, 3 to 0, 1, 2?
The first animation now occurs automatically without a tap or click. The first and second taps or clicks now will apply the emphasis and exit animations.

What is the difference between the With Previous and After Previous settings?
The With Previous setting starts the effect simultaneously with any prior animation; the After Previous setting starts the animation after a prior animation has ended. If the prior animation is fast or a short duration, it may be difficult for a viewer to discern the difference between these two settings.

- Tap or click the Duration up arrow (ANIMATIONS tab | Timing group) several times to increase the time from 00.50 second to 02.00 seconds (Figure 3–62).

- Tap or click the Preview button to view the animations.

Q&A What is the difference between the duration time and the delay time?
The duration time is the length of time in which the animation occurs; the delay time is the length of time that passes before the animation begins.

Can I type the speed in the Duration box instead of tap or clicking the arrow to adjust the speed?
Yes. Typing the numbers allows you to set a precise timing.

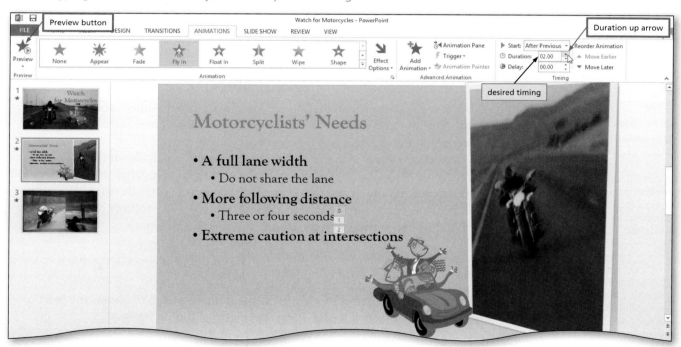

Figure 3–62

4

- Tap or click the Delay up arrow (ANIMATIONS tab | Timing group) several times to increase the delay time from 00.00 seconds to 04.00 seconds (Figure 3–63).

- Tap or click the Preview button to view the animations.

◄ Q&A Can I adjust the delay time I just set?
Yes. Tap or click the Delay up or down arrows and run the slide show to display Slide 1 until you find the time that best fits your presentation.

Figure 3–63

To Modify Emphasis and Exit Timings

BTW

Distributing a Document

Instead of printing and distributing a hard copy of a document, you can distribute the document electronically. Options include sending the document via email; posting it on cloud storage (such as SkyDrive) and sharing the file with others; posting it on a social networking site, blog, or other website; and sharing a link associated with an online location of the document. You also can create and share a PDF or XPS image of the document, so that users can view the file in Acrobat Reader or XPS Viewer instead of in PowerPoint.

Now that the entrance animation settings have been modified, you then can change the emphasis and exit effects for the car illustration. The emphasis effect can occur once the entrance effect has concluded, and then the exit effect can commence. With gravity's effect, the car should be able to roll more quickly down the lower part of the slide, so you will shorten the duration of the exit effect compared with the duration of the entrance effect. The animation sequence should flow without stopping, so you will not change the default delay timing of 00.00 seconds. The following steps modify the start and duration settings for the emphasis and exit animations.

1 Tap or click the tag numbered 1, which represents the emphasis effect, on the left side of the car illustration.

2 Tap or click the Start arrow (ANIMATIONS tab | Timing group) to display the Start menu and then tap or click After Previous to change the start option.

3 Tap or click the Duration up arrow (ANIMATIONS tab | Timing group) several times to increase the time to 03.00 seconds.

4 Tap or click the tag numbered 1, which now represents the exit effect, tap or click the Start arrow, and then tap or click After Previous.

5 Tap or click the Duration up arrow several times to increase the time to 04.00 seconds.

6 Preview the Slide 2 animation (Figure 3–64).

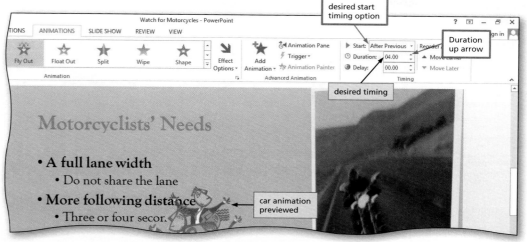

Figure 3–64

To Animate Content Placeholder Paragraphs

1 INSERT & ADD EFFECTS | 2 MODIFY PLACEHOLDERS | 3 MODIFY & COPY ILLUSTRATIONS
4 ADD MEDIA | 5 ANIMATE SLIDE CONTENT | 6 CUSTOMIZE SLIDE ELEMENTS

The car illustration on Slide 2 has one entrance, one emphasis, and one exit animation. You decide to add similar animations to the five bulleted paragraphs in the Slide 2 content placeholder. *Why? For a special effect, you can add several emphasis animations to one slide element.* The following steps add one entrance and one emphasis animation to the bulleted list paragraphs.

• Double-tap or click the Slide 2 content placeholder border so that it displays as a solid line (Figure 3–65).

Figure 3–65

2

• Tap or click the More button (shown in Figure 3–65) in the Animation group (ANIMATIONS tab | Animation group) to expand the Animation gallery (Figure 3–66).

Figure 3–66

• Tap or click the Fade entrance effect in the Animation gallery (second effect in first row) to add and preview this animation.

• Change the Start option to With Previous.

• Change the Duration time to 02.00 seconds (Figure 3–67).

Q&A Do I need to change the delay time?

No. The paragraphs can start appearing on the slide when the car exit effect is beginning.

• Tap or click the Add Animation button (ANIMATIONS tab | Advanced Animation group) and then tap or click the Font Color emphasis animation effect (last effect in the third row).

• Change the Start option to After Previous.

• Preview the Slide 2 animation.

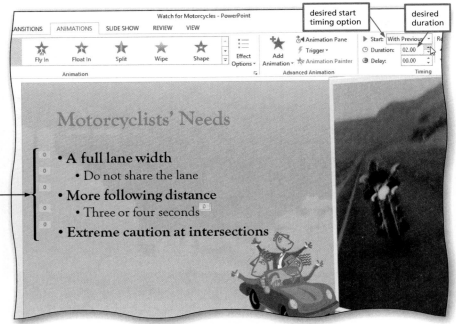

Figure 3–67

• Tap or click the Add Animation button and then click the Underline emphasis animation effect (the first effect in the fourth row), as shown in Figure 3–66.

Q&A Why do the animation effects display differently in the Animation gallery on my screen?

The width of the Animation gallery and the order of the animations may vary, especially if you are using a tablet.

• Change the Start option to With Previous (Figure 3–68).

Q&A Why is a second set of animation numbered tags starting with 0 displaying on the left side of the content placeholder?

They represent the three animations associated with the paragraphs in that placeholder.

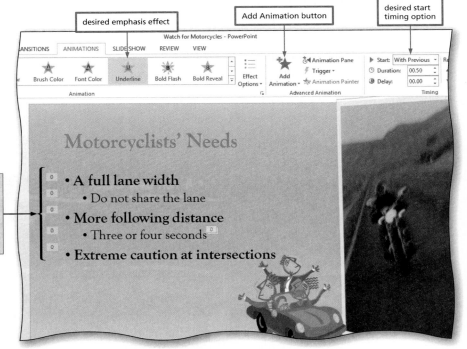

Figure 3–68

Customizing Slide Elements

PowerPoint's varied themes and layouts help give presentations a unified and aesthetically pleasing look. You may, however, desire to modify the default settings to give your slides a unique quality. One of the easier methods of developing a custom show is to change a theme for one or more slides, not an entire presentation. Similarly, you can change the variant for one or more slides to give a coordinating look to the slides in your deck. One other method of altering your slides slightly is to change the default colors associated with a particular theme.

The animated elements on Slide 2 help emphasize the need for drivers to pay particular attention to motorcyclists. Changing the theme colors for that slide to red calls even more attention to the importance of following the guidelines expressed in the bulleted list.

To Change the Theme and Variant on One Slide

1 INSERT & ADD EFFECTS | 2 MODIFY PLACEHOLDERS | 3 MODIFY & COPY ILLUSTRATIONS
4 ADD MEDIA | 5 ANIMATE SLIDE CONTENT | 6 CUSTOMIZE SLIDE ELEMENTS

The Office theme applied to the presentation is appropriate for this topic. The font and placeholder locations are simple and add variety without calling attention to the design elements. The following steps change the theme and variant for Slide 2. *Why? To call attention to the important material in the bulleted list on Slide 2, you can apply an equally effective theme that has a few design elements. You then can modify this new theme by changing the variant on one slide.*

- With Slide 2 displaying, display the DESIGN tab and then tap or click the More button (DESIGN tab | Themes group) to expand the Theme gallery (Figure 3–69).

Experiment

- If you are using a mouse, point to various document themes in the Themes gallery and watch the colors and fonts change on Slide 2.

Figure 3–69

- Press and hold or right-click the Retrospect theme (seventh theme in the first row) to display a shortcut menu (Figure 3–70).

Figure 3–70

3

- Tap or click 'Apply to Selected Slides' to apply the Retrospect theme to Slide 2.
- Press and hold or right-click the gray variant (third variant in the row) to display a shortcut menu (Figure 3–71).

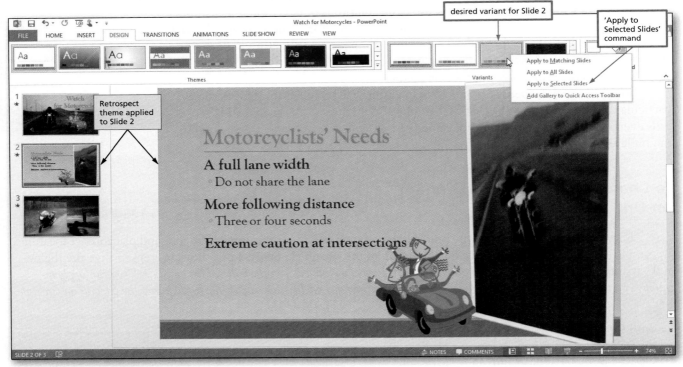

Figure 3–71

4

- Tap or click 'Apply to Selected Slides' to apply the gray variant to Slide 2 (Figure 3–72).

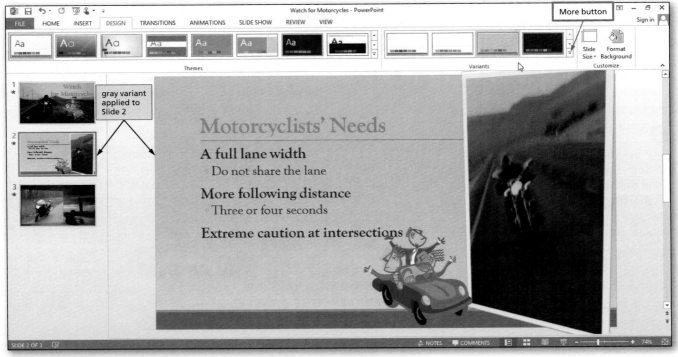

Figure 3–72

To Change the Theme Colors

Every theme has 10 standard colors: two for text, two for backgrounds, and six for accents. The following steps change the theme colors for the Watch for Motorcycles slides. *Why? You can change the look of your presentation and add variety by applying the colors from one theme to another theme.*

1

- Tap or click the More button (shown in Figure 3–72 on the previous page) in the Variants group to expand the gallery.
- Tap or point to Colors in the menu to display the Colors gallery (Figure 3–73).

Experiment

- If you are using a mouse, point to various color rows in the gallery and watch the colors change on Slide 2.

Figure 3–73

2

- Tap or click Red in the gallery to change the Slide 2 colors (Figure 3–74).

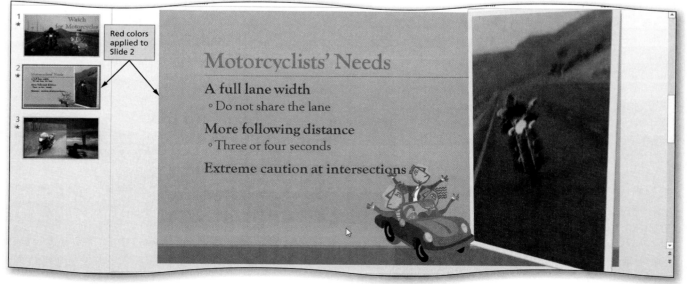

Figure 3–74

To Run a Slide Show with Media

All changes are complete, so you now can view the Watch for Motorcycles presentation. The following steps start Slide Show view.

1 Tap or click the 'Start from Beginning' button to display the title slide and listen to the motorcycle engine sound. Allow the audio clip to repeat several times.

2 Tap the screen or press the SPACEBAR to display Slide 2. Watch the car and bulleted list animations.

3 Tap the screen or press the SPACEBAR to display Slide 3. Watch the video clip.

4 Tap the screen or press the SPACEBAR to end the slide show and then tap or press the SPACEBAR again to exit the slide show.

1 INSERT & ADD EFFECTS | 2 MODIFY PLACEHOLDERS | 3 MODIFY & COPY ILLUSTRATIONS
4 ADD MEDIA | 5 ANIMATE SLIDE CONTENT | 6 CUSTOMIZE SLIDE ELEMENTS

To Preview and Print a Handout

Printing handouts is useful for reviewing a presentation. You can analyze several slides displayed simultaneously on one page. Additionally, many businesses distribute handouts of the slide show before or after a presentation so attendees can refer to a copy. Each page of the handout can contain reduced images of one, two, three, four, six, or nine slides. The three-slides-per-page handout includes lines beside each slide so that your audience can write notes conveniently. The following steps preview and print a presentation handout with two slides per page. *Why? Two of the slides are predominantly pictures, so your audience does not need full pages of those images. The five bulleted paragraphs on Slide 2 can be read easily on one-half of a sheet of paper.*

1
- Tap or click FILE on the ribbon to open the Backstage view and then tap or click the Print tab.
- Tap or click the Previous Page button to display Slide 1 in the Print gallery.
- Tap or click 'Full Page Slides' in the Settings area to display the Full Page Slides gallery (Figure 3–75).

Q&A Why does the preview of my slide appear in color?
Your printer determines how the preview appears. If your printer is capable of printing color images, the preview will appear in color.

Figure 3–75

• Click 2 Slides in the Handouts area to select this option and display a preview of the handout (Figure 3–76).

Q&A The current date displays in the upper-right corner of the handout, and the page number displays in the lower-right corner of the footer. Can I change their location or add other information to the header and footer?
Yes. Click the Edit Header & Footer link at the bottom of the Print gallery, click the Notes and Handouts tab (Header and Footer dialog box), and then decide what content to include on the handout page.

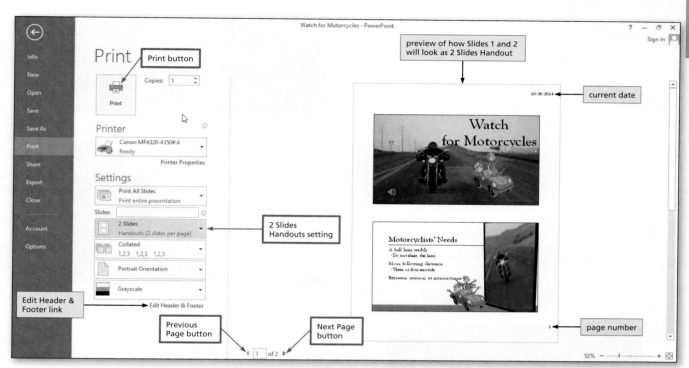

Figure 3–76

BTW

Conserving Ink and Toner

If you want to conserve ink or toner, you can instruct PowerPoint to print draft quality documents by tapping or clicking FILE on the ribbon to open the Backstage view, tapping or clicking Options in the Backstage view to display the PowerPoint Options dialog box, tapping or clicking Advanced in the left pane (PowerPoint Options dialog box), sliding or scrolling to the Print area in the right pane, placing a check mark in the 'Use draft quality' check box, and then tapping or clicking the OK button. Then, use the Backstage view to print the document as usual.

- Click the Next Page and Previous Page buttons to display previews of the two pages in the handout.

- Click the Print button in the Print gallery to print the handout.

- When the printer stops, retrieve the printed handout (Figure 3–77).

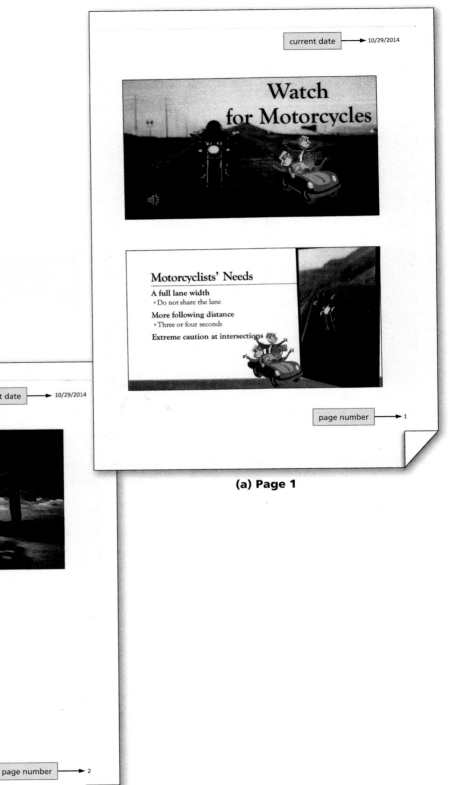

Figure 3–77

To Save the Presentation, Sign Out of a Microsoft Account, and Exit PowerPoint

You have made several changes to the presentation since you last saved it. Thus, you should save it again. The following steps save the presentation, sign out of your Microsoft account, and exit PowerPoint.

1 Tap or click the Save button on the Quick Access Toolbar.

2 If you wish to sign out of your Microsoft account, open the Backstage view, tap or click the Account tab to display the Account gallery, and then tap or click the Sign out link, which displays the Remove Account dialog box. If a Can't remove Windows accounts dialog box appears instead of the Remove Account dialog box, click the OK button and skip the remaining steps.

3 Tap or click the Yes button (Remove Account dialog box) to sign out of your Microsoft account on this computer.

4 Tap or click the Back button in the upper-left corner of the Backstage view to return to the document.

5a If you have one PowerPoint presentation open, tap or click the Close button on the right side of the title bar to close the open document and exit PowerPoint.

5b If you have multiple PowerPoint presentations open, press and hold or right-click the PowerPoint app button on the taskbar and then tap or click 'Close all windows' on the shortcut menu, or press ALT+F4 to close all open presentations and exit PowerPoint.

BTW

Quick Reference
For a table that lists how to complete the tasks covered in this book using touch gestures, the mouse, ribbon, shortcut menu, and keyboard, see the Quick Reference Summary at the back of this book, or visit the Quick Reference resource on the Student Companion Site located on www.cengagebrain.com. For detailed instructions about accessing available resources, visit www.cengage.com/ct/studentdownload or see the inside back cover of this book.

Chapter Summary

In this chapter you have learned how to adjust photo colors and effects, modify placeholders, modify and copy illustrations, add and format media, animate slide content, customize slides, and print a handout. The items listed below include all the new PowerPoint skills you have learned in this chapter, with the tasks grouped by activity.

Add Media to Increase Interest and Visual Appeal
Insert a Video File (PPT 167)
Trim a Video File (PPT 169)
Add Video Options (PPT 170)
Insert an Audio File (PPT 170)
Add Audio Options (PPT 172)
Add a Video Style (PPT 173)
Resize a Video (PPT 175)

Adjust Photo Colors and Effects
Color a Photo (PPT 150)
Add an Artistic Effect to a Photo (PPT 152)
Change the Stacking Order (PPT 153)

Animate Slide Content Using Effects and Timing
Change Views (PPT 157)
Animate an Illustration Using an Entrance Effect (PPT 176)
Change Animation Direction (PPT 177)
Animate an Illustration Using an Emphasis Effect (PPT 177)
Animate an Illustration Using an Exit Effect (PPT 178)

Preview an Animation Sequence (PPT 180)
Modify Entrance Animation Timing (PPT 180)
Animate Content Placeholder Paragraphs (PPT 183)

Customize Slide Colors and Themes
Change the Theme and Variant on One Slide (PPT 185)
Change the Theme Colors (PPT 187)

Modify Illustrations to Create Unique Clips
Ungroup an Illustration (PPT 160)
Change the Color of a Clip Object (PPT 161)
Delete a Clip Object (PPT 163)
Regroup Objects (PPT 165)
Copy a Clip from One Slide to Another (PPT 166)

Modify Placeholders to Customize Slide Appearance
Resize a Placeholder (PPT 154)
Align Paragraph Text (PPT 154)
Move a Placeholder (PPT 155)
Delete a Placeholder (PPT 156)
Add a Text Box (PPT 156)
Preview and Print a Handout (PPT 188)

CONSIDER THIS

What decisions will you need to make when creating your next presentation?
Use these guidelines as you complete the assignments in this chapter and create your own slide show decks outside
of this class.

1. Determine if adjusting photo colors and effects can increase visual appeal.

    a) Change color saturation.

    b) Change tones.

    c) Recolor the image.

2. Vary paragraph alignment.

    a) Themes dictate whether paragraph text is aligned left, center, or right in a placeholder, but you can modify these design decisions when necessary. Moving placeholders and changing paragraph alignment can help create a unique slide.

    b) Different effects are achieved when text alignment shifts in a presentation.

3. Use multimedia selectively.

    a) Locate video, music, and sound files that are appropriate for your audience and that you have permission to use.

    b) Use media files only when necessary, however, because they draw the audience's attention away from the presenter and toward the slides.

    c) Using too many multimedia files can be overwhelming.

4. Use animation sparingly.

    a) PowerPoint audience members usually take notice the first time an animation is displayed on the screen, so be certain the animation will help focus on the precise points being presented during a particular time of the presentation.

    b) Avoid using animation for the sake of using animation. Use animation only when necessary to add emphasis.

    c) Animation overuse annoys and desensitizes audience members.

    d) Carefully decide how text or a slide element enters and exits a slide and how it is displayed once it is present on the slide.

5. Use handouts to organize your speech and to distribute to audiences.

    a) Determine if a handout with two slides per page will help unify your message when you distribute copies to an audience.

How should you submit solutions to questions in the assignments identified with a **symbol?**

Every assignment in this book contains one or more questions identified with a ✳ symbol. These questions require you to think beyond the assigned presentation. Present your solutions to the questions in the format required by your instructor. Possible formats may include one or more of these options: write the answer; create a document that contains the answer; present your answer to the class; discuss your answer in a group; record the answer as audio or video using a webcam, smartphone, or portable media player; or post answers on a blog, wiki, or website.

Apply Your Knowledge

Reinforce the skills and apply the concepts you learned in this chapter.

Resizing a Photo by Entering Exact Measurements, Formatting a Video Border, Moving a Placeholder, and Animating a Photo and Title Using an Entrance Effect

Note: To complete this assignment, you will be required to use the Data Files for Students. Visit www.cengage.com/ct/studentdownload for detailed instructions or contact your instructor for information about accessing the required files.

Instructions: Run PowerPoint. Open the presentation, Apply 3-1 Trees, from the Data Files for Students.

The six slides in the presentation, shown in Figure 3–78, discuss the importance of pruning trees and the methods used to prune the trees. The document you open is composed of slides containing photos, illustrations, and a video. You will apply artistic effects or modify some of these graphic elements. You also will move placeholders. In addition, you will animate photos and a title using an entrance effect.

Perform the following tasks:

1. On the title slide, color the photo by selecting Saturation: 200% from the Color Saturation area (the fifth effect), and apply the Paint Brush artistic effect (the third effect in the second row) to the photo, as shown in Figure 3–78a. Increase the photo size to 6.47" × 9.73" and apply the Soft Edge Oval picture style (the sixth style in the third row). Then apply the Float In Entrance effect, change the duration to 3.00, and change the start timing setting to With Previous. Move the photo to the top of the slide, as shown in the figure.

(a) Slide 1
Figure 3–78 (Continued)

Continued >

Apply Your Knowledge *continued*

2. Change the title font to Arial Black, increase the font size to 60 point, and then change the font color to Light Green (the fifth color in the Standard Colors row). Move the title placeholder to the lower-left corner of the slide as shown in the figure. Apply the Fly In from Top Right Entrance effect to the title text font and change the duration to 2.00. Change the start timing setting to After Previous.

3. On Slide 2, change the title text font to Arial Black and then change the font color to Dark Blue (the ninth color in the Standard Colors row). Use the Format Painter to format the title text font on Slides 3 through 6 with the same features as the title text font on Slide 2. Increase the size of the list font on Slide 2 to 24 point, change the font color to Dark Blue and then bold this text. Move the list placeholder to the lower-right area of the slide, as shown in Figure 3–78b.

4. Increase the size of the illustration to approximately 3.42" × 3.17", apply the Thick Matte, Black picture style (the first style in the second row), and then move the illustration to the location shown in the figure.

5. On Slide 3, increase the left and right placeholder text fonts to 28 point, and bold them. Change the font color in the left placeholder to Green (the sixth color in the Standard Colors) and change the font color in the right placeholder to Blue (the eighth color in the Standard Colors), as shown in Figure 3–78c.

6. On Slide 3, change the Drop Shadow Rectangle picture style to the Metal Frame picture style (the third style in the first row), and change the picture border color to Gold, Accent 5 (the ninth color in the first Theme Colors row) on both photos. Apply the Fly In from Left Entrance effect to the left photo, change the duration to 1.25, and change the start timing setting to After Previous. Apply the Fly In from the Right Entrance effect to the right photo, change the duration to 1.25, and then change the start timing setting to With Previous.

7. On Slide 4, increase the size of the video to 5.3" × 9.41" and move the video to the location shown in Figure 3–78d. Add a 6 pt Red, Accent 2 border (the sixth color in the first Theme Colors row) and then apply an Offset Diagonal Bottom Right Video Effect (the first effect in the Outer Shadow area) to the video, as shown in Figure 3–78d.

8. Increase the size of the photo to approximately 3.76" × 4.69" on Slide 5. Apply the Double Frame, Black picture style (the seventh style in the first row) to the photo, and then move the photo to the location shown in Figure 3–78e. Also move the list placeholder to the lower-right area of the slide as shown.

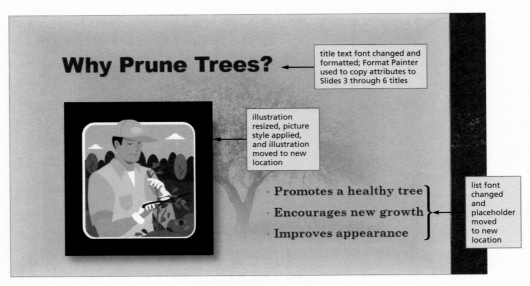

(b) Slide 2

Figure 3–78

(c) Slide 3

(d) Slide 4

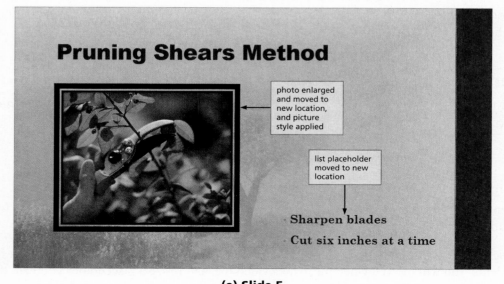

(e) Slide 5

Figure 3–78 (Continued)

Continued >

Apply Your Knowledge *continued*

9. On Slide 6, increase the font size of the subtitle text font to 32 point, change the font color to Red, Accent 2 (the sixth color in the first Theme Colors row), center the text and then move this placeholder so it is centered under the title text font, as shown in Figure 3–78f.

10. On Slide 6, increase the size of the illustration to approximately 5.53" × 4.24", apply the Reflected Bevel, Black picture style (the fourth style in the fourth row), and change the color to Red, Accent color 2 Light (the third effect in the third row in the Recolor area). Move the illustration to the location shown in the figure.

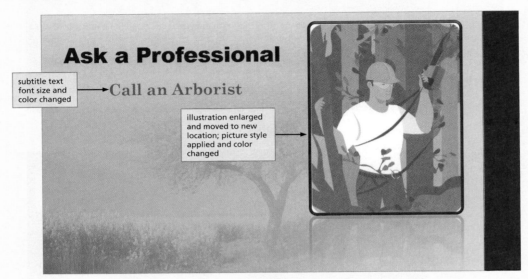

(f) Slide 6

Figure 3–78 (Continued)

11. If requested by your instructor, add your father's first name as a second line under the subtitle.

12. Apply the Wind transition in the Exciting category to Slides 2, 5, and 6. Change the duration to 3.50 seconds.

13. Save the presentation using the file name, Apply 3-1 Tree Pruning.

14. Submit the revised document in the format specified by your instructor.

15. ✳ In Step 2, you moved the title placeholder to the bottom of the title slide and changed the color. How did this style improve the slide? On Slide 3, you applied entrance effect animations to the two photos and changed the placeholder text fonts to different colors. Why?

Extend Your Knowledge

Extend the skills you learned in this chapter and experiment with new skills. You may need to use Help to complete the assignment.

Changing Theme Colors, Inserting a Video File, Trimming a Video File, Resizing a Placeholder, and Inserting an Audio File

Note: To complete this assignment, you will be required to use the Data Files for Students. Visit www.cengage.com/ct/studentdownload for detailed instructions or contact your instructor for information about accessing the required files.

Instructions: Run PowerPoint. Open the presentation, Extend 3-1 Tortoise, from the Data Files for Students. You will insert a video file, trim a video file, and resize a placeholder to create the presentation shown in Figure 3–79.

Perform the following tasks:

1. Change the theme variant to Green and choose the Sand texture fill (the third texture in the second row) to format the background on all slides. Also change the transparency to 33%.

2. On Slide 1, change the title text font to Cooper Black, increase the size to 80 point, and add the Small Caps font effect. Hint: Font effects are located in the Font dialog box (HOME tab | Font group). Also change the font color to Green, Accent 2, Darker 50% (the sixth color in the sixth Theme Colors row) and then center the text. Decrease the size of the title placeholder to approximately 1.33" × 5.49" and move this placeholder to the left side of the slide, as shown in Figure 3–79a.

3. Increase the text font size of the subtitle text font to 40 point, and center the text. Decrease the size of the subtitle placeholder to approximately 0.66" × 5.24" and move this placeholder under the title placeholder, as shown in the figure.

4. Increase the size of the photo to approximately 7.49" × 5.01", apply the Soft Edge Rectangle picture effect (the sixth effect in the first row), and then move the photo to the right side of the slide, as shown in Figure 3–79a.

5. On Slide 1, change the volume to low on the audio file (Gentle Nature), start it automatically, play across slides, and hide during the show.

6. Slide 2, change the title text font to Cooper Black, decrease the font size to 40 point, change the font color to Green, Accent 2, Darker 50% (the sixth color in the sixth Theme Colors row), and align the text left. Use the Format Painter to apply these attributes to the title text font on Slides 3 and 4. Apply the Bevel Perspective Level, White picture style (the third style in the fourth row) to the photo and move it to the upper-right corner of the slide, as shown in Figure 3–79b.

7. Copy the turtle illustration from Slide 4 and paste it on Slide 2 and move to the location shown. Apply the Fly Out To Right Exit effect to the illustration and change the duration to 4.00. Change the start timing setting to After Previous. Delete the turtle illustration from Slide 4.

8. On Slide 3, align the title font to the top of the placeholder. Hint: placeholder alignments are located on the Align Text dialog box (HOME tab | Paragraph group). Move the title placeholder to the top of the slide, as shown in Figure 3–79c.

(a) Slide 1

Figure 3–79 (Continued)

Continued >

Extend Your Knowledge *continued*

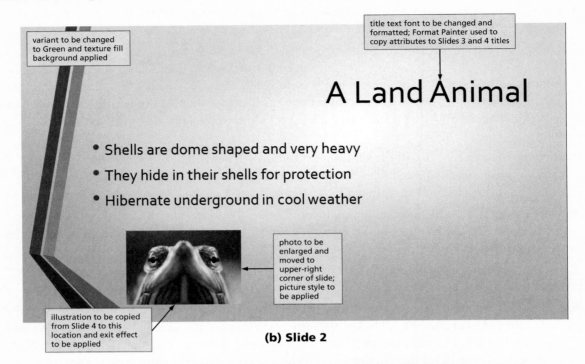

variant to be changed to Green and texture fill background applied

title text font to be changed and formatted; Format Painter used to copy attributes to Slides 3 and 4 titles

A Land Animal

- Shells are dome shaped and very heavy
- They hide in their shells for protection
- Hibernate underground in cool weather

photo to be enlarged and moved to upper-right corner of slide; picture style to be applied

illustration to be copied from Slide 4 to this location and exit effect to be applied

(b) Slide 2

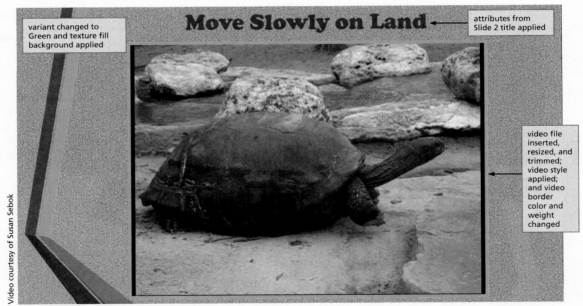

variant changed to Green and texture fill background applied

Move Slowly on Land

attributes from Slide 2 title applied

video file inserted, resized, and trimmed; video style applied; and video border color and weight changed

Video courtesy of Susan Sebok

(c) Slide 3

Figure 3–79

9. Insert the video file, Turtle, from the Data Files for Students. Resize this video file to approximately 6.34" × 8.45" and move the video to the location shown in the figure. Apply the Moderate Frame, Black video style (the second style in the first row in the Moderate area). Change the color of the border to Lime, Accent 1 (the fifth color in the first Theme Colors row) and change the border weight to 6 pt. Trim the video so that the Start Time is 00:09.650 and the End Time is 00:39.755. Start this video automatically.

10. On Slide 4, increase the size of the photo and apply the Reflected Bevel, Black picture style (the fourth style in the fourth row) to the photo, as shown in Figure 3–79d.

(d) Slide 4
Figure 3–79 (Continued)

11. Apply the Fly In From Right Entrance effect to the title text font and change the duration to 5.00. Change the start timing setting to After Previous. Delete the turtle illustration from Slide 4.

12. If requested by your instructor, insert a text box on Slide 4 under the turtle picture and add the name of your current or previous pet.

13. Apply an appropriate transition to all slides.

14. Save the presentation using the file name, Extend 3-1 Slow Tortoise.

15. Submit the revised document in the format specified by your instructor.

16. ✳ In this assignment, you inserted an audio file to play across the slides. How did this enhance the presentation?

Analyze, Correct, Improve

Analyze a presentation, correct all errors, and improve it.

Correcting Formatting, Coloring a Photo, Changing Animation Direction, and Inserting and Moving a Text Box
Note: To complete this assignment, you will be required to use the Data Files for Students. Visit www.cengage.com/ct/studentdownload for detailed instructions or contact your instructor for information about accessing the required files.

Instructions: Run PowerPoint. Open the presentation, Analyze 3-1 Bulb Flowers, from the Data Files for Students. This presentation contains five slides and explains how to plant bulb flowers. Modify the slides by making the indicated corrections and improvements.

1. Correct

a. Change the variant to green (the third one), as shown in Figure 3–80 on the next page.

b. Decrease the font size of the Slide 1 title text font to 66 point and change the font color to Yellow (the fourth color in the Standard Colors).

c. On Slide 1, change the volume of the audio file to low and hide during show.

Continued >

Analyze, Correct, Improve *continued*

d. If requested by your instructor, change your first name on Slide 1 to your grandmother's first name.

e. On Slides 2 and 3, adjust the photo sizes and move them so they do not overlap text and are the appropriate dimensions for the slide content.

f. On all slides, adjust text font sizes and text font colors so they are the appropriate size and enhance the presentation.

2. Improve

a. On Slide 1, change the Color Saturation of the photo to Saturation: 200% (the fifth color in the first row).

b. On Slides 2 and 3, change the picture style for all photos to Reflected Rounded Rectangle (the fifth style in the first row).

c. On Slide 4, change the picture border to Lavender, Accent 4 (the eighth color in the first Theme Colors row) on the photo and then change the border weight to 6 pt.

d. On Slides 4 and 5, change the From Bottom Left Entrance effect to the From Bottom Right Entrance effect on the titles.

e. Increase the size of the video on Slide 5 so that it is as large as possible and move it so it is aligned above the caption. Change the volume on the video to Medium on Slide 5. Also change the video option to start automatically.

f. Save the presentation using the file name, Analyze 3-1 – Planting Bulb Flowers.

g. Submit the revised document in the format specified by your instructor.

3. ✸ Which errors existed in the starting file? How did changing the picture styles help? When you adjusted the photo sizes, how did you determine their final sizes?

Figure 3–80

In the Labs

Design and/or create a presentation using the guidelines, concepts, and skills presented in this chapter. Labs 1 and 2, which increase in difficulty, require you to create solutions based on what you learned in the chapter; Lab 3 requires you to create a solution, which uses cloud and web technologies, by learning and investigating on your own from general guidance.

Lab 1: Changing the Stacking Order, Adding Audio Options to an Audio File, and Animating a Photo, Illustration, and Title Using Entrance Effects

Problem: Open the presentation, Lab 3-1 Kangaroos, from the Data Files for Students. You are studying Australia in your Geography class and on a recent vacation you visited a zoo that had kangaroos. You thought it would be interesting to put together a presentation for your class about some of the unique things about kangaroos like how long a joey stays in its mother's pouch. Create the slides shown in Figure 3–81.

Note: To complete this assignment, you will be required to use the Data Files for Students. Visit www.cengage.com/ct/studentdownload for detailed instructions or contact your instructor for information about accessing the required files.

Instructions: Perform the following tasks:

1. On Slide 1, increase the size of the photo, and apply the Soft Edge Oval picture style (the sixth style in the third row), and move the photo to the location shown in Figure 3–81a.

2. Apply the Grow and Turn entrance effect to the title text font. Change the start timing option to With Previous and the duration to 03.50 seconds.

3. Increase the size of the kangaroo illustration and bring the illustration to the front of the photo. Apply the Bounce entrance effect to the illustration and change the start timing option to After Previous and the duration to 03.50 seconds, as shown in Figure 3–81a.

4. Select the audio file, Happiness Music, on Slide 1 and change the volume to low, start Automatically, play across slides and loop until stopped. Also hide this audio file during the show.

5. On Slide 2, increase the size of the kangaroo illustration so that it measures approximately 3.27" × 5.24" and apply the Bounce entrance effect. Change the start timing option to With Previous and the duration to 03.00. Move the illustration to the lower-right corner of the slide, as shown in Figure 3–81b on the next page.

(a) Slide 1

Figure 3–81 (Continued)

Continued >

In the Labs *continued*

6. On Slide 3, apply the Simple Frame, Black picture styles (the second style in the second row) to both photos. Apply the Orange, Accent 6 fill (the last color in the first Theme Colors row) to each rounded rectangle shape. Also change the font color in these shapes to Black and then bold them, as shown in Figure 3–81c.

7. On Slide 4, change the size of the video so that it measures approximately 6.53" × 8.9", and move the video to the location shown in Figure 3–81d. Change the video style to the Beveled Perspective Left (the first style in the first Intense area row), change the border color to Orange, Accent 1 (the fifth color in the first Theme Colors row), and then change the border weight to 10 pt, as shown in the figure. Have the video start Automatically.

8. Trim the end of the video by leaving the Start Time at 00:00 and changing the End Time to 00:33.394.

9. On Slide 5, apply the Bevel Rectangle picture style (the seventh style in the third row) to the koala photo, apply the Bevel Perspective picture style (the first style in the fourth row) to the opossum photo. Move the two photos to the locations shown, and bring the opossum picture forward, as shown in Figure 3–81e.

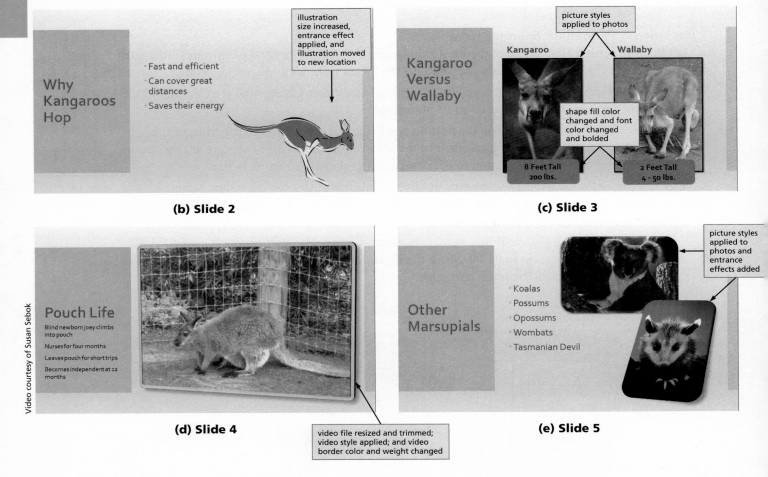

(b) Slide 2

(c) Slide 3

(d) Slide 4

(e) Slide 5

Figure 3–81

10. Apply the Fade entrance effect to the two photos. Change the start timing option to After Previous and the duration to 02.50.

11. If requested by your instructor, insert a text box on Slide 5 and add the name of the street where you lived as a child.

12. Save the presentation using the file name, Lab 3-1 Kangaroos and Wallabies.

13. Submit the document in the format specified by your instructor.

14. ✹ On Slide 1, why did you bring the kangaroo illustration to the front of the photo? Why did you trim the end of the video instead of the beginning of the video on Slide 4?

Lab 2: Ungrouping a Clip, Changing the Color of a Clip Object, Deleting a Clip Object, and Regrouping Objects

Problem: On your recent vacation in Mexico, you saw a muster of peafowl residing on the resort grounds. You found them to be very tame and interesting. And you were especially amazed at the beautiful plumage of the male peafowl or peacock. You belong to the local Audubon Society, and next month it is your turn to make a presentation. You thought the members would enjoy seeing a presentation of the peafowl you saw during your vacation. You decide to create the presentation shown in Figure 3–82.

Note: To complete this assignment, you will be required to use the Data Files for Students. Visit www.cengage.com/ct/studentdownload for detailed instructions or contact your instructor for information about accessing the required files.

Instructions: Perform the following tasks:

1. Open the presentation, Lab 3-2 Peacocks, from the Data Files for Students.

2. On Slide 1, apply the Rotated, White, picture style (the third style in the third row) to the photo. Increase the size of the photo so that it measures approximately 7.02" × 4.61" and move the photo to the location shown in Figure 3–82a.

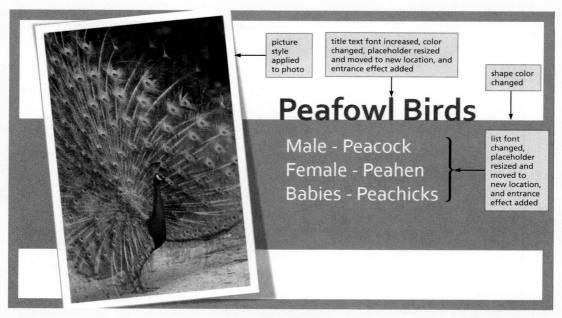

(a) Slide 1
Figure 3–82 (Continued)

Continued >

In the Labs continued

3. Increase the title text font to 60 point, and change the color of the title text font to Purple (the tenth color in the Standard Colors). Decrease the size of the title placeholder to approximately 1.11" × 6.33" and position the title on top of the rectangle, as shown in the figure. Apply the Fly In From Left entrance effect to the title, change the start timing option to After Previous, and change the duration to 03.00.

4. Change the color of the purple rectangular shape on Slide 1 to Turquoise, Accent 1 (the fifth color in the first Theme Colors row).

5. Increase the subtitle text font to 36 point, decrease the size of the subtitle placeholder to approximately 1.78" × 5.93", and move the placeholder to the position shown in the figure.

6. Apply the Fly In From Left entrance effect to the first line of the subtitle, change the start timing option to After Previous and the duration to 02.25. Apply the Fly In From Left entrance effect to the second line of the subtitle and then change the start timing option to After Previous and the duration to 02.25. Apply the same animation settings to the third line of the subtitle text.

7. On Slide 2, increase the size of the video to approximately 5.57" × 7.42", apply the Canvas, White video style (the fourth style in the second row in the Intense area) to the video, change the video border color to Turquoise, Accent 1 (the fifth color in the first Theme colors row), and then change the border weight to 6 pt, as shown in Figure 3–82b. Trim the video so that the Start Time is 00:01.147. Change the volume to Low, and start the video automatically. Move the video to the left side of the slide, as shown in the figure.

8. Apply the Soft Edge Oval picture style (the sixth style in the third row) to the photo, enlarge it, and move it to the bottom-right corner of the slide as shown.

9. On Slide 3, select the peacock illustration and zoom in to the three oval spots at the end of the peacock's feathers. Ungroup this illustration. Select the green oval spot on the left feather and change the color to Turquoise, Accent 3 (the seventh color in the first Shape Fill Theme Colors row). Regroup the clip, as shown in Figure 3–82c on the next page.

10. Change the volume on the audio file to low, play across slides, and hide during the show.

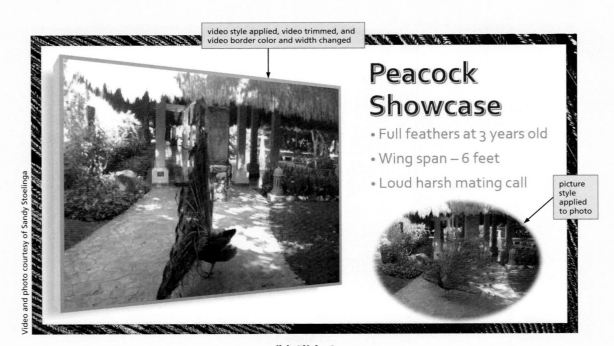

(b) Slide 2

Figure 3–82

(c) Slide 3

(d) Slide 4

Figure 3–82

11. On Slide 4, apply the Reflected Rounded Rectangle picture style (the fifth style in the first row) to the upper-right photo and apply the Bevel Rectangle picture style (the seventh style in the third row) to the photo at bottom-center of the slide, as shown in Figure 3–82d on the next page.

12. Apply the Appear entrance effect to the two photos. Change the start timing option to After Previous.

13. If requested by your instructor, insert a text box at the lower-right corner of Slide 3 and type the color of your eyes in the text box.

14. Change the transition to Fade in the Subtle category to all slides. Change the duration to 3.00 seconds.

Continued >

In the Labs *continued*

15. Save the presentation using the file name, Lab 3-2 Peacock Plumage.

16. Submit the revised document in the format specified by your instructor.

17. ✹ In Step 4, you changed the color of the rectangle shape from purple to turquoise. How did that color change improve the title slide? Why did you change the volume on the audio file to low?

Lab 3: Expand Your World: Cloud and Web Technologies
Inserting Video Files from the Web

Problem: The Watch for Motorcycles presentation you created in the chapter has a video you inserted from the Data Files for Students. The rider in this video demonstrated proper riding techniques and had appropriate riding attire. Many organizations promoting motorcycle safety have created videos and posted them to online websites. PowerPoint allows you to insert online videos easily in a manner similar to how you inserted the Motorcycle Rider file. You are going to search for and then insert one of these online videos into the Watch for Motorcycles presentation.

Note: To complete this assignment, you will be required to use the Data Files for Students. Visit www.cengage.com/ct/studentdownload for detailed instructions or contact your instructor for information about accessing the required files.

Instructions:

1. Open the Watch for Motorcycles file, insert a new Slide 4 with the Title and Content layout, and then type **Safety Tips** as the title text. Use the Format Painter to copy the font formatting from Slide 2 to the new Slide 4 title. Center this title text.

2. Format the Slide 4 background with a gradient or texture fill.

3. Tap or click the Insert Video icon in the content placeholder to display the Insert Video dialog box. If necessary, tap or click the YouTube button at the bottom on the dialog box to add that website to the list of file locations.

4. Tap or click the YouTube search box and then type **motorcycle safety tips** as the search text.

5. When the search results are displayed, browse the video frames and tap or click one that appears to fit the theme of this presentation. View the title of the video, its length, and its source in the lower-left corner of the dialog box. Then, tap or click the View Larger (magnifying glass) icon in the lower-right corner of the video frame to view a preview of the video.

6. Tap or click the Insert button to insert the video on Slide 4.

7. Add a style to the video and then resize the frame. Start this file automatically during the presentation and have it play full screen, if possible.

8. If requested to do so by your instructor, add the city where you were born to the Slide 4 title text.

9. Save the presentation using the file name, Lab 3-3 Watch for Motorcycles Expanded.

10. Submit the assignment in the format specified by your instructor.

11. ✹ What criteria did you use to select a particular YouTube video? What decisions did you make to choose a background format?

✳ Consider This: Your Turn

Apply your creative thinking and problem-solving skills to design and implement a solution.

1. Design and Create a Presentation about Canal Locks

Personal

Part 1:   Your family belongs to a small boat club with 10 members. The club has planned a canal cruise next summer. Everyone knows there are different water levels on this canal. As the president of your club, you were asked to get all the information necessary about how the 10 boats will pass through the locks. Some of the members of your club have admitted they know very little about canal or river locks. Last summer when you went to one of the lock sites, you took a video and asked the person manning the locks some questions. You learned that the locks are manned 24 hours a day between May and October. He explained how the locks are similar to a flight of stairs. There are two sets of gates (top and bottom) and the chamber where your boat enters. The gates close and water is added or drained to meet the next level. Use the concepts and techniques presented in this chapter to prepare a presentation with a minimum of four slides that explores this subject. Select a suitable theme, add media including the video named Locks Video available in the Data Files for Students and search for an appropriate audio file to add interest to your presentation. The presentation should also contain photos and illustrations. The Data Files for Students contains five photos and illustrations called Locks1, Locks2, Locks3, Locks4, and Locks5. You can add your own digital photos or videos or photos from Office.com if they are appropriate for this topic. Apply picture styles and effects. Add a title slide and closing slide to complete your presentation. Submit your assignment in the format specified by your instructor.

Part 2:   ✳ You made several decisions while creating the presentation in this assignment: where to place text, how to format the text (for example, font, font size, and adding font effects), which graphical image(s) to use, what styles and effects to apply, where to position the graphical image, how to format the graphical images, and which shapes to use to add interest to the presentation. What was the rationale behind each of these decisions? When you reviewed the document, what further revisions did you make and why? Where would you recommend showing this slide show?

2. Design and Create a Presentation about Garter Snakes

Professional

Part 1:   You work part-time as a teacher's assistant in an elementary school science class. The teacher decided that a garter snake would make an excellent reptile addition to the classroom. She assigned you the task of getting a garter snake and setting up its habitat. You learned that they are harmless and non-venomous, they eat bugs and small rodents, they can grow to between 1 foot (0.3048 m) and 2 feet (0.6096 m) long. They can help control mice or insect problems. You will need a container with a secure lid, preferably a glass aquarium. You decide to put together a presentation to teach the class about garter snakes and how to care for them. Use the concepts and techniques presented in this chapter to create a presentation with at least four slides. Select a suitable theme and then include a title slide, photos, illustrations, and an audio file to add interest to the presentation. The Data Files for Students contains a video called Snake1 and five photos and illustrations called Snake2, Snake3, Snake4, Snake5, and Snake6. One or more of the illustrations can be ungrouped, and you can change the color to add some visual interest to the presentation. Submit your assignment in the format specified by your instructor.

Part 2:   ✳ You made several decisions while creating the presentation in this assignment: where to place text, how to format the text (such as font and font size), which graphical image(s) to use, what styles and effects to apply, where to position the graphical images, and which shapes to use to add interest to the presentation. What was the rationale behind each of these decisions? When you reviewed the document, what further revisions did you make and why? Where would you recommend showing this slide show?

STUDENT ASSIGNMENTS

Consider This: Your Turn *continued*

3. Design and Create a Presentation about Bird Watching
Research and Collaboration

Part 1: Millions of people across the country enjoy watching birds. Some belong to clubs, and some join bird watching tours in their cities and also in other states and countries. Some plan holidays and family trips around the migration habits of their favorite birds. It is an inexpensive hobby and a good reason to get some exercise outdoors and enjoy nature. The activity is very relaxing and is a great social activity. You have decided to start a bird watching club with some of your friends and neighbors. There are 12 members of your club, so you divide into three groups of four members. One group will go to the library and do some research on the various species of birds in your area. The second group will research what kind of binoculars are best for beginners. The third group will take some video and photos at the local nature center so that you can put together a presentation about bird watching to share with your new club members. After gathering all the information and photos about bird watching, use the concepts and techniques presented in this chapter to prepare a presentation with a minimum of four slides that explore the subject of bird watching. Select a suitable theme, include a title slide, bulleted lists, shapes, and WordArt. The Data Files for Students contains one video called Bird Watching and six photos and illustrations called Birds1, Birds2, Birds3, Birds4, Birds5, and Birds6. Change the color for at least one photo. Apply a transition in the Subtle area to all slides and increase the duration. Submit your assignment in the format specified by your instructor.

Part 2: ✺ You made several decisions while creating the presentation in this assignment: where to place text, how to format the text (such as font, font size, and where to use WordArt), which image(s) to use, what styles and effects to apply, where to position the images, which styles to use, and which shapes to use to add interest to the presentation. What was the rationale behind each of these decisions? When you reviewed the document, what further revisions did you make and why? Where would you recommend showing this slide show?

Learn Online

Reinforce what you learned in this chapter with games, exercises, training, and many other online activities and resources.

Student Companion Site Reinforcement activities and resources are available at no additional cost on www.cengagebrain.com. Visit www.cengage.com/ct/studentdownload for detailed instructions about accessing the resources available at the Student Companion Site.

SAM Put your skills into practice with SAM! If you have a SAM account, go to www.cengage.com/sam2013 to access SAM assignments for this chapter.

Index

Note: Please note that boldfaced page numbers indicate key terms.

Quick Reference Summary

Task	Page Number	Ribbon	Other On-Screen Areas	Shortcut Menu	Keyboard Shortcut
Animation, Add	PPT 176	ANIMATIONS tab | Animation group			
Animation, Add to Existing	PPT 177	Add Animation button (ANIMATIONS tab | Advanced Animation group)			
Animation, Change Direction	PPT 177	Effect Options button (ANIMATIONS tab | Animation group)			
Animation, Delete	PPT 179				Tap or click number associated with animation, DELETE
Animation, Modify Timing	PPT 180	ANIMATIONS tab | Timing group			
Animation, Preview Sequence	PPT 180	Preview button (ANIMATIONS tab | Preview group)		Play Selected button (Animation task pane)	
Audio File, Insert	PPT 170	Audio button (INSERT tab | Media group)			
Audio Options, Add	PPT 172	AUDIO TOOLS PLAYBACK tab | Audio Options group			
Clip Object, Delete	PPT 163	Cut button (HOME tab | Clipboard group)		Cut	
Clip Object, Change Color	PPT 161	Shape Fill arrow (DRAWING TOOLS FORMAT tab | Shape Styles group)		Fill button; or Format Shape, Fill & Line icon, FILL, Solid fill, Color button (Format Shape task pane)	
Copy	PPT 101, PPT 166	Copy button (HOME tab | Clipboard group)		Copy	CTRL+C
Document Properties, Change	PPT 48	Properties button (FILE tab | Info tab)			

Microsoft PowerPoint 2013 Quick Reference Summary *(continued)*

Task	Page Number	Ribbon	Other On-Screen Areas	Shortcut Menu	Keyboard Shortcut
Document Properties, Print	PPT 122	FILE tab, Print tab, Print All Slides button, Document Info, Print button			
Document Theme, Change Color Variant	PPT 5	Choose color variant (DESIGN tab | Variants group)			
Document Theme, Choose	PPT 5	FILE tab, New tab; More button (DESIGN tab | Themes group)			
Exit PowerPoint	OFF 42, PPT 55	Exit (FILE tab)	Close button on title bar	Right-click PowerPoint app button on taskbar, click Close window	ALT+F4 or CTRL+Q
Font Size, Decrease	PPT 100	Decrease Font Size button or Font Size arrow (HOME tab | Font group)	Decrease Font Size button or Font Size arrow on mini toolbar	Font, Size arrows (Font dialog box)	CTRL+SHIFT+LEFT CARET (<)
Font Size, Increase	PPT 12	Increase Font Size button or Font Size arrow (HOME tab | Font group)	Increase Font Size button or Font Size arrow on mini toolbar	Font, Size arrows (Font dialog box)	CTRL+SHIFT+RIGHT CARET (>)
Font, Change	PPT 98	Font arrow or Font dialog box launcher (HOME tab | Font group)	Font arrow on mini toolbar	Font	CTRL+SHIFT+F
Font, Change Color	PPT 13	Font Color button or Font Color arrow or Font dialog box launcher (HOME tab | Font group)	Font Color button or Font Color arrow on mini toolbar	Font, Font Color button on Font tab (Font dialog box)	CTRL+SHIFT+F
Format Painter, Use	PPT 101	Double-click Format Painter button (HOME tab | Clipboard group), select text with format you want to copy, select text to apply previously selected format; press ESC to turn off Format Painter	Format Painter button on mini toolbar		
Handout, Print	PPT 188	Full Page Slides button (FILE tab | Print tab), select layout in Handouts section, tap or click Print button			CTRL+P
Illustration, Regroup	PPT 165	Group button, Regroup command (DRAWING TOOLS FORMAT tab | Arrange group)		Group, Regroup	
Illustration, Ungroup	PPT 160	Group button, Ungroup command (PICTURE TOOLS FORMAT tab | Arrange group), click Yes to convert to Microsoft Office drawing, click DRAWING TOOLS FORMAT tab, Group button, Ungroup		Group, Ungroup	CTRL+SHIFT+G
Illustration, Placeholder, or Shape, Move	PPT 39, PPT 155		Drag		ARROW KEYS move selected image in small increments
List Level, Increase	PPT 19	Increase List Level button (HOME tab | Paragraph group)	Increase List Level button on mini toolbar		TAB

Microsoft PowerPoint 2013 Quick Reference Summary *(continued)*

Task	Page Number	Ribbon	Other On-Screen Areas	Shortcut Menu	Keyboard Shortcut
List Level, Decrease	PPT 19	Decrease List Level button (HOME tab | Paragraph group)	Decrease List Level button on mini toolbar		SHIFT+TAB
Move to Another Slide in Normal View	PPT 29		Next Slide or Previous Slide buttons on vertical scroll bar; drag scroll box on vertical scroll bar; click slide thumbnail in Thumbnail pane Touch Mode: Tap desired slide in Thumbnail pane		PAGE DOWN (next slide); PAGE UP (previous slide)
Move to Another Slide in Slide Show View	PPT 50		Click to display next slide; click Next Slide or Previous Slide icons on Slide Show toolbar Touch Mode: Swipe forward or backward on slide		PAGE DOWN (next slide); PAGE UP (previous slide); RIGHT ARROW or DOWN ARROW (next slide); LEFT ARROW or UP ARROW (previous slide)
Notes, Add	PPT 115		Notes icon on status bar; type notes in Notes pane		
Notes, Print	PPT 121	FILE tab, Print tab, tap or click Notes Pages (Print Layout area), tap or click Print button			CTRL+P
Open Presentation	OFF 54	Open (FILE tab)			CTRL+O
Paste	PPT 101, PPT 166	Paste button (HOME tab | Clipboard group)		Paste	CTRL+V
Picture, Add an Artistic Effect	PPT 152	Artistic Effects button (PICTURE TOOLS FORMAT tab | Adjust group)		Format Picture, Effects icon, ARTISTIC EFFECTS (Format Picture pane)	
Picture, Add Border	PPT 88	Picture Border arrow (PICTURE TOOLS FORMAT tab | Picture Styles group)			
Picture, Change	PPT 85	Change Picture button (PICTURE TOOLS FORMAT tab | Adjust group)		Change Picture	
Picture, Color or Recolor	PPT 150	Color button (PICTURE TOOLS FORMAT tab | Adjust group)		Format Picture, Picture icon, PICTURE COLOR (Format Picture pane)	
Picture, Correct	PPT 87	Corrections button (PICTURE TOOLS FORMAT tab | Adjust group)	Picture Corrections Options (Corrections gallery)	Format Picture, Picture Corrections (Format Picture dialog box)	
Picture, Insert	PPT 31	Pictures button or Online Pictures button (INSERT tab | Images group)	Pictures icon or Online Pictures icon in slide		
Picture, Move	PPT 39		Drag		ARROW keys to move in small increments

Microsoft PowerPoint 2013 Quick Reference Summary *(continued)*

Task	Page Number	Ribbon	Other On-Screen Areas	Shortcut Menu	Keyboard Shortcut
Picture Border, Change Color or Weight	PPT 88–89	Picture Border arrow (PICTURE TOOLS FORMAT tab | Picture Styles group)		Format Picture, Fill & Line, Line (Format Picture pane)	
Picture Effects, Apply	PPT 90	Picture Effects button (PICTURE TOOLS FORMAT tab | Picture Styles group)		Format Picture, Effects (Format Picture pane)	
Picture Style, Apply	PPT 87	More button (PICTURE TOOLS FORMAT tab | Picture Styles group)			
Placeholder, Delete	PPT 156			Cut	select placeholder, DELETE or BACKSPACE
Placeholder, Move	PPT 155		Drag		
Placeholder, Resize	PPT 154		Drag sizing handles		
Print a Presentation	PPT 52	Print button (FILE tab | Print tab)			CTRL+P
Resize	PPT 36, PPT 93, PPT 175	Enter height and width values (PICTURE TOOLS FORMAT tab | Size group or DRAWING TOOLS FORMAT tab | Size group or VIDEO TOOLS FORMAT tab | Size group)	Drag sizing handles	Format Picture or Format Shape or Format Video, Size & Properties icon	
Run PowerPoint	OFF 46, PPT 4		PowerPoint 2013 tile on Start menu; search for PowerPoint 2013 using Search charm on Charms bar		
Save a Presentation	PPT 82	Save (FILE tab)	Save button on Quick Access toolbar		CTRL+S or SHIFT+F12
Save a Presentation with a New Name	PPT 15	Save As (FILE tab)			
Shape, Add	PPT 92, PPT 94	Shapes button (Insert tab | Illustrations group); Shapes More button (HOME tab | Drawing group) or DRAWING TOOLS FORMAT tab | Insert Shapes group			
Shape, Apply Style	PPT 95	Quick Styles button (HOME tab | Drawing group); Shape Styles More button or Format Shape dialog box launcher (DRAWING TOOLS FORMAT tab | Shape Styles group)		Format Shape	
Slide, Add	PPT 15	New Slide button (HOME tab | Slides group)		New Slide	CTRL+M
Slide, Arrange	PPT 42	Slide Sorter button (VIEW tab | Presentation Views group), drag thumbnail to new position	Drag slide in Thumbnail pane to new position, click Slide Sorter icon on status bar, drag thumbnail to new position		
Slide, Delete	PPT 79			Delete (touch screen) or Delete Slide	DELETE

Microsoft PowerPoint 2013 Quick Reference Summary *(continued)*

Task	Page Number	Ribbon	Other On-Screen Areas	Shortcut Menu	Keyboard Shortcut
Slide, Duplicate	PPT 41	New Slide arrow (HOME tab | Slides group), Duplicate Selected Slides		Duplicate Slide	
Slide, Format Background	PPT 109-111	Format Background button (DESIGN tab | Customize group)		Format Background (Format Background pane)	
Slide, Insert Picture as Background	PPT 108	Format Background button (DESIGN tab | Customize group)		Format Background, Picture or Texture Fill, Insert from File (Format Background pane)	
Slide, Select Layout	PPT 23	Layout button or New Slide arrow (HOME tab | Slides group)			
Slide Number, Insert	PPT 118	Insert Slide Number button (INSERT tab | Text group) or Header & Footer button (INSERT tab | Text group), click Slide number check box			
Slide Show, Start	PPT 49	Slide Show button (SLIDE SHOW tab | Start Slide Show group)	Slide Show button on status bar; 'Start from Beginning' button in Quick Access toolbar		F5
Slide Show, End	PPT 51		Tap or click black ending slide	End Show	ESC or HYPHEN
Spelling, Check	PPT 117	Spelling button (REVIEW tab | Proofing group)	Spell Check icon on status bar	Spelling (or click correct word on shortcut menu)	F7
Stacking Order, Change	PPT 153	Bring Forward or Send Backward button (PICTURE TOOLS FORMAT tab | Arrange group)		Send to Back or Bring to Front	
Synonym, Find and Insert	PPT 114	Thesaurus button (REVIEW tab | Proofing group)		Synonyms	SHIFT+F7
Text, Add Animation	PPT 183	More button, ANIMATIONS tab | Animation group			
Text, Add Shadow	PPT 100	Text Shadow button (HOME tab | Font group)			
Text, Align Horizontally	PPT 154	Align Text buttons (HOME tab | Paragraph group)	Align Text buttons on mini toolbar; Paragraph dialog box launcher (HOME tab | Paragraph group), Indents and Spacing tab (Paragraph dialog box), Alignment arrow	Paragraph, Indents and Spacing tab (Paragraph dialog box), Alignment arrow	CTRL+R (right), CTRL+L (left), CTRL+E (center)
Text, Bold	PPT 21	Bold button (HOME tab | Font group)	Bold button on mini toolbar	Font, Font tab (Font dialog box), Font style arrow, Bold	CTRL+B
Text, Change Color	PPT 13	Font Color button or Font Color arrow or Font dialog box launcher (HOME tab | Font group)	Font Color button or Font Color arrow on mini toolbar	Font, Font Color button (Font dialog box)	CTRL+SHIFT+F
Text, Delete	PPT 43	Cut button (HOME tab | Clipboard group)		Cut	DELETE or CTRL+X or BACKSPACE

Microsoft PowerPoint 2013 Quick Reference Summary *(continued)*

Task	Page Number	Ribbon	Other On-Screen Areas	Shortcut Menu	Keyboard Shortcut
Text, Find and Replace	PPT 113	Replace button (HOME tab | Editing group)			CTRL+H
Text, Italicize	PPT 11	Italic button (HOME tab | Font group)	Italic button on mini toolbar	Font, Font style arrow (Font dialog box), Italic	CTRL+I
Text, Select	PPT 11		Drag to select; double-click to select word; triple-click to select paragraph Touch Mode: Tap to position insertion point and drag selection handles		CTRL+SHIFT+RIGHT ARROW (select word); CTRL+SHIFT+DOWN ARROW (select paragraph)
Text Box, Add	PPT 156	Text Box button (INSERT tab | Text group)			
Theme, Change	PPT 26, PPT 185	More button (DESIGN tab | Themes group)			
Theme, Download	PPT 77	Choose category from Suggested searches (FILE tab, New tab), choose theme, tap or click Create button			
Theme Colors, Change	PPT 187	More button (DESIGN tab | Variants group), Colors			
Transition, Add	PPT 45	More button (TRANSITIONS tab | Transition to This Slide group)			ALT+A, T
Transition, Change Duration	PPT 46	Duration box or arrows (TRANSITIONS tab | Timing group)			
Transparency, Change	PPT 109	Background Styles button (DESIGN tab | Background group), Format Background, move Transparency slider		Format Background, Transparency slider	
Undo Changes	PPT 8		Undo button (Quick Access toolbar)		CTRL+Z
Video File, Insert	PPT 167	Video button (INSERT tab | Media group)	Insert Video icon in slide		
Video File, Trim	PPT 169	Trim Video button (VIDEO TOOLS PLAYBACK tab | Editing group), drag video start/end points or edit Start Time and End Time boxes		Trim	
Video Options, Add	PPT 170	VIDEO TOOLS PLAYBACK tab | Video Options group		Format Video, Video icon (Format Video task pane), VIDEO, Presets button	
Video Style, Add	PPT 173	More button (VIDEO TOOLS FORMAT tab | Video Styles group)			
View, Change	PPT 157	View buttons (VIEW tab | Presentation Views group)	View buttons on status bar (Normal, Slide Sorter, Reading View, Slide Show)		
WordArt, Add Text Effects	PPT 104	Text Effects button (DRAWING TOOLS FORMAT tab | WordArt Styles group)			
WordArt, Apply Text Fill	PPT 106	Text Fill arrow (DRAWING TOOLS FORMAT tab | WordArt Styles group)			

Microsoft PowerPoint 2013 Quick Reference Summary *(continued)*

Task	Page Number	Ribbon	Other On-Screen Areas	Shortcut Menu	Keyboard Shortcut
WordArt, Change Outline Color or Weight	PPT 106-107	Text Outline arrow (DRAWING TOOLS FORMAT tab | WordArt Styles group)			
WordArt, Insert	PPT 103	WordArt button (INSERT tab | Text group)			
Zoom for Viewing Slides	PPT 10	Zoom button (VIEW tab | Zoom group)	Zoom slider on status bar; Zoom In or Zoom Out buttons on Zoom slider; change percentage in Zoom level box on left side of slider Touch Mode: Pinch two fingers to zoom out; stretch two fingers apart to zoom in		

Important Notes for Windows 7 Users

The screen shots in this book show Microsoft Office 2013 running in Windows 8. If you are using Microsoft Windows 7, however, you still can use this book because Office 2013 runs virtually the same way on both platforms. You will encounter only minor differences if you are using Windows 7. Read this section to understand the differences.

Dialog Boxes

If you are a Windows 7 user, the dialog boxes shown in this book will look slightly different than what you see on your screen. Dialog boxes for Windows 8 have a title bar with a solid color, and the dialog box name is centered on the title bar. Beyond these superficial differences in appearance, however, the options in the dialog boxes across both platforms are the same. For instance, Figures 1 and 2 show the Font dialog box in Windows 7 and the Font dialog box in Windows 8.

Figure 1 Font Dialog Box in Windows 7

Figure 2 Font Dialog Box in Windows 8

Alternate Steps for Running an App in Windows 7

Nearly all of the steps in this book work exactly the same way for Windows 7 users; however, running an app (or program/application) requires different steps for Windows 7. The following steps show how to run an app in Windows 7.

Running an App (or Program/Application) Using Windows 7

1. Click the Start button on the taskbar to display the Start menu.
2. Click All Programs and then click the Microsoft Office 2013 folder (Figure 3).
3. If necessary, click the name of the folder containing the app you want to run.
4. Click the name of the app you want to run (such as Excel 2013).

Figure 3 Running an App Using the Windows 7 Start Menu